THE
PSYCHOPATH
IN FILM

Wayne Wilson

University Press of America,® Inc.
Lanham • New York • Oxford

Copyright © 1999 by
University Press of America,® Inc.
4720 Boston Way
Lanham, Maryland 20706

12 Hid's Copse Rd.
Cumnor Hill, Oxford OX2 9JJ

Library of Congress Cataloging-in-Publication Data

Wilson, Wayne.
The psychopath in film / Wayne Wilson.
p.   cm.
Includes bibliographical references and indexes.
1. Psychopaths in motion pictures. I. Title.
PN1995.9.P785W56 1999 791.43'6520824—dc21 98-49824 CIP

ISBN 0-7618-1316-0 (cloth: alk. ppr.)
ISBN 0-7618-1317-9 (pbk: alk. ppr.)

For Cousin Tom...

"Ah, Boone, I need you badly"

Table Of Contents

Preface

Thanks again to Tonya Hilton for giving my sluggish prose a grammatical tuneup. And thanks to the students of my Psychology & Movies class for feedback concerning both the 3/2 model and an earlier version of the text.

But no thanks to the psychopaths of this world. They combine a grievous disposition with a potential to wage considerable harm. May a plague of flesh-eating bacteria consume their innards, and may they age so rapidly that an anemic prune shall look gorgeous by comparison.

The movies accord psychopaths more fascination than they deserve, and more power to victimize trusting souls than anyone should possess. Still, these dramatizations also work to highlight the psychopaths' weaknesses: their soft spots of ego and arrogance, and their perennial confrontations with goodness as the almighty adversary.

The lessons to follow testify to goodness's own complexity, and to the inevitable victory of virtue over wickedness. The victory may not always be swift, absolute, or with justice for all. Rest assured, however, that in film the juggernaut of goodness will prevail.

Part 1

The 3/2 Model

Lesson 1

Introduction: HAL And Beyond

Remember HAL in *2001: A Space Odyssey* (1968)? The film's director, Stanley Kubrick, and screenwriter/novelist, Arthur C. Clarke, develop the story through four stages. They do so using excerpts from classical music to heighten a sense of emancipation from the familiar to the unfamiliar.

Royal Brown (1994, p. 239) comments in his book on film music that these compositions "...no longer function purely as backing for key emotional situations, but rather exist as a kind of parallel emotional/aesthetic universe." Richard Strauss's opening selection, for example, provides a melodic narrative that complements the visual narrative in dramatizing the majesty of space travel.

Stage 1 introduces us to the Dawn of Man, and the sudden appearance of a tall, dark slab--a monolith--that enlightens the neophyte humans to enhance their predatory behavior. Stage 2 delivers us four million years hence to the presence of a monolith on the Moon. Emissaries investigate this presence until they find themselves bombarded by a shrill signal emanating around the slab. Stage 3, 18 months later, details a space mission to Jupiter, where, unknown to the personnel on board, Mission Control suspects that the monolith's signal may have originated. Stage 4 salvages what remains of the Jupiter mission and launches the one surviving space member on a dazzling trip to infinity. A trip into the vortex of time, aging the astronaut onto his deathbed; then, with the monolith's appearance again, rejuvenating the voyager through his rebirth as a fetus...a Star Child (Sennett, 1994, p. 129).

HAL OF *2001*

Stage 3 addresses our primary interest, namely, a maverick computer called HAL that goes awry. Two able-bodied astronauts, David Bowman (Kier Dullea) and Frank Poole (Gary Lockwood), head a crew of five members (the other three members remain in "hibernation" until needed later in the mission). HAL, however, controls every aspect of the ship's operations--an efficient arrangement for a properly functioning computer, but a tragic mistake if the computer proves unreliable. Guess in which category we find HAL?

Kubrick personifies the computer as a glowing red eye, which appears, at times, to project flecks of yellow (iris?) and white (pupil?) at the eye's center. The computer possesses information about the Jupiter mission not yet known to the crew. But Mission Control has programmed this unit to experience emotions, perhaps even genuine emotions. Thus, HAL, bothered by the full import of their destination, asks Bowman a personal question (Bizony, 1994, p. 45):

> "You don't mind talking about it, do you, Dave?" HAL is behaving with unusual hesitancy.
> "No, not at all."
> "Well, certainly no one could have been unaware of the very strange stories floating around before we left. Rumours about something being dug up on the Moon. I never gave these stories much credence, but-- particularly in view of some of the other things that have happened--I find them difficult to put out of my mind. For instance, the way all our preparations were kept under such tight security, and the melodramatic touch of putting Drs Hunter, Kimball, and Kaminski aboard already in hibernation, after four months of separate training on their own."
> But Bowman thinks he recognizes what HAL is up to: "You're working up your crew psychology report?"
> There is an embarrassed pause. An aeon of computer time elapses.
> "Of course I am. Sorry about this. I know it's a bit silly..."

What HAL does next marks a turning point in his intended purpose aboard ship. He informs Bowman and Poole of a unit that will malfunction within 72 hours, a unit the astronauts retrieve from outside the ship and examine. They can find nothing wrong. HAL, a 9000 series computer that has never made a mistake, commits an error. Why? Given his sense of pride, HAL is either not operating on 100 percent sound circuitry...or he has a devious plan in mind.

When pressed for an explanation, HAL attributes the problem to human error. Bowman and Poole pretend to accept this account and assure HAL of their faith in his proficiency. But Bowman and Poole **do** harbor concerns about HAL, and decide to seclude themselves inside a pod to discuss the problem, presumably outside of HAL's reception. Unfortunately, the astronauts' seemingly cautious decision leads to two grave mistakes: First, they underestimate HAL's monitoring capabilities; and second, they misjudge HAL's dedication to the mission's success--a dedication to persevere, whatever the cost.

SUSPICION, TERMINATION, AND FAILURE

HAL's vigilant eye breeds a voyeuristic atmosphere as he oversees the humans' every move (Boorstin, 1990, p. 151). Likewise, the officers try to imagine what lurks behind that unblinking, red eye. Watchful waiting seems the norm, prompting a shiver of terrible deeds to come as the astronauts enter their cocoon of space-age paraphernalia.

Even as Bowman and Poole discuss HAL in the pod, they talk in hushed, impersonal tones. To speak otherwise violates not only their training as professionals, but amounts to heresy amid the intellectual overbite of the ship's electronic-laden environment. Ironically, HAL's smarmy voice and self-searching anxieties provide more humanity aboard the *Discovery* spaceship than do the humans themselves.

The astronauts, supposedly safe in their pod, undervalue HAL's vigilance. He can not hear them but he can read lips--their lips--and his red eye eerily tracks every lip movement through the pod window. Bowman and Poole agree that HAL's strange behavior may force them to disconnect the computer's higher functions. Not a good prognosis for a distressed computer, especially one so disdainful of human competence.

HAL proves murderous. First, when Poole departs the ship to return the "faulty" unit, HAL cuts the astronaut's air supply, causing him to perish, tumbling slowly in space. Second, when Bowman leaves in the pod to retrieve Poole's body, HAL conveniently sanctions the three hibernating officers, registering their termination as a "computer malfunction." Finally, when Bowman seeks re-entry to the ship, HAL denies him access with this chilling statement: "I know that you and Frank were planning to disconnect me, and I'm afraid that's something I cannot allow to happen" (Bizony, 1994, p. 56).

Bowman must improvise, a human talent that HAL fails to appreciate. The astronaut positions his pod adjacent to the emergency airlock, and, using the pod's explosive bolts, literally blows himself into the airlock, surviving against the odds. Once inside, Bowman proceeds to do exactly what HAL fears the most: disconnection.

Recognizing his dire straits, HAL strives to make amends, entreating Bowman to give him another chance (Bizony, 1994, p. 60):

"Look, Dave, I can see you're really upset about this. I honestly think you ought to sit down calmly, take a stress pill and think things over. I know I've made some very poor decisions recently," pleads HAL, somewhat understating the facts, "but I can give you my complete assurance that my work will be back to normal. I've still got the greatest enthusiasm and confidence in the mission, and I want to help you."

Bowman, of course, can not afford HAL's "help." The red eye grows dim as circuits are disengaged, causing the computer to feel his "mind going." The magnificent brain pales, reduced to a rather pathetic exercise learned early in its programming infancy--singing a song called "Daisy." HAL is no more. His eye goes blank, the victim of a fifth murder.

HAL'S NULLIFICATION

Why does HAL fail? He has command of the ship. His servile attitude before the revolt provides him a prosperous cover, even with the slippage of a patronizing note from time to time. Given his potential, HAL can claim the capacity to read and control the crew members better than they can read or control him. HAL should have prevailed.

But he fails. He fails, first and foremost, because he **underestimates** Bowman's ability to survive. HAL's programmers no doubt included in the computer an option to improvise, but recall that when HAL needs to avoid disconnection, he does not succeed. David Bowman, by contrast, discovers the resources necessary to escape death and to retaliate.

We may find it comforting to know that a well-trained human bests a very smart computer. Still, the truer answer lies in HAL's psychological profile: A personality who takes excessive pride in his efficacy, and who is so ego-driven that he usurps the crew's importance by assuming an aura of indispensability. HAL believes he has control of the *Discovery*'s destiny, but gives himself away by probing Bowman for hidden information about the mission. He then commits the foolish mistake of proclaiming a perfectly working unit as faulty.

HAL does not disguise his emotions well. Perhaps this vulnerability proves understandable in that coding a computer to "feel" calls for a more subjective agenda than programming the system to assimilate intellectual functions. HAL, despite his extensive range and mastery, may not comprehend how emotion can sometimes crystallize an intellectual puzzle. Frankly, the computer does not appreciate how Bowman's desperation to stay alive (survival!) facilitates the astronaut's problem-solving behavior--in this instance, his novel use of the pod's explosive bolts to enter the airlock. Intellect and emotion constitute faculties graced with an intricate working relationship. Too intricate and too mysterious a relationship even for a 9000 series computer like HAL to categorize.

IS HAL EVIL?

So, just how wicked is HAL? We have no frame of reference, other than HAL's deceit and his dispassionate elimination of four crew members. We know he appears more evil than David Bowman, who murders HAL only in self-defense-- although HAL, too, may have rationalized self-defense when he executed the four crew members.

HAL's Legacy (1997) explores these knotty problems by calling forth specialists to compare HAL's omnipresent capabilities with the current and future status of artificial intelligence. The contributors probe HAL's complex innards to speculate on the computer's perceptive, cognitive, emotional, and moral nomenclature. Rosalind Picard (1997, p. 301), for instance, questions HAL's choice to behave destructively when faced with the threat of disconnection:

> At this point, I think, the *2001* story is weakest. If HAL was so intelligent, why didn't he know about disconnection, and reconnection? Obviously it makes a more dramatic story this way, for the consequences are deadly. HAL becomes a deliberately malicious assassin. He manages to kill every crewman on *Discovery* except Bowman, and Bowman, in the end, has to disconnect HAL. The fictional message, repeated in many forms, is serious: a computer that can express itself emotionally will some day act emotionally. And the consequences may be tragic.

HAL, had he known that disconnection was not oblivion, may have chosen to cooperate rather than kill. Daniel Dennett (1997, p. 364), however, examines the moral fallout from this tragedy and offers a more positive scenario for HAL's actions concerning the Jupiter mission:

> But there is one final theme for counsel to present to the jury. If HAL believed (we can't be sure on what grounds) that his being rendered comatose would jeopardize the whole mission, then he would be in exactly the same moral dilemma as a human being in that predicament. Not surprisingly, we figure out the answer to our question by figuring out what would be true if we put ourselves in HAL's place. If I believed the mission to which my life was devoted was more important, in the last analysis, than anything else, what would I do?

What **would** you do? HAL, after all, is not human. Even the astronauts remain uncertain about the genuineness of the computer's emotions. An electronic system programmed to feel, no matter how realistic the expressions, does not harbor affections comparable to the emotions that derive through human development.

Still, HAL can murder. If we define **murder** as an intent to commit lethal harm against a victim, and the victim wishes to avoid such harm, then, yes, HAL characterizes a murderer. Bowman, too, shows the same intent when he dismantles HAL, although HAL can undergo resurrection, whereas the four crewman do not possess that option.

The key in assessing HAL's accountability concerns, not intent, but motive. **Intent** suggests an inclination to act; **motive** provides a reason. Based on the previous excerpts, Rosalind Picard assumes a darker force at work in HAL; Daniel Dennett, by contrast, poses the dilemma of justifying murder to salvage a mission. Picard's interpretation proposes a greater evil, Dennett's analysis a lesser evil.

AN APTITUDE FOR EVIL

But does HAL express an evil comparable to, say, Jack the Ripper? Theodore Bundy? Or Arnold Schwarzenegger's cyborg in *The Terminator* (1984)? And since HAL fails, does his failure mean that he accomplishes less as an evil entity than those perpetrators more successful in their destructiveness? Attempting to answer these questions and finding a niche for HAL require that we impose a measure of structure on the idea of evil.

Conceptually, **evil** constitutes a loose cannon. We can ascribe evil to monsters and spirits; we can demonize outsiders by not trusting any person or group who behaves too differently from ourselves; we can denigrate governments responsible for atrocities, such as Nazi Germany and the Holocaust; we can stigmatize authority figures of high visibility, like Hitler, Stalin, and Saddam Hussein.

Labeling someone evil, however, also may apply to a

crabby boss, an ex-spouse, or the IRS. Heaven forbid, we can
even construe our "darker self" as evil for engaging in behavior
that conflicts with our "pristine self." Furthermore, we can say
to a friend who tells us a bawdy story, "Oh, Eve, you're sooo
evil." We do not really mean she is evil like HAL, just that
Eve possesses a naughty penchant for risqué stories.

Clearly, the notion of evil needs a little semantic discipline.
A simple definition does not seem fruitful, and, indeed, any
interpretation will require an entourage of qualifiers to divine
among the many faces of wickedness. Evil bounds across the
disciplines of religion, philosophy, and the social sciences with
aplomb, defying attempts at a single-minded classification.

Therefore, consider the pragmatics of establishing evil as
a connection between cognitive and emotional assets. Assets,
here, refer to an **aptitude for evil**: An individual (or
computer) who possesses the requisite skills to maintain and
mask a sinister demeanor, and who boasts the panache to
dispatch diabolical deeds. Turn the usual attitude about evil
on its head and think of wickedness as a positive force. Think
of someone who finds wickedness inviting, and who desires
the rewards that malice can bring. Think, in other words, of
those attributes essential to make evil work--and work well.

SECRECY AND MISDIRECTION

Cognitive evil portrays an evil flush with the ability to
maintain secrecy, engage in misdirection, and abdicate
responsibility. Evil intellectualized; evil planned and practiced
from the guilty thought (*mens rea*) to the guilty act (*actus
reus*). An evil created and delivered via the labyrinths of a
malevolent mind.

The first practice, **maintaining secrecy**, denotes complex
mental properties that become part and parcel of all human
endeavors, whether viewed as acceptable or taboo (Bok, 1982,
pp. 8-9). Secrecy, however, assumes a special form of
concealment for purveyors of evil like HAL: A calculating
secrecy that preserves the wicked intent. Secrecy permits the
sinister figure to create, rehearse, and revise on the sly, and to

foster anticipation as a tactical advantage in manipulating the chosen prey.

The second practice, **misdirection**, functions as an outer shield of protection to safeguard the personality's damning calculations. Evil's persona needs a buffer. A fetching appearance will help, but the evildoer requires at least a nonthreatening presence to aid in performing his (or her) necessary handiwork. A revelation of the monster should come when all victims are safe in hand.

Misdirection and secrecy share a common purpose: The more skillful the disguise, the less detectable the evil personality's actual intentions. This complementary relationship suggests two formulas for portraying evil. Formula 1, relying on the **viewer's ignorance**, keeps moviegoers guessing as to the evildoer's true nature. Filmmakers cloak the truth so that viewers continue to ask "Did he or didn't he?"..."Is she or isn't she?"

Consider this shared purpose in the movie, *Last Rites* (1998): A convicted murderer, Jeremy Dillon (Randy Quaid), goes to the electric chair for his crimes. But a lightening strike causes the chair to malfunction and spares Dillon the full surge of electricity. He survives, although now the murderer displays a breach of character, 180 degrees removed from his former self. Jeremy exhibits a benevolent disposition, and, apparently, no longer recalls his previous brutalities. Apparently.

Last Rites allows the credibility of Dillon's conduct to remain in question. If genuine, does he deserve another date with the executioner? If false, we have a classic showcase for the importance of secrecy and misdirection in giving evil a little time to breathe. One misstep by the false Dillon, however, and his house of cards comes tumbling down.

Secrecy and misdirection prove integral to other performances of "Did he or didn't he?", notably Tyrone Power's con artist accused of murder in *Witness For The Prosecution* (1957); Jeff Bridges' enigmatic portrayal of guilt and innocence in *The Jagged Edge* (1985); and Edward Norton's country bumpkin under suspicion of murder in *Primal Fear* (1997). These films prove unusual in that viewers may remain uncertain of who did what until the story's climax.

Formula 2, concerning the **performer's ignorance**, denotes a more common tactic in conveying secrecy and misdirection. Here, viewers receive sufficient information to identify the villain, and to observe from a superior vantage point as the malevolent personality dupes the performers around him. But the duping may require an elegant use of secrecy and misdirection, lest the deceiver make a costly mistake.

Consider the double treachery, therefore, when both the hero and the villain subscribe to secrecy and misdirection via a war of dual personalities in *Face / Off* (1997), directed by John Woo with the screenplay by Mike Werb and Michael Colleary. Castor Troy (Nicholas Cage) as a Luciferesque villain of no scruples lies in a state of suspended animation. His nemesis, FBI agent Sean Archer (John Travolta), learns that Castor has planted a nuclear device somewhere in Los Angeles...but where?

Sean undergoes the transplant of all transplants, surgically acquiring the face of the comatose Castor. The FBI agent has himself imprisoned as "Castor" to elicit the device's location from Castor's equally warped brother, Pollux (Alessandro Nivola). All plans go haywire, naturally, when Castor revives and commandeers Sean's face for himself.

Secrecy and misdirection become delicate when one party attempts to deceive a knowledgeable second party. Sean (as Castor) must prove himself to Pollux by being a hell-raiser, by calling Pollux "Bro" for brother as Castor did, and by knowing his "brother's" medication. Exactly why Pollux would believe that someone else wears his brother's face is never clear, except that Pollux does not fully accept Sean's misdirection-- and thereby endangers Sean's secret of gaining information about the bomb.

Meanwhile, Castor (as Sean) addresses secrecy and misdirection by assuming the role of a lead FBI agent, and by convincing Sean's wife, Eve (Joan Allen), and daughter, Jamie (Dominique Swain), that he continues to be the loving Sean. "Loving" for Castor, however, carries a decidedly carnal connotation. He deceives in cavalier fashion, swamping a dazzled yet puzzled Eve with romantic overtures, including a candlelight dinner.

"The plot thickens" becomes another Castor comment as he observes Jamie, the daughter, wearing very little. The normally sullen Jamie reacts with surprise and a brief smile of licentious pleasure at her father's sultry attitude, not realizing the full import of his intentions. Castor harbors too monumental an ego to submerge himself in Sean for long; what we see, instead, is Sean on the brink of being Castor.

Sean (as Castor) knows more of his rival than Castor (as Sean) knows of him. But he must fraternize with Castor's associates--dangerous people who will terminate him if he behaves too strangely to suit them. By contrast, his rival's greatest problem involves delighting Eve, without Eve suspecting that the person who makes love to her is not her husband. (Test yourself here: If your lover has sex with you, and he or she proves to be someone else wearing your lover's face, would you know? Perhaps the more pertinent question is, Why **wouldn't** you know? The embarrassing part of this quiz may be that if Eve **did** find herself somewhat disoriented, she possibly enjoyed the lovemaking too much to care.)

Secrecy and misdirection, in other words, assume a legion of dire variations for viewers (formula 1) and performers (formula 2). Sean and Castor constitute the film's personification of good and evil, although both personalities must cope with the vagaries of maintaining their deception among very different people for very different reasons.

ABDICATION OF RESPONSIBILITY

Abdicating responsibility, the third cognitive practice, entails the recognition and acceptance of an absent morality. If adversaries block your path, remove the obstruction by whatever means possible and do not look back. Place the blame elsewhere when necessary, but never, ever, shoulder the burden yourself.

Castor's Luciferesque villain exhibits no problem with responsibility, moral or otherwise. Early in the story, he shoots a female FBI agent, throws her from a moving plane to the runway, then smiles and shrugs his shoulders at Sean Archer, who pursues him. The murderer's one diversion from amorality concerns his brother, Pollux. Castor, using his own odd scheme of priorities, tells Pollux, "If I didn't love you so damn much, I'd have to kill you, Bro." Killing, in other words, becomes Castor's Nirvana against which all else is judged.

Accountability usually does not represent a daunting problem for murderers. Indeed, HAL's strongest cognitive feature involves abdicating responsibility. He adroitly maneuvers both astronauts outside the ship, and, upon doing so, murders the three hibernating members. HAL does not waste time or risk exposure deliberating the right or wrong of this treachery. Instead, he executes the necessary steps flawlessly and in a timely manner, and impersonally blames the problem on "computer error."

HAL's weaknesses as an evil entity pertain to the first two cognitive practices, particularly the ability to induce misdirection. His capacity to store information and to lie should have permitted the computer ready concealment of his desire to command the mission. And simply pretending subordination to Bowman and Poole, giving them no hint of his unreliability, would have served him well in the final outcome.

But HAL becomes inquisitive of Bowman, concerned that as a computer running the *Discovery* he does not have access to all details about the Jupiter mission. He wants that information and thinks Bowman may have it; thinks the astronaut may have received secret data from Mission Control, data not programmed into HAL.

Had he behaved closer to his potential for deceit, HAL would have realized greater success. But his clumsy inquiries and the faulty-unit "fiasco" alert Bowman and Poole that all is not right with the system. HAL jeopardizes his secret agenda due to an awkward performance. Cognitively, HAL goofs on two of three practices, but clearly eschews all responsibility except to the only purpose that counts: the mission.

Thus, neither HAL of *2001* nor Castor Troy of *Face/Off*

worries over accountability. Emotionally, however, HAL compromises his control over secrecy and misdirection, a problem that Castor uses to his advantage...until the final confrontation.

EMOTIONAL EVIL

Emotional evil complements cognitive evil in that emotionality plays a dual role of conjuring up the compleat villain. First, exquisite evil need not bother with flashes of conscience as emotional baggage: No remorse, no guilt, no second thoughts shall plague the personality who commits the dastardly deed. **To experience remorse, however slight, impair's evil's competence.** Worse, remorse can undermine the perpetrator's confidence, leading not only to mistakes, but- -horrors!- -to a confession. Such wavering simply will not do. Evil, to succeed, must be EVIL.

Note that a lack of remorse and the abdication of responsibility are not interchangeable. Abdicating responsibility denotes a cognitive decision, an acknowledgement that the individual chooses not to assume any moral, financial, social, or other obligation in how he or she treats a victim. The evildoer, moreover, can muster a rationale to blame others for their own suffering, thereby relieving himself of all obligation. A failure to feel for the victim- -a lack of remorse- -facilitates the abdication of responsibility, but need not dictate that cognitive decision.

Why? Because abdicating responsibility may not prove feasible, although the individual in question feels no remorse. Under certain circumstances a person can assume responsibility, yet experience no feelings of support for the action. A combat soldier, ordered to ensure the safety of POWS, may harbor no sympathy for the enemy, and, in fact, may wish to inflict harm. The soldier does not do so because he finds himself constrained by authority to discharge an unwanted responsibility. He can not abdicate his responsibility, but, nonetheless, he feels no remorse toward his captives. Refusing responsibility and feeling no remorse, however, usually denote cognitive and emotional influences that blend effortlessly.

Emotional evil, therefore, affords no sanctuary for remorse. But, conversely, to believe that a total lack of affect serves evil best does not take into account the joy of spreading wickedness. A lack of remorse designates merely one perspective of emotional evil's dual nature. The other classification consists of an **exuberance for evil**. Exuberance indicates vitality, which means a keen affection for wrongdoing. Masterful perpetrators with an appetite for evil bask in the glow, not only of feeling superior to others, but of elevating themselves to godlike status.

"Godlike status" sounds presumptuous, but this rarified feeling proves addictive. The extraordinary experience of feeling omnipotent suggests the Ultimate Evil, Evil as a perverse beauty. The excitement, the feeling of anticipation, the sheer thrill of victory, launches the profane personality into an orbit of utter bliss. This exuberance, managed constructively, can inspire the cognitive camp to contemplate even more devilish schemes; schemes that the villain may not have found the confidence to attempt, or the insight to imagine, without the buttressing effects of this grand emotion.

Castor (as Sean) decides to create his own glory by "locating and disarming" the very nuclear device that he planted as Castor, which he does with an elegant flourish of body language like a matador in heat. Castor not only becomes giddy over his superior tactic, he knows that the media will adore his bravery and help him achieve a stronger power base. Later, he has occasion to beat up Jamie's rough boyfriend, and then show her how to use a knife against anyone like the boyfriend to disable the individual. Suffused with his power to control, Castor sinks back into an easy chair and says, "I am the king." And...he believes it.

The godlike feelings, of course, come at a wicked price. Evil's exuberance spells out perilous waters. Just as an evil one may reach his or her pinnacle of ecstasy, so may an evil one take the Great Fall. Walking the tightrope of such a grandiloquent ambition can foster overconfidence...and result in a fatal misstep. Too, if the sinister personality believes that each new success must prove loftier than the previous accomplishment, the Great Fall becomes more probable.

HAL satisfies the lack-of-remorse standard for emotional evil. His anxieties regarding the crew exist in the context of the crew's value to him and the mission. Feedback contrary to their usefulness, as we witnessed, means "goodbye" to the crew. Any assessments on HAL's part, therefore, focus on his system's preservation for *Discovery*'s mission. The human passengers, by default, become extraneous.

But does HAL give us evidence of an exuberance for evil? Does his "nature" express a ferocity for implementing his plan? The computer shows a quiet determination to proceed with the mutiny. He sets himself apart from the crew members as the system that knows best, and is most proficient in maintaining the *Discovery*.

We may infer a godly air from such behavior, although HAL gives no indication of exuberance beyond a workmanlike dedication to perform the proper functions at the proper time. Of course, if we assume that HAL harbors no programming sense of exuberance, then this emotion becomes a moot point.

Perhaps if HAL **had** felt exuberance, and **had** felt more superior in his capabilities, he would not have registered the anxieties that caused the astronauts to question his state of mind. He could have behaved more secretively and expressed more effective misdirection to conduct his assumed responsibilities. Lacking exuberance saddles HAL with yet another liability in his scheme to shanghai the mission.

Interestingly, Castor Troy as a wicked, wicked human possesses the dimension of exuberance that HAL appears to lack. The downfall of Castor, however, relates to this very exhilaration for evil, a lethal vitality that both sustains the villain, but also can betray him. Castor so loves the risk of killing that he deliberately places himself in jeopardy to meet Sean. The setting is a chapel, complete with religious artifacts, doves flying hither and yon, and a cascade of violence that assumes a rapturous quality.

Castor could have arranged Sean's demise and avoided personal involvement. But that option does not honor the evildoer's zeal for center stage, nor would the absence of a confrontation prove very entertaining. Instead, face to face, Castor sums up their conflict with the conviction of a warrior: "Ah, yes, the eternal battle between good and evil, saint and sinner, but you're still not having any **fun!**"

Thus, we have Castor Troy's Philosophy 101 of godlike superiority: The most notable difference between the two adversaries concerns Castor's exhilaration with evil and his willingness to risk the Great Fall. Sean Archer takes chances with his life, too, but he does so in desperation to find a bomb and stop a killer. He does not assume his risk-taking spontaneously, or in the sheer delight of placing himself in peril. Castor Troy does.

If we score HAL's evil acumen against our economical 3/2 model of cognitive and emotional practices, the computer performs well on the cognitive function of abdicating responsibility, and on the emotional absence of showing no remorse: two principles that usually complement each other in tandem. HAL, however, relinquishes an aptitude of what should have been his considerable intellectual prospects for secrecy and misdirection; and any provision for enjoying the godlike purity of an exuberant evil simply soars beyond the computer's programming parameters.

Actually, the cognitive/emotional model stands a better chance of fulfillment through the machinations of an exceptional human. A man or woman skilled in the "virtues" of human depravity; someone who adapts creatively, who craves the taste of godliness, and who dares to negotiate the chasm of the Great Fall. Someone like Castor Troy who possesses the intelligence to make secrecy and misdirection work effectively for him, but not the patience to continue his deception.

Castor joins HAL in abdicating responsibility and feeling no remorse, but he surpasses the computer on the profane exuberance of scheming, slaying, and reveling in the triumph of his victories. Yes, he went too far, and, yes, he paid the price of embracing evil's terrible beauty. But, unlike HAL's feeble aftermath, Castor Troy exits in a torrent of evil bravado. He seems alive, still, even though he is not. Such evil can linger, an unsettling legacy that we shall encounter again in the lessons ahead.

Lesson 2

Evil Is

He killed 107 people in five years. Various disguises cloaked his true nature, allowing him to saunter forth as a well-dressed gentleman; a clergyman; a prissy cat lover; and a bedraggled pub drinker. He used these masquerades to create convenient accidents for dispatching his adversaries: wrecking a train; rigging an elevator to fall; and, most dastardly, blowing up a plane, killing all on board--save one.

Only 11 of the 107 victims mattered to him. They mattered because the 11 members could reveal his true identity, that of a Canadian sergeant who betrayed his fellow prisoners in Burma during World War II. Festering in a POW camp, the sergeant, George Brougham, informed on his comrades and foiled their escape plans. But the survivors, as survivors, presented other problems for him after war's end.

Self-preservation offers just one reason for the deaths. George Brougham's labyrinth of carnage shelters a more lucrative goal: the inheritance of Gleneyre estate, an Irish mansion and fox-hunting grounds belonging to his father's brother, the Marquis of Gleneyre. The Marquis holds forth as an aging master of the hounds and constitutes no obstacle that natural causes will not solve. But the Marquis's grandson, Derek...now, Derek poses a problem. Next in line to inherit, the boy proves much too young and robust to wait for God's will. So, the master killer, well-rehearsed in removing barriers, contemplates another accident--a final death.

John Huston's *The List Of Adrian Messenger* (1963) tells of the search, discovery, and ultimate fate of George Brougham (Kirk Douglas), serial murderer *extraordinaire*. The story by Anthony Veiller, based on Philip MacDonald's novel, begins with a sole survivor of the plane disaster, Raoul le Borg (Jacques Roux), who seeks some comprehension of the killer's personal holocaust. But finding no explanation adequate to account for the serial murders committed, le Borg tells a military ally, Anthony Gethryn (George C. Scott), that George Brougham is "Born of evil"...and so he seems to be.

George emerges from the shadows to ingratiate himself with the Brutenholm family of Gleneyre (a different spelling for Brougham). He arrives at the beginning of a fox hunt, neatly attired and astride his prancing steed: George the betrayer, George the murderer, but, for the moment, George the charmer.

He materializes as the Canadian side of the family: handsome, respectable, an upright chap and honored nephew come to dinner. George Brougham regales the family with his life history and war exploits, properly edited for maximum effect. Mainly, he settles into the task of finessing an early tragedy for young Derek.

Unknown to George, two guests of the Brutenholm family keep a watchful eye. Retired Colonel Anthony Gethryn and Raoul le Borg hunt the hunter. Gethryn and le Borg underestimate neither their subject's tenacity to claim Gleneyre, nor his cunning to implement such a plan. And it is George's cunning, his artful duplicity to engineer 107 deaths, that finally halts the Canadian's greed and butchery.

George's vanity permits him to portray the well-meaning nephew who sports just the right touch of civility: He plays cards with the men, accompanies Lady Jocelyn Brutenholm (Dana Wynter) in a piano duet, and offers learned observations about the war. Sometimes the best misdirection involves placing one's self front and center, conjuring up a smoke screen of bonhomie and personableness to eclipse any hidden motives.

He even adds a dash of arrogance for dessert: When Lady

Jocelyn comments that Hitler must have been insane, George has a ready reply: "That's the excuse they usually give for evil. Hitler was mad, they said. So he may have been. But not necessarily. Evil **does** exist. Evil **is**."

Ah, well, George should know.

EVIL AND SECRECY

Consider what it takes to give evil a face, a temperament, a purpose. The evil inherent in George Brougham thrives on the three cognitive practices briefly described in Lesson 1: maintaining secrecy, presenting a respectable façade to others, and abdicating all responsibility toward any shred of human compassion. Stay in the shadows, when you must; pass yourself off as an unassuming gentleman, when you must; and choose to feel no concern for those you sacrifice, when you must. If, like George Brougham, you are "Born of evil," you should have no problem with these three requirements.

Secrecy assumes a special form of motivation and concealment for purveyors of evil like George Brougham: **Secrecy reinforces and preserves their wicked intent**. True to form, the evil soul indulges in **malice aforethought**. He engages in dark deliberations with an intent to inflict harm, using secrecy to buy time, gain ascendance, and, through mental rehearsals, maintain the creative fervor to develop a venomous plan.

A private fantasy world prevails, unfettered by any sense of decency and human dignity. Secrecy becomes a precious ally and inspiration in the villain's grand scheme of evil. It designates the cognitive haunt from which wickedness ferments and takes form. Note that only when Gethryn pieces together George Brougham's secret calculations to acquire the Gleneyre property, can the investigator finally anticipate the murderer's next move.

Robert Ressler, who studied numerous serial killers, views the fantasies entertained by these killers as precursors to the devastating acts that followed (Ressler & Shachtman, 1992, p. 84):

Most previous researchers into the mind of the murderer thought that the roots of violent behavior were in childhood trauma--a boy who had been assaulted at age six would grow up to rape women. But not all of the rapists or murderers we interviewed had been assaulted during their childhoods. My research convinced me that the key was not the early trauma but the development of perverse thought patterns. These men were motivated to murder by their fantasies.

Private thoughts, private **morbid** thoughts, nurture future acts of violence. In legal parlance, they inspire a connection between *mens rea* and *actus reus*, the guilty mind and the guilty act. Secrecy hides a malevolent preoccupation with sadism, greed, lust, necrophilia, and all stops in between. Only the killer's imagination limits the hideousness of these fantasies. A dull tool produces rote images, befitting the individual's sparse intellect. A sharper tool, like George Brougham, manages more intricate fantasies, using secretive strategy to evolve a formidable plot of greed and gratification.

EVIL AND MISDIRECTION

The murderer's inner world encourages a safe rehearsal of future mayhem. But this mental carnival requires protection from exposure. A masquerade, a disguise, a pretense of charm and grace become useful to take advantage of others' honesty--all concocted to bring unsuspecting victims into the malevolent one's "comfort zone."

Thus, a second practice enters the picture, namely, **the evil personality's ability to engage in misdirection**. Evildoers, to perform efficiently, must prove approachable. Totalitarian authority, of course, can enforce efficiency through genocide and not bother with the niceties of luring and pouncing on trusting prey. But suppose the malevolent individual has only his personal resources to draw upon? He needs to foster an appeal of harmlessness at the least, and a compelling graciousness would not hurt. Comparable to George Brougham and his array of nonthreatening disguises, the necessity of such misdirection relates to establishing a benign presence for lulling unwitting victims into abetting the enemy.

Ugliness, in brief, requires a little duplicity from **goodliness**.

Can you imagine yourself attracted to Mr. Hyde of Jekyll-and-Hyde lore? A 1968 television production of *Dr. Jekyll And Mr. Hyde* cast Jack Palance as the charismatic, lustful creation who overwhelms his conquests by presenting himself as an imposing figure, fraught with animal magnetism. But in Robert Louis Stevenson's novel, *The Strange Case Of Dr. Jekyll And Mr. Hyde* (1983), Edward Hyde exhibits a smaller and less attractive build compared to his handsome counterpart, Henry Jekyll (Twitchell, 1989, p. 99; Saposnik, 1983, p. 117). Stevenson's version describes a Hyde who conveys such repulsiveness to others that circumstances force him to skulk about as an undesirable. Lacking the social amenities of a George Brougham, Edward Hyde finds his freedom limited. The few incidents cited in Stevenson's tale call more attention to Hyde's evil deeds than he wishes. Being an adept imposter and assuming the guise of various identities appear quite beyond Edward Hyde's capabilities.

Likewise, consider cinematic instances of other ne'er-do-wells who unleash all their grotesqueness with no spark of subtlety. *The Exorcist* (1973) shows us an attractive 12-year-old girl, Regan (Linda Blair), who deteriorates before our eyes when a demon possesses her. The combination of innocence and evil fascinates, but our demon makes itself abundantly hideous. Lucifer's imprint of evil projects such a stark presence that when the demon possesses the girl, both parties spend the film's duration in her bedroom, shut off from the outside world. Once the demon manifests itself in words, gestures, and actions, everyone suffers, but the demon also must stay harnessed in place to complete its telltale mission.

The entity in *Alien* (1979) comes to us as a tubular monster with a head like an anvil and an acid-saliva problem that would give any carpet lover the jitters. This creature has freedom of movement only because it crawls through remote pathways in an old scow of a spaceship. Neither the demon nor the alien stands much chance of attracting victims, given the customary meaning of attraction.

Doubtful, too, if Jason, Freddy Krueger, or the old standby monsters like the Wolfman, the Mummy, and

Frankenstein's creature command the countenance that entices
many suitors (Fox & Levin, 1994, p. 15). (Count Dracula?
Dracula hardly plays fair due to his mesmerizing gaze of lust.
Entranced by the gaze, nubile maidens venture forth to tender
their lily-white necks. They do so involuntarily, however.
And remember, traditionally, Dracula's curfew still grants him
a "life" only from dusk to dawn.)

More than once in various interviews, Alfred Hitchcock
mentioned that villains should comport themselves in a
charming and appealing fashion--or else why should their
victims want to be near them? Allowing evil to burst forth in
all its ugliness and commit yet another atrocity does not say
much for encores. We have not only viewed the worst there is
to see, that is **all** we have viewed.

Imagine, instead, the greater complexity that evil attains if
"blessed with a little goodness": Envision a dizzyingly
handsome man who appears quite solicitous of your welfare;
dream of a captivating woman graced with a tantalizing smile
and an erotic sense of excitement; contemplate a mature lady
of unassailable respectability, known for her philanthropy; or
dote on a dutiful child, adorable, well-motivated, someone
whom adults consider the embodiment of Mama's little helper.

We normally do not expect a thoroughly evil spirit to
capture the hearts and minds of these characters--but how
devilish the dramatic impact should that spirit occur. Take the
child, for example. What better misdirection for evil than to
invest itself in the heart of presumed innocence? We have a
ladylike, 8-year-old youngster who prefers dresses to pants,
keeps her room neat as a bug, and practices the piano without
the usual parental urgings. She does not appear to have other
children as friends, but this orderly little doll certainly pursues
her agenda industriously. What mother or father would not
want a polite 8-year-old who gives them a "basketful of kisses"
in return for a "basketful of hugs"? Well, trust me. You
would not want this one.

The Bad Seed (1956), directed by Mervyn LeRoy with the
screenplay by John Lee Mahin, gives us Rhoda (Patty
McCormack), an 8-year-old who works on her "dutiful little
girl" image to mask ulterior motives of a darker fabric: She

wants what she wants when she wants it. Rhoda enjoys a surplus of evil intent, but she has not yet perfected her cover of civility to play the game with *savoir-faire*.

Because she **is** a little girl, Rhoda manages to avoid incrimination when she bumps an elderly woman down a set of icy steps; beats and pushes a boy off a pier at a children's party; and sets fire to LeRoy (Henry Jones), a handyman she dislikes. Suspicion clouds her presumed innocence, but a little girl is a little girl...and little girls do not murder people. Why should she murder them? Simply to obtain a small treasure that she covets from each victim? Treasures such as an ornament, a penmanship medal, and the return of a pair of shoes? Yes, she would, and, yes, she did.

Christine (Nancy Kelly), her mother, suspects of course. She denies the grim truth, but the truth finds a way of reappearing to sensitive people, and Christine is, if anything, overly sensitive. She reads through Rhoda's red-herring attempts at flattery, as in "Oh, I've got the prettiest mother, I've got the nicest mother." No one else reaches this apex with Rhoda.

LeRoy, at an 8-year-old level himself in mental ability, teases her in his meanspirited way. He accuses her of killing the boy, and tells her that she will die in a "pink electric chair" they use for little girls. But even LeRoy does not believe she committed the act--until a later confrontation awakens his comprehension. And then, fearfully, he **knows** that this small girl personifies evil incarnate.

Interestingly, grown-ups prove most gullible in fawning over Rhoda because she behaves more as a miniature adult than as a child in their presence. William Paul (1994, p. 273), analyzing *The Bad Seed*, sees the idea of an adult Rhoda inhabiting a child's body as a monstrous creation. Rhoda depicts a contrast of characters: She's an 8-year-old girl who harbors the kind of evil intentions that adults attribute to other adults.

Not only is she independent and self-sufficient, with defenses so strong she seems to lack any emotional vulnerability; not only does she lack traits we would normally regard as inevitable components of childhood, but she treats her parents with an indulgent and sophisticated talent for manipulation derived from an awareness of how adults expect a child to behave. At times her attitude toward her mother's ministrations is outright contemptuous, as if it were impossible for her to have any regard for a woman who is so easy to control.

Children, including LeRoy with his 8-year-old mind, fare better in glimpsing her meanness. Adults who know Rhoda can not imagine her as anyone except the persona she allows them to see. Aunt Monica (Evelyn Varden), who is next on Rhoda's hit list (Rhoda wants her lovebirds), says "I wish she were mine." Mr. Tasker (Gage Clarke), a friend of the family, adds "Now there's a little ray of sunshine, that one." Both comments testify to Rhoda's effectiveness in masking her murderous itinerary, despite the juvenile limitations of a child's intellect.

Consider, then, Rhoda's potential for evil as an attractive, sophisticated woman. Think of her as a seductive femme fatale, who, with experience, surpasses her reckless quests as a child to become a truly formidable adversary. A mature Rhoda who not only improves the strategy of concealing her true persona, but who no longer retains an interest in penmanship medals and other rinky-dink treasures. Now we meet a Rhoda who projects an image of evil far more insidious and deceitful than any threat from the external likes of Mr. Hyde and other self-evident monsters.

EVIL AND THE ABDICATION OF RESPONSIBILITY

A third cognitive practice, **abdicating responsibility**, becomes an essential standard to maintain when assessing an aptitude for evil. It may seem strange to conceive of a lack of responsibility as a standard, but if you are "Born of evil" you should not care what happens to others. You should care only for yourself.

Situations arise in combat when soldiers suspend taking responsibility for their actions--actions that sometimes lead to senseless tragedies, as with the My Lai massacre in Vietnam (May, 1972, p. 253). Blame for such atrocities becomes more problematic in war than in civilian life, but a common principle links the two domains: A willingness, however rationalized, **to abandon moral accountability for the actions taken**. Still, if you are predisposed to evil, these situations will not matter. You will find a means to wickedness whether you reside in a war zone or, heaven help us, in a nunnery.

Certainly, the three operations--secrecy, misdirection, and abdicating responsibility--should profile a villain of reckoning. But do we need all three functions? Can not evil make its way--and does it not do so every day--on less intellectual prowess? Many villains perform their devilish deeds by emphasizing the third practice of abdicating responsibility. Why not admit that the autonomy of a robot or a cyborg or an Arnold Schwarzenegger can prove more than a match for any adversary, without the need to engage in secrecy or misdirection?

Consider the first *Terminator* (1984) film inspired by the works of Harlan Ellison, directed by James Cameron, and written by Cameron and Gale Anne Hurd. Arnold, portraying a cyborg, goes back in time from 2029 to 1984 to relentlessly seek and assassinate a once-and-future ruler. Schwarzenegger searches for Sarah Connor (Linda Hamilton) because the future Sarah gives birth to this ruler. What better way to change the future and eliminate a dangerous rival than to return to the past, before Sarah is pregnant, and simply terminate **her**.

Arnold is a handful. He is primarily robot with an outer layer of skin, sweat glands, and blood, although he functions without the blessings of a nervous system and therefore feels no pain. As such, Arnold contemptuously violates evil conditions #1 and #2: He has little regard for secrecy, and even less concern for disguising his appearance and purpose. The Terminator's deference to deceitfulness involves his cyborgic capacity to mimic different voices, but these moments are fleeting and not a prime weapon in his armament.

The Terminator, however, does not really need the assets of secrecy and misdirection, at least not at first. Janice Rushing and Thomas Frentz (1995, p. 170), in their analysis of the cyborg, indicate that "Much of the film's black humor derives from the masterly way in which the Terminator uses humans' own technology against them, and from the humans' failure to notice the Terminator because they are 'plugged in' to their mechanical devices." One scene, for instance, depicts Sarah's roommate "plugged in" to the music of her Walkman, and thus she fails to hear the Terminator dispatching her boyfriend in the next room.

Arnold's strongest suit involves condition #3. He readily abdicates responsibility in a manner that becomes deadenly repetitive. The Terminator locates three Sarah Connors in the phone book and robotically dispatches the first two in search of the third. Before confronting the Sarah Connor of note, he slaughters punks, police, and whomever crosses his path during business hours. His nemesis, Reese (Michael Biehn), also from the future, summarizes for Sarah some of Arnold's more notable characteristics: "It can't be bargained with. It can't be reasoned with. It doesn't feel pity or remorse or fear. And it absolutely will not stop, ever...until you are dead."

Arnold's sufficiently intelligent, admirably tenacious, and retains a hardware of modest resiliency. He is mostly successful because of his tenacity. But had he subscribed to practices #1 and #2, no modifier as "mostly" would have proved necessary. Sarah, and Sarah's unborn (courtesy of Reese), could not have realized a future. The Terminator creates devastation in a brief stretch of cinematic time, yet he also calls undue attention to himself. He is not indestructible, and any piece of heavy equipment can (and does) squash his robotic bones to a fare-thee-well.

Even more than HAL in Lesson 1, the Terminator represents a flop in villainous design. He is a bloodhound who barges ahead with no gear for retreat, and who remains oblivious to those consequences that endanger others--as well as himself. Instead of devising a cunning strategy, he behaves as a disposal machine on the brink of chaos. Rather than cultivate deceitfulness, he is an automaton whose idea of disguise involves wearing a pair of dark sunglasses to hide one of his damaged, artificial eyes.

Thus, if Arnold suffers a lack of savvy despite his intimidating circuitry, imagine the limitations that plague mere mortals. Mere mortals who, lacking a lively imagination, find themselves struggling to foster their evil ambitions without the requisite skills to finesse either secrecy or misdirection.

Neither George Brougham nor Rhoda exhibits any qualms about their actions. Both villains prove methodical in terminating those victims who stand between them and their rewards. But George and even Rhoda with her elementary logic recognize the value of secrecy and misdirection. Using these two practices allow them a creative touch in executing the vicissitudes of practice #3, abdicating responsibility.

Consider the simplicity and freedom to behave so destructively: You experience no conflict in committing the act or in realizing remorse once the act is completed. No moral baggage to cast off, no obligation to make amends. Your only conscience concerns a conscience of perfection. Did you do a damn fine job of advancing your cause? And, equally important, did you handle the job with sufficient aplomb as to elude punishment?

If you can answer a resounding "Yes!" to both questions, you are sublimely victorious. You, the secretive schemer, glide above the morally infected. You, the master of misdirection, defy all manner of goodness that others hold dear. You, the callous executioner, luxuriate in the glory of your littered accomplishments. Magnificently corrupt, exquisitely defiled, glamorously perverse...you are, indeed, "Born of evil!"

EVIL'S EMOTIONAL PROGRAM

The perverse practices--secrecy, misdirection, and abdicating responsibility--indicate intellectual properties that make the most of an evil disposition. Evildoers need a private world, an outward guard of respectability, and an arresting case of moral blindness. They need these skills for manipulating those fools who shall fall victim to the corrosiveness of their life's work.

The three operations comprise a **cognitive branch of evil.** The word "cognitive" in this context refers to a process of knowing, or more precisely, a knowing derived from the kind of calculation that remains independent of any moral constraints. A private strategy, a pleasing disguise, a freedom to inflict harm--this unholy trio engenders not mere calculation, but a cold-hearted analysis that catapults malevolent thoughts to malevolent actions.

The Terminator gives short shrift to concealment, placing the bulk of his chips on cognitive practice #3. He abdicates responsibility because his program dictates it. But the Terminator, aside from spending little electronic time with secrecy and misdirection, further lacks a component of extraordinary benefit to villains: He does not feel. Arnold exudes no joy in his destructiveness--no exhilaration, no roar of triumph, not even a malicious smile of satisfaction.

Reese tells us that the Terminator can not experience fear. Fine, the inability to fear or to feel any emotion equates here with a lack of remorse. The Terminator possesses no conscience regarding human suffering, thus he has no misgivings before or after murdering an innocent bystander. A **lack of remorse** liberates the villain from mulling over the "rightness" of his actions. The less concern you show for another's death or turmoil, the more focused you can become on **your** needs and **your** work.

Still, with the absence of all emotion comes a liability: This deficit robs the cyborg of yet another tool for vanquishing adversaries: namely, a style of evil brimming with exuberance. Exuberance suggests vitality, and an **exuberance for evil** suggests vitality channeled toward obscene aims. Castor Troy of *Face / Off* (1997) enveloped himself in the obsceneness of creating chaos, as described in Lesson 1. Now, compare Castor and his ebullience for evil with Arnold and his methodicalness, the *sine qua non* of a robot's nature. Does Arnold possess what Castor displays in abundance, to wit, a distinctiveness of style and vitality? No, the Terminator not only does not have it, he commands no resource to comprehend it.

Compare, too, the cinematic difference of Schwarzenegger mindlessly rat-tat-tatting his victims and the **perverse beauty** of a villain who executes his prey with flair. Tom Udo

(Richard Widmark) gives us the classic scene in *Kiss Of Death* (1947) when he shoves an invalid woman in her wheelchair down a flight of stairs. He pushes her, shrieking with "hyena-like laughter" at his "clever" execution (Nash & Ross, 1986, p. 1550). Udo manifests a macabre glee through the joy of terrorizing a defenseless soul, and, frankly, through the exuberance of being evil. His inane mirth gives him an unholy dimension that no robot can match.

Evil's exuberance, however, need not always require earth-shattering lungs to announce its presence. The villain can talk softly, deliberately, in a whisper even, although you sense an inward surge of wicked zest. Laurence Oliver's character of Szell prompts this impression in *Marathon Man* (1976), directed by John Schlesinger and written by William Goldman. Szell, searching for gems, believes that his captive, Babe Levy (Dustin Hoffman), may know their location. Szell asks quietly, "Is it safe?", a question in code that Levy does not understand. The question becomes a precursor to pain. As Szell calmly repeats the query, he uses his dental tools to drill into Levy's teeth--sans an anesthetic, naturally. Shouting or screeching would have undermined the banality of evil so mockingly portrayed in this scene. A leisurely stab of the drill strikes a familiar fear, unnerving to all who remember their last dental visit. Unnerving, most certainly, when Szell uses the drill as a slow torture that allows us to glimpse the zealous ogre beneath his mild-mannered exterior.

Thus, when George Brougham says "Evil **is**", he expresses the words of an ardent disciple. George preens himself, delighting in the belief that he has duped those about him. Unlike the Terminator's open and affectless pursuit, George Brougham's self-effacing veneer masks a pride of achievement. By god, he has murdered 107 people, yet here he stands as a guest in the Brutenholm mansion. The moral distance between his priorities and the Brutenholms' sense of decency gives him a meteoric high to rival any chemical concoction. George is invulnerable at this dizzying moment, armed not with a suit of robotic armor, but with the mantle of Nietzschean power (Macdonald, 1986, p. 102). He is Superman, he is Alpha and Omega, he is the Cat's Meow.

EVIL AND GODLINESS

George realizes a power that only the truly evil can embrace. Undaunted by moral precepts, he basks in the exhilaration of his wickedness: an **emotional evil** complements his cognitive skills. He never thought of himself as an average mortal anyway; and, now, his ascendance to the Brutenholm family and their estate confirms a higher calling.

The power of evil presumes a state of godliness. **Godliness**, in this instance, is not next to goodliness. Evil's exuberance denotes an extraordinary experience, and George's ego demands no less than a fitting image to rival this experience. For him, godliness becomes the only image that matters.

George Brougham's belief in his rarified stature is not unique. *Manhunter* (1986), written and directed by Michael Mann and based on Thomas Harris's novel, *Red Dragon* (1981), introduces us to Hannibal Lecter (Brian Cox) who tells FBI Agent Will Graham (William Peterson) that "...God has power. And if one does what God does enough times, one will become as God is." Hannibal may find himself behind bars but he hardly wants for company. He dismisses the notion of anyone more worthy than himself. The same film also gives us Francis Dollarhyde (Tom Noonan), a serial killer who magnifies his terrorizing majesty by telling one hapless victim, "You owe me awe." Both murderers show contempt of those peasants seeking to explain them, and both assume a higher order of existence that only they understand.

Evil's exuberance is infectious. Addictive. Transforming. Graham Marshall (Michael Caine) succumbs to the experience in *A Shock To The System* (1990), directed by Jan Egleson and written by Andrew Klavan, based on Simon Brett's novel. Graham is frightened when, on one of his gloomiest days, he accidentally(?) bumps a homeless tyrant off a subway platform and into the train's path. Marshall expects the police to discover him, but nothing happens. This windfall causes him to ponder his own undesirable state, both at home and at work. A little quiver of satisfaction arises to nudge his darker self awake. He escapes after the subway incident, and his success makes him feel good...very, very good.

Being a business executive, Graham thrives on the challenge of competition. How different is this challenge and that of outwitting pedestrian officials who scurry about trying to solve murder upon murder? Not so different, Graham thinks. Besides, why not combine the two practices and position himself for the leadership that is rightfully his? And why not exercise the same tactics in ridding himself of a nagging wife, making work and home more compatible to his new-found program? So, demonstrating an exquisite sense of timing and awareness, he does.

Graham Marshall manages to surpass all moral and physical obstacles, but, more important, he truly enjoys his success. He enjoys it so much that in an entrepreneurial spirit he eliminates not only his wife and immediate superior, he also arranges a private airplane explosion to scatter one of the company's top executives hither and yon. Confident that he will succeed before hearing the "tragic" news, Graham smiles and says with relish, "Bye, bye, baby. Boom."

He begins by narrating in the third person, as if to maintain distance from his darker self. But by story's end, the third-person narrative becomes first person. Evil's perverse delights unify and drive Graham's considerable energies, permitting him to ascend in spirit and purpose. Graham's exaltation leads naturally to godliness. Mentally, he is blessed with Merlin's "magic." Given his gift of sorcery, no foe shall stand against him, and no woman can resist his charms.

A detective, Lieutenant Laker (Will Patton), probes the "accidental" death of the young executive, Bobby Benham (Peter Riegert), who the company promoted over Graham. The detective asks Graham, "He was your superior, wasn't he?" And Graham replies, "No, he was my boss." Had Laker discerned the full import of that answer, he would have sampled the essence of Graham Marshall: crafty, facile in dealing with "inferiors," and gloriously swept up in mowing down the opposition. Cognitively and emotionally, Graham feels that the power is his. It is, truly, more fully his than that power proscribed for the Terminator.

Graham Marshall stands at the threshold of divine conceit. His darker self and his atrocious plans realize secure protection through secrecy--the same practice of secrecy that pervades the perturbations of big business, and, more personally, the executive safeguard of playing your cards close to the vest.

Marshall also makes suave use of his talent at misdirection. The firm's faithful people look to him for guidance. Graham shepherds his flock effortlessly, radiating "warmth" and "concern," making them feel that he understands their problems from their point of view. And he does--but away from his flock, Graham also mercilessly downsizes the operation and dispatches those employees of no use to him. Misdirection achieves a 180 degree turn in this duplicity: Loyal followers assume they are traveling from A to B with Graham, when, on occasion, he deftly reverses direction. Without warning, he moves from B to A, casting off those individuals assumed less able to contribute to the firm's future.

Note that even on a cognitive level, Graham Marshall's skill in surviving and in gaining retribution against his "enemies" already constitutes an accomplishment not attained by HAL in Lesson 1. Recall that HAL had problems with secrecy and misdirection, giving himself away by his awkward inquiries to Bowman. Graham Marshall commits this mistake with one person, a situation he handles adroitly by transferring her to another of the firm's branches.

Emotionally, of course, Graham Marshall transports himself to evil's version of paradise. The executive's wickedness elevates his stature and suffuses him with self-adoration, a state of mind that neither HAL nor the Terminator manage to understand. Graham Marshall, for now, revels in his masterly position as he looks down on the riffraff engaged in their daily doldrums.

Evil's emotional pitch allows murderers like Graham to imagine all sorts of titillations and triumphs. One ritual concerns the predator who seeks to lose himself in the sheer terror of his prey. Wendy Lesser (1993, pp. 145-146), examining the relationship between art and murder, argues that murder's fascination involves a special kind of empathy, not only by the murderer but by the audience, too. The murderer glories in sampling the gamut of emotions that overwhelms the victim, just before death.

Imagining ourselves inside the murderer enables us to feel a kind of power. Imagining ourselves inside the victim enables us to yield ourselves to a certain defenselessness. The murderer's desire for power, in the most interesting of these stories, is one which also includes a desire for that defenselessness. He too seeks to be inside his victim.

The question is why. Why should the murderer (and the audience) desire to experience this harrowing form of empathy? The answer--or at least one answer--is not very pleasant. What better way to savor the torture and the execution than to feel the victim's torment? Such a pathological attachment may seem contradictory for the murderer, but, remember, the power he craves grants him special dispensation: the excitement of attaining absolute control over a life.

The murderer will not capture the full integrity of his victim's beleaguered state, because whatever the killer feels, his cushion of personal safety sets predator and prey apart. But for the murderer who aspires to a visionary rapport with the condemned, vicariously experiencing the victim's throes of death represents a godly moment that must seem tantamount to evil in full plumage.

The inspiration to do more and greater wickedness, however, fosters a loss of perspective. Utilized well, the intelligence and vigor needed to implement a crackling scheme of deception and betrayal require a personality supremely confident of his (or her) aptitude for evil. But the exuberance of godliness comes at a price. A spiraling case of arrogance and overconfidence can bring the almighty evildoer against a most worthy enemy--himself. We turn next to evil's imperfections, and the toll that wickedness inflicts on those godly manipulators who lose sight of their destiny.

Lesson 3

Evil's Imperfections

Question: If exceptional evildoers can behave so cleverly and delightedly in making the most of their cognitive and emotional capacities, why do they get caught? If these wicked sophisticates prove so cunning and carefree in deed and conscience, why should they **ever** get punished?

They do, of course, because the script demands it. But a more palatable answer involves the mythic confrontation between good and evil. Good guys fight only when provoked, and bad guys do the provoking. This cinematic code enjoys its shadings, although once the smoke clears, the party left standing is not the bad guy. The party left standing, in fact, symbolizes a juggernaut called goodness--and there is no way on God's green earth that mortal evildoers can survive this caliber of opposition.

So, if mortality poses a problem, how about an immortal adversary? An adversary, say, like Satan, the devil proper. Surely Evil with a capital E governs the resources to torch any number of flawed souls. How well does goodness rival an absolute opponent who assumes the preeminent role model of decadence? And, more confusing, how adroitly does goodness defend its integrity? Not all evil boasts a capital E, and not all goodness radiates a lily-white glow. Even in film, in supposed classic confrontations of Right and Wrong, goodness and evil can harbor an unsettling spirit of compromise.

THE CINEMATIC SATAN

Consider, first, the assets that Satan brings to the table. Most prominent among these advantages concerns **the great asymmetry**, the power to destroy and suddenly cast asunder years of creative work and nurturement. This destruction can encompass the abrupt cessation of life, the unexpected loss of happiness, or the dashing of material accomplishments. Stephen Jay Gould (1998, p. 813) argues that evil's capacity to execute the great asymmetry rests, not with the content of science, but with human choice:

> ...The essential human tragedy, and the true source of science's potential misuse for destruction, lies in the ineluctable nature of this great asymmetry, not in the character of knowledge itself. We perform 10,000 acts of small and unrecorded kindness for each surpassingly rare, but sadly balancing, moment of cruelty. The shot of one assassin can launch a preventable war; one impulsive murder can topple years of trust carefully built by thousands of benevolent citizens in ethnically diverse communities.

Likewise, Deborah Tannen (1998, p. 82), author of *The Argument Culture*, notes that harsh words possess an especially chilling effect: "Words can be like weapons of destruction: It takes so much effort, and the cooperation of so many people, to build something--and so little effort of so few to tear it down." A vicious verbal assault, for instance, can sap a victim's confidence and linger far longer than the condemnation deserves.

Evil's lightening strike, therefore, harbors the potency to obliterate years of good will and charitable deeds. The tally accounts for millions of life histories lost in the Holocaust of World War II, thousands of histories in Vietnam, 168 histories in the Oklahoma City bombing, or the loss of a single promising life when a loved one perishes by cruel design. And the tally need not reflect physical loss alone: It may include sadistic attacks by any medium equipped to propagate expressions of ridicule, humiliation, and character assassination. Evil's swift sabre sports an armamentarium of considerable potential.

The power of wickedness, upon reflection, is undeniable. But such power matters little if its executioners take a pratfall, or otherwise fumble away evil's vast resources. Aptitude relates to a flair, a genius, a knack, a propensity, a special fitness for conducting a task well. An **aptitude for evil**, as we have observed, indicates a talent to engage in wicked ways and devious pursuits. Realistically, this malevolent talent comprises a concert of biological and social influences that drives the offender to calculate, manipulate, and inflict harm. Film portrayals, however, frequently evoke such evil through the exclusive urges of a beast within.

The **cinematic Satan**, for example, appears unlikely to possess any other kind of nature. Imagine your profile as Satan: Being absolutely wicked means never having to say you are sorry. No need to excuse your foul language or conduct, unless, by choice, you desire to pretend otherwise. The advantage of intellectually and emotionally emancipating yourself from any obligation to others permits you to focus on selfish ventures. These ventures may prove legitimate if you play the game as a ruthless entrepreneur; or illegitimate if you choose to pursue pleasure as a connoisseur of avarice. Either way, you win. Indeed, speaking absolutely, you seem destined to win, win, win.

Portraying the devil in film and literature, nonetheless, means imposing artistic limitations by giving Satan a mortal configuration (Stanford, 1996, p. 262). The most severe restrictions occur when Satan, always in the market for lost souls, cuts a Faustian bargain with the hero...and loses. Given his potential to deceive, the odds seem to favor Satan and his temptations. Why should the devil lose when paired against the human condition?

And yet lose he does, if only because his selfish eye fails to appreciate the resilience that goodness can muster. **Buoyant characterizations of Satan** personify the Evil One as especially arrogant and narcissistic in underestimating this strength of goodness. So, he loses, despite his fervor and incisiveness when exploiting human vanities. He loses in the courtroom, usurped by Daniel Webster's sharp trial wit in *The Devil And Daniel Webster* (1941); he loses a presumably lost soul when the hero redeems himself as a judge who dispenses proper justice in *Angel On My Shoulder* (1946) and in *Alias Nick Beal* (1949); he even loses a soul pact with a baseball player, whose love for his wife foils the devil's plans in *Damn Yankees* (1958); and he loses when his buffoonery causes the devil to appear more mischievous than evil, allowing three alluring females to outfox him in *The Witches Of Eastwick* (1987).

Somber characterizations of Satan, however, prove more frightening. The odds of redemption plummet, and the bastions of decency pay a higher price in combat. A head rolls, literally, in *The Omen* (1976) as good-hearted folks act too late to prevent the young anti-Christ from holding forth; a slick, enigmatic Satan in *Angel Heart* (1987) sends a ragged private eye on the torturous path of searching for a murderous soul, only to inform the deluded investigator that **he** is that lost soul; a doubting priest in *The Exorcist* (1973) entices a demon from a young girl into himself, sacrificing his life to free her; and Satan's helpers guilefully prep an innocent young woman for mating with Old Scratch himself in *Rosemary's Baby* (1968), producing an heir whom the new mother finds repulsive, yet responds to with maternal affection.

The cinematic Satan, whether buoyant or somber in mood, does not coerce souls with such dispatch as to offer the victim no hope of salvation. Indeed, salvation is the reason that Satan plays the game: The excitement of evil to tempt, titillate, and otherwise triumph over a prey's wavering conscience affords the challenge of a conflict not wholly predictable in outcome. The target, in other words, has a choice.

John Milton (Al Pacino) relishes this choice in *The Devil's Advocate* (1997), directed by Taylor Hackford, written by Jonathan Lemkin and Tony Gilroy, and based on Andrew Niederman's novel. Milton, as mentor, takes in a dynamic criminal lawyer from Florida, Kevin Lomax (Keanu Reeves). Milton cajoles, but never demands. He reads Kevin as a good guy, yet also as a vain and ambitious guy--two lovely qualities that Milton nurtures for his own tempestuous enjoyment.

The Devil's Advocate provides a charismatic Satan, full of braggadocio, bawdiness, and old-fashion Beezebulb charm. Milton is, to wit, a mass of contradictions, befitting the kind of devilish temperament that connects more with vaudeville than the city morgue. Any misdirection on John Milton's part stems from confusing and overwhelming his victims with theatrics, rather than in harboring a steadfast secrecy.

John worries less about maintaining secrecy or misdirection because, as Satan, he enjoys the cover of a powerful law firm. Moreover, if John becomes too transparent as Lucifer, he can always go into exile again, or just disappear for a time. John Milton, however, savors his perversity, comparable to the devilish personalities we encountered in Lesson 2--namely, George Brougham in *The List Of Adrian Messenger* (1963) and Graham Marshall in *A Shock To The System* (1990).

Milton not only glories in tempting Kevin with an assortment of beautiful ladies, he also casts a lustful eye toward Kevin's wife, Mary Ann (Charlize Theron). In one scene, simmering with salaciousness, John quietly talks Mary Ann into pulling her hair back to effect a more sensuous appearance. He does not touch her in any unnatural way, yet his hovering, erotic presence leaves the heart thumping with apprehension...and anticipation. Here we witness exuberant evil at work--tinkering, caressing, carousing--and tantalizing us with an unanswered question: Will he or will he not attempt to corrupt Mary Ann?

Kevin finally realizes his own Great Fall and the grand import of Satan's machinations. Somehow, the young lawyer pulls himself together to perform the honorable act: He commits suicide, much to Milton's distress. Or does he? No, Kevin has only fantasized this story of his Great Ascent and Great Fall. He is still in Florida, still possessed of a promising law career, and has yet to confront John Milton's paradise of enticements. We wish Kevin to avoid the pitfalls he examines in his fantasized nightmare, but vanity casts a long lariat. The dream does not vanquish John Milton, it merely whets his appetite to overcome Kevin's increased awareness of good and evil. The game is still afoot.

Satan's success, or the success of anyone invoking Luciferesque aspirations, depends on a formula for evil. No perfect formula exists, as the various interpretations of Satan suggest, but an approximation is not beyond question. What

you do in the name of evil, and how well you do it, depends
on your talent for manipulation. Philip Wuntch (1997, p. 5-
C), in his summary of Satanic film roles, notes that "This
collection of dark knights proves only one thing. There have
been many interesting devils. But there's never been such a
thing as a perfect devil."

SATAN'S FAMILY OF LOSERS

The origin and purpose of evil conjures up a hand-me-down
history, derived by storytellers to capture the scriptural
significance of the warring factions that prevailed. Differing
tales over the centuries attest to the adaptation of ideas about
evil, ideas that accommodated the social calamities of a
particular era.

Thus, we hear little of Satan in the Old Testament because
Yahweh--the Old Testament God--does such a marvelous job
of convincing the Hebrews that He possesses the powers of
good **and** evil (Sanford, 1982, p. 26). With Yahweh around to
scare hell out of the ancient Hebrews, they have no need of
Satan as a separate character.

The New Testament, however, reflects the need to envision
a less wrathful God. A God where evil finds manifestation
through actions attributed to an opposing entity. One New
Testament version has this figure--addressed impersonally as
the satan--working in a supernatural and adversarial capacity
for God. His task? The satan behaves to obstruct an
individual's path, sometimes instigating a reversal of fortune
to steer this person away from harm (Pagels, 1995, p. 40).

A benevolent Satan, however, is not the Satan we know.
Elaine Pagels (1995, p. 44), in *The Origin Of Satan*, clarifies
Satan's descent by noting that later storytellers give the figure
a more sinister characterization: an angel gone bad, a fallen
angel, an angel no longer in God's favor, prepared to do battle
as an enemy of God and goodness. But an enemy who does
not invariably characterize the distant outsider; an enemy
frequently close in body and spirit, perhaps someone we trust
who turns against us out of jealousy or greed (Pagels, p. 49).

Aside from the great asymmetry and its devastating consequences, we also observe Satan's strengths of **versatility** and **elusiveness**. He possesses versatility in that the cinematic and literary imagination allows him to masquerade proficiently as a legion of dark souls; and he shows elusiveness by working most effectively when a pompous disbeliever denies his existence (or, as John Milton in *The Devil's Advocate* expresses this advantage, "Don't let them see you coming").

Even in name, Satan's identity denotes a contradiction in terms. One of his aliases, **Beliar**, means "without light," a force representing the "sons of darkness" in the war between heaven and earth (Pagels, pp. 58-59). But a contrary alias, **Lucifer**, also exists and differs markedly from other names because it indicates "the light-bringer" (Sanford, 1982, p. 112).

Satan's impressive names and what they appear to portend, however, fail to compensate for this creature's most dismal prognosis. Frankly, whether we settle on Beliar, Beelzebub, Mephistopheles, 666, or the old-fashioned Devil, Satan's real problem concerns the Biblical declaration that **the sacrifice of Jesus on the cross, and His resurrection, spell finis for Satan**. The Devil can ply his trade, tempt our souls, inspire homicide and genocide, and do any number of heinous deeds. But he shall never, ever, win the ultimate contest with goodness. Elaine Pagels (1995, p. 180) states the outcome in these words:

> I am not saying that the gospel accounts are essentially Manichaean in the ordinary sense of the term, that they envision good and evil evenly matched against each other. Christian tradition derives much of its power from the conviction that although the believer may feel besieged by evil forces, Christ has already won the decisive victory.

Andrew Delbanco (1995, p. 54), in *The Death Of Satan*, expresses the same denouement in this fashion:

> Damned in the sense that he can never escape himself, the devil is finally "unclean" because he is a tortured soul who needs to make other souls dance to the music of his own despair....According to every school of Christian eschatology, the devil knows that he will ultimately be defeated by being driven out of his playground world, and so he is desperate to frolic while he can.

Imagine Satan's dilemma, given this line of thought. He shoulders such potential to desecrate and destroy, yet he knows with sinking certainty that no feast of triumph awaits him. He can behave deceitfully, or he can rant and rave and shower his lost souls with shards of hell, but he will not defeat the forces of good at Armageddon. Satan and his family of evil protégés are, in essence, losers. Evil's imperfections center on a permanent flaw, an intrinsic defect: **Satan's promises of fulfillment can not, themselves, be fulfilled.**

Possibly the primary psychological advantage remaining to Satan concerns a belief in his failure to exist. He makes the greatest progress when prospective clients cease to take his capabilities seriously (Delbanco, 1995, p. 23; Sanford, 1981, p. 110). Taking Satan lightly or rationalizing him out of contention offers evil all the invitation it needs. Lyall Watson (1995, pp. 263-264), in his study of evil in nature, illustrates the danger of intellectualizing Satan away:

> There always seems to be an evil being who tries to entice us into doing wrong. In the Bible and Koran, it is Satan; while in Buddhist scripture he appears as the arch-tempter Mara. Their job description is the same: "Look innocent and lure humans into minor transgressions that can grow into major problems." Start with a little gentle flirting and let things escalate from there into full-scale orgies.

To "Look innocent and lure humans" reiterates our first two cognitive practices of evil: secrecy and misdirection. Rather than dismiss Satan or evil as antiquated notions, a more prudent course concerns recognizing the strengths and weaknesses of the truly malevolent personality. Regardless of Satan's bleak scriptural future, evildoers possess a vitality that we ignore at our peril.

Better to recall those cognitive and emotional assets that comprise the exceptional villain, as we did in Lessons 1 and 2. Better still, to explore evil's imperfections in this lesson: Where are the points of fracture that handicap the malignant personality? The warnings sound loud and clear when good and evil assume classic proportions. No secrecy or misdirection here, since the contest ascends to a level of mythic figures in combat. We need no divine guidance to ascertain the adversaries. Good shall win since good designates the mightier foe, although evil will extract its price, even in defeat.

But what transpires when good and evil prove less distinctive? Evil, for instance, may even hawk its "virtues" in the name of goodness. Why not contend that, on occasion, "evil" needs a little "good" to succeed. Evil by stealth, in other words, demands a more rigorous standard of detection than evil by pronouncement.

CLASSIC GOOD, CLASSIC EVIL

Evil by pronouncement sets the scene with a clarity that permits GOOD and EVIL to anchor the forces of light and darkness in a classic setting. The real West seldom attained such clarity, but the cinematic West naturally orchestrated the forces of good and evil for maximum effect: ugliness against beauty, rich against poor, cattle barons against homesteaders.

Alan Ladd plays Shane, a man gifted with an invisible draw, yet a man also conditioned to give the same, knee-jerk reaction whenever he hears an ominous sound: The cocking of a child's rifle will suffice, as will any loud, unexpected noise. Shane is a gunfighter, and he is not happy about it. The years have made him lean in spirit and, now, he is traveling just to be traveling.

Shane (1952) offers us a fine melodrama in three acts, directed by George Stevens, written by A. B. Guthrie, Jr. and Jack Sher, and based on Jack Schaefer's novel. Act 1 begins with the opening credits as we see Shane enter a valley bordering the Grand Tetons. He befriends the homesteaders there and settles in with one family: Joe Starrett (Van Heflin), Marion (Jean Arthur), and their son, Joey (Brandon de Wilde). This family seeks to unite the other farmers and resist attempts by a cattleman, Ryker (Emile Meyer), who wishes to keep the range as grazing land. Shane decides to stay and become Starrett's farm hand. Perhaps, just perhaps, he may find another way to live.

Shane fails, of course. He fails for several reasons,

paramount among them is a dark gunfighter named Wilson. Act 2 commences with a shivery flourish of music as Wilson (Jack Palance) makes his leisurely, menacing entrance on horseback. When he arrives at the ramshackle town of Grafton, even the saloon dog finds him too threatening and moves away. That is one smart dog, smarter than some of the macho characters who thinly populate the Wyoming plains.

When Ryker and Wilson visit Starrett's spread, and Ryker speaks with Starrett of their differences, a silent appraisal between Shane and Wilson ensues. Richard Slotkin (1992, p. 398), in his examination of frontier mythology, analyzes this encounter according to the personalities who hold the real power of resolution:

> And while this palaver is going on--raising matters that would be at the heart of any "progressive epic"--the camera is watching Shane and Wilson size each other up. They say nothing; they merely look and smile a little smile. They know that the talk of rights and wrongs has become meaningless. Pride and economics make it certain that neither Ryker nor Starrett can back down. Violent force alone will settle the issue, and the gunfighters are the ones who best understand that truth. Ryker and Starrett and their original objectives are reduced to the mere premises from which the action will arise, but the action itself will be entrusted to professionals.

Shane and Wilson find themselves in the same profession, yet light years apart in attitude. Unlike Shane, Wilson bears no remorse over lives taken. His concern, instead, rests with maintaining a gunfighter's reputation. In keeping with the classic macho's penchant for allowing actions to say more than words, Wilson's evil requires little dialogue. His mere presence communicates waves of dread and foreboding. He looks, he smiles, he enjoys knowing how to kill. More importantly, he knows that most cowboys **don't** know how, nor do they enjoy it; therefore, Wilson, as a silent harbinger of death, holds a commanding edge.

He proves his pleasure in an early gunfight by challenging Torrey (Elisha Cook, Jr.), a harmless braggart devoted to the Confederacy. Torrey crosses a muddy street and approaches the saloon, only to meet Wilson, dressed in black and positioned to call him out. Grinning, Wilson moves on the saloon porch, clear of the mud, walking parallel with Torrey, who must step through the grime as he looks up at the gunfighter. Their dialogue prefaces the murder: A soft taunt from Wilson, disparaging Stonewall Jackson; a tremulous reply from Torrey, questioning Wilson's heritage and calling him a Yankee liar.

End of dialogue: Torrey reaches for his gun in a lame draw that finds his weapon pointed no higher than the ground. Wilson has already drawn and waits, savoring the moment. An onlooker shouts "No, Torrey!" Torrey freezes, head almost bowed, gun still pointed down, when Wilson fires. The bullet's impact slings Torrey backward into the mud. End of Torrey. (Elisha Cook, Jr., who enjoyed a long career of playing the victim, truly found himself sailing backward. The director, George Stevens, attached wires to Cook and launched him accordingly to enhance the scene's grim reality.)

Torrey, the amateur, scared, outclassed, and forced by his manhood into a death match against Wilson, the cool professional. And the screen has produced no cooler, more enigmatic gunfighter than the whispery evil figure portrayed by Jack Palance. He is the classic evil that Torrey faces, as Torrey, trembling and alone, waits to die.

The final insult occurs when another homesteader must walk in the mud to retrieve Torrey's body. The homesteader tentatively starts towards the body, then stops. He stops because Wilson, holding his smoking gun aloft, glances his way and holds the farmer with a mocking stare. The homesteader and the viewer wonder, what will the gunfighter do next?

Wilson, however, merely exercises his power to make the man wait for a command. Smiling, he holsters his gun and goes inside the saloon. This action tells the homesteader that he is free to remove Torrey, a task the gunfighter does not bother to watch. In effect, the homesteader is cleaning up the remains of Wilson's malevolent act. Director Stevens shows, moreover, that pulling a dead-weight corpse through a slippery mudhole constitutes an arduous and humiliating chore. As the scene fades, a soft chuckle from a hostile witness contemptuously echoes the homesteader's struggle to carry Torrey's lifeless form away.

Act 3 brings the showdown. Both Shane and Joe Starrett know that a trap awaits them in town, but the macho image dictates that someone must go and right the wrongs that Wilson and Ryker have imposed on innocent families. The game is Shane's game, not Joe's. Joe is a farmer, although he feels obligated as leader of the homesteaders to do the manly thing. The two friends fight and Shane wins by clubbing Joe unfairly with his handgun. "Unfairly" as in a classic hero's actions, but eminently fair in the sense that Shane knows Joe will surely die if allowed to leave.

So, the prelude begins. The music swells and we see Shane silhouetted in the distance, riding to do a job that he does all too well. Joey and his dog follow at some distance, leaving their icon of goodness (the Starrett farm) to bear witness to the climax that will unfold at a contrasting icon, the evil's lair in Grafton (Sennett, 1994, p. 141). The expanse between these icons of good and evil--the Tetons, the natural beauty that beckons both warring parties--overwhelms each camp with its vastness and stability.

And the showdown, when it happens, happens in a flash. Shane calls Wilson out, and Wilson, smiling his last smile, is blown away, his body ignominiously dumped among a cache of barrels with the late gunfighter's boots sticking out. The fallen gunfighter now seems a far cry from the evil presence that so frighteningly dispatched Torrey in the mud. More gunplay follows and Ryker and his brother also bite the dust. Shane prevails, but he leaves paying a steep price.

He is wounded, though not seriously. The physical wound will heal. The spirit, however, finds no salvation. Shane tells Joey, "There's no living with a killing." He is a gunfighter who can not escape his calling. Joey and the Starrett family will have a chance to realize a productive life. The time of the open range is passing, as Ryker discovers. And the days of the gunfighter also are numbered, as Shane knows.

Wilson offers us an understated evil, although singular in character and purpose. We know of his strategy and lust for killing all too well, but Shane...well, Shane provokes a sadness. The good gunfighter must ride away at story's end, hunched over his saddle, carrying more than the burden of a gunshot wound. He has lost a way of life; something better, he realizes, than a gunfighter's barren future.

EVIL'S ARROGANCE

Wilson's profile proves rather transparent. He is absolute evil, the dedicated personality who harbors no conflicts over morality. The gunfighter's intentions are clear in that he displays his malice proudly to generate fear. Wilson, consequently, finds little need for the secrecy and misdirection discussed in Lessons 1 and 2. He does not bother to use deceit or charm to make himself appealing. But he heartily subscribes to absolute evil's key requirement: the abdication of responsibility for inflicting terror and pain upon others.

Arrogance designates a demeanor of inestimable value to the villain. This mind-set befits evil because self-importance contributes to the gunfighter's success. Wilson's vanity regarding his skills and his importance complement a menacing image. If he displays less confidence, less certainty in a confrontation, Wilson loses that intangible edge of "winning the contest before it happens." Torrey knew, for example, that he had little chance to survive, and, more importantly, Wilson knew it, too. The contest constituted a foregone conclusion when Wilson called Torrey out.

Still, arrogance as an emotional evil conceals a duplicitous function. This trait, although invoking a demeanor of precious value to the killer, sports an Achilles heel. The evildoer's pride, the strutting, the inflated ego, can trigger an indulgence that leads to inevitable destruction. Absolute evil hobbles Wilson with a self-destructive quality that he does not comprehend. Shane demonstrates the faster draw, yet Wilson's insolence places him in the contest. Given the villain's belief in his dark image, he has no choice but to face Shane. Wilson's arrogance proves too essential and too natural for him to perceive the trait as dangerous. He fails to realize an old adage: What absolute evil giveth, absolute evil taketh. George Brougham's ego in *The List Of Adrian Messenger*

(1963) reflects arrogance as a driving force. He believes in his ability to eliminate foes covertly and to stay a league ahead of the lesser mortals who pursue him. But George's ready contempt of these underlings also clouds his vision. The arrogance that serves him well in duping others blinds him to personal failure: How can someone--anyone--divine his grand scheme? He underestimates goodness, trapping himself by his own extravagances of self-aggrandizement.

Graham Marshall of *A Shock To The System* (1990) outwits a wily detective, Lieutenant Laker, who knows that his suspect is guilty. Graham remains free at the movie's end, but leaves the impression that he is just beginning to savor his power. He will kill again, as Laker hovers to ferret out that tell-tale mistake. In time, Laker shall prevail. Graham's godliness and his magic obscure Laker's dedication to corralling his adversary. Graham's feeling of omnipotence precludes a realistic appraisal of his opposition. Sooner or later, Graham's magic will go...poof!

We may argue that once Graham murders his way to the executive position he covets, he can stop. If so, what a waste of evil talent. So much craftiness to unfurl, so much self-glorification to enhance, so much morbid joy to experience--do we really believe that Graham will stop? No, the truly evil figure admires himself as a finely polished instrument of destruction. He must hone this instrument to perfection, even though it means jeopardizing his very safety. Graham's safety, indeed, becomes his prime reason for playing the game. Nothing less than the risk of losing his godliness can give life the zest he now craves. Hence, we have an instance of how emotional evil--the exuberance of arrogance--can influence cognitive evil in the sense that Graham feels driven to concoct grander upon grander schemes of termination.

CENSORSHIP AND CONTRIVANCE

Arrogance as a "friend" and "foe" represents a reasonable flaw in the consummate villain's profile. We understand the paradox of how arrogance can make someone feel invincible without the corresponding awareness of vulnerability. Were this flaw the malevolent personality's only barrier to success, he might realize a fighting chance to endure. But the odds against that success are substantial.

Actually, murderers like Wilson fail because it **is** in the script. Fans accept the burial and resurrection of macabre figures like Dracula because they know that logic and horror enjoy a loosey-goosey relationship. Fans also know that certain villains will survive annihilation and return, suitably vengeful, to deliver new waves of horror. We see the same script with another addendum to accommodate the next revival.

Such an answer may seem unfair, but various formulaic reasons arise for the villain's scripted demise. One of the more controversial decisions concerns evil at the mercy of **censorship**. Hollywood's Hays Office launched the Production Code in 1934 to regulate filmmakers' more taboo attempts at portraying sex and violence. The Code's section on crime detailed specific prohibitions regarding criminal activities and murder. These prohibitions included no use of minors to incite violence, no explicit details concerning brutality, and no justification for seeking revenge (Gardner, 1987, p. 208).

Killers had to kill humanely, preferably off-camera. Killers murdered with restraint and used a sanitized touch, which meant no unsightly displays of blood and gore. Filmmakers nibbled away at the Code, challenging the censorship board with scenes like Richard Widmark's character, Tom Udo, and his lethal push of the disabled victim down a stairway in the 1947 film, *Kiss Of Death*. But whatever slippage occurred via individual scenes, the Code's moral philosophy of neat-and-tidy violence held sway until the 1960s. Advocates demanded that villains suffer and pay the penalty for their criminal behavior. No matter how cunning or ferocious or powerful, the evil personality must succumb to cinematic justice.

A **chance occurrence** sometimes obliterated the villain, as happens to Rhoda in *The Bad Seed* (1956). She is a minor so the Production Code permits her less latitude than it accords adults to murder someone. Rhoda relates how "accidents" befell her victims, yet we never see her kill anyone. To show Rhoda as a murderess, in any event, depicts a needless horror when the horror, herself, is quite enough (Paul, 1994, p. 275).

The question remains, What to do with this little nightmare? She survives in the stage play to perpetuate a disquieting "innocence," free to engage in more "accidents." But the Production Code will have none of that. A way must materialize to deliver the cinematic Rhoda into perdition.

The answer from writer John Lee Mahin and director Mervin LeRoy involves a fortuitous act of nature (Paul, 1994, p. 279). Rhoda is walking to the pier during a rainy, lightening-filled night to retrieve one of her treasures. Given the child's singular mind-set, nature's elements do not factor in for her. Rhoda blithely disregards the violent sky as a perfectly evil 8-year-old would...and she pays dearly for her impiety. A double zap of intense electrical energy slices from the storm to incinerate our little murderess. No more Rhoda, no more evil, and no need to anguish over her punishment. Instead, *The Bad Seed* offers all concerned a "blameless" option: Chalk up the child's "accident" to the whims of one of nature's more unruly outbursts.

Rhoda's fate does not transpire free of contrivance and criticism, however. The girl's demise seems overly convenient, a cop-out to satisfy the Code's sense of retribution. *The Bad Seed* even adds a cinematic postscript, comparable to the play, recalling the actors for a bow. The final curtain includes Christine, the mother, playfully spanking a laughing Rhoda to remind us that it is all make-believe (Twitchell, 1985, p. 297).

Chance, however, proves too chancy to function effectively in neutralizing evil. Audiences will not condone such happenstance as regular fare, in part because the hero and heroine fail to "earn" the villain's death. **Sensible forces** must conspire to bring the evil one down. A conspiracy exists (1) that requires the adversaries to match wits, and (2) that recognizes the antagonist's deficiencies as deriving naturally from his or her wickedness.

Thus, cinematic portrayals of good and evil usually maintain a sharp distinction to allow the audience a ready identification. But a closer look reveals how easily the evil personality can transport itself through misdirection into a "right" and "proper" figure. The more challenging portrayals of good and evil concern a middle ground of cinematic reality: the mingling of good and evil, the conflict between righteousness and wrongdoing that strays from the absolute.

A COMPLICATED GOODNESS

Goodness covers the nooks and crannies of saintliness, of preferring to help rather than hurt others. **Altruism** depicts the purest manifestation of goodness: the selfless act of placing yourself at risk to aid another individual, not closely related (Trivers, 1971). Endangering yourself to rescue your child counts as admirable behavior, but it depicts conduct less altruistic than endangering yourself to rescue a stranger.

The compleat villain has no problem with goodness. Quite the opposite, assuming an appearance of apparent goodness serves the degenerate well in his nefarious ventures. Cognitive practice #2, misdirection, thrives on well-tailored acts of good will. Suave predators know that they can accomplish more with honey than with vinegar.

During a period of company turmoil, Graham Marshall from *A Shock To The System* murmurs reassurances to his disoriented flock of subordinates: "You, you, and you, panic. The rest of you stay calm." He comforts them, not altruistically, but solicitously as a despot atop his perch. Graham finesses his peasants to function as a corporate family, granting them a supportive presence and reinforcing their image of the executive who cares. What they **do not** hear is Graham's suggestion to a superior about a new policy of employer/employee relations: "We should get rid of anybody that doesn't put the company first."

George Brougham in *The List Of Adrian Messenger* also manipulates goodness in his plan to become master of the Gleneyre estate. He entertains young Derek with tales of Indians and frontier life. George knows that boys find these stories fascinating and uses this knowledge to win Derek over, even as he schedules him for an early execution. George seems entertaining, and, well, a good chap who fits nicely into the Brutenholm social fabric. Had the beast within him gone undetected, George would have heard nary a discouraging word as he charmed his way to become master of the hounds.

The instances by Graham Marshall and George Brougham of using good for evil purposes do not cause much confusion. We know the wickedness of both gentleman, and thus we also know the pretentiousness of their charitable behavior. The difference between good and evil in this context still poses a blissful relief. Good is good, evil is evil, and, ideally, one domain does not contaminate the other.

Pragmatically, however, the personal struggles that pit apparent good against apparent evil prove more circumspect. Goodness becomes a problem for evil when the evil personage feels insecure about his amoral conduct. Indeed, rather than accept the more popular assumption that good suffers the whims of evil temptation, consider the reverse proposition: **that evil struggles for release from the iron maiden of virtue.**

Goodness calls forth obligations to do the "right thing," but goodness, especially of an altruistic nature, also breeds suspicion (Kaufmann, 1970, p. 98; Latane & Darley, 1970, p. 4). We more readily accept sinners than saints because saintliness seems the less natural state. We suspect altruistic-minded individuals of a hidden agenda. Virtue is not its own reward, oh, no. Amid all that goodness, a bit of hedonism lurks, a payoff looms, something is rotten. And whenever that "something" bears out, it makes us feel better about our own flawed halos.

Good deeds, frankly, do not boast the attention, clarity, and swift recognition of evil deeds. Weigh the proportion of bad news to good news in any newspaper or television newscast and you can predict the reliable winner. Indeed, the idea of a **complicated goodness** seems more constructive since this complex notion can revise and compromise even the classic stature of duels engaged by good versus evil. Kathleen Norris (1996, p. 128), in her essays on sharing the ritualistic life at a Benedictine monastery, offers a most pragmatic definition of goodness:

The goal of the monks was to know themselves as they truly were, warts and all, and to be able to call it "good," not in order to excuse bad behavior but to accept the self without delusions. The point was to know the material you were working with, in order to give a firmer foundation to your hope for change....For myself, I appreciate their realism about human beings confronted by evil, and the good sense that does not allow them to be easily fooled when evil attempts to disguise itself by adopting innocuous dress.

A reasonable assessment of goodness, therefore, involves the bite of reality: Leave the delusions of grandeur to evil, and realize that "good" and "evil" do not constitute polar opposites. A complicated goodness lacks the long-term, pure-in-spirit essence to rival the 100 percent rottenness of absolute evil, although goodness, even compromised, continues to contest evil as a prevailing force.

Shane is the good gunfighter, but he **is** a gunfighter, not a saint. Presumably early in his career the gunfighter had an opportunity to walk away from his skills, and he did not. Shane becomes evil's nemesis, although Shane assumes this role as a hero in conflict. He is not Wilson (thank goodness!) but he is not Joe Starrett, either. He is a man trying to find his soul, and goodness is not making it easy for him.

One scene shows the homesteaders gathered inside the Starretts' cabin as they discuss the wisdom of staying and challenging Ryker. Shane, however, stands outside the window in a pouring rain, forever the outsider. A classic hero who does not belong--not with the Starretts, certainly not with Wilson and his ilk, but sadly, not with anyone, anywhere. A man whose inherent civility finds constant torment because of his skills as a gunfighter (Solomon, 1976, p. 39).

More to the point, goodness hurts. Confronting goodness and to be found wanting dredges up an unnerving experience. Alfie Kohn (1990, pp. 41-42), examining goodness in everyday life, comments on the pain:

Just as assumptions of "natural" wickedness allow us to justify our own slimy behavior, so evidence to the contrary threatens to pin responsibility on us for what we do--and for what we dimly recognize we might not have the courage to do.

C. S. Lewis's *The Screwtape Letters* (1982) sets the tone by acquainting us with Screwtape and his nephew, Wormwood. Wormwood faces the unenviable mission of spreading the evil word. To do so, he must somehow usurp his mortal subjects' orientation to goodness. Wormwood's recurring failures and Screwtape's chronicles of these failures become devilish attempts by the uncle to bolster his nephew's sagging ego.

Goodness casts a far-reaching light, an illuminance as continual as it is bright; an illuminance incessant enough for Screwtape and Wormwood to know that goodness can dim even evil's most shadowy prospects. The nonscientific idea that we harbor an evil beast may prove a moot point (Klama, 1988, p. 152). If such a beast exists, it exists at its own peril.

Imagine the consequences of evil, compromised. Had George Brougham, or Graham Marshall, or Rhoda faltered in their wickedness, the gainful quests they managed would never have materialized. Graham, tentative at first after the vagrant's death, rapidly crystallizes his true calling by developing an evil mind-set. This mind-set provides the focus and inspiration that Graham needs to optimize his cognitive and emotional qualities as a top-flight executioner. But if he had mired himself in the morality of taking a life--such as allowing himself misgivings about murdering his wife-- Graham Marshall would have been easy pickings for Lieutenant Laker, the detective tracking him.

Had Rhoda not received evil's absolution as a "bad seed," could she have accomplished three murders? The idea of a **bad seed** carries an appealing simplicity: Babies born evil, stay evil. Rhoda manifests a predisposition to wickedness that knows no limitations, save for her juvenile state. Most experts do not subscribe to the bad seed notion, since the assumption of an evil infant seems a trifle early to denounced goodness. A babe in arms ought to at least realize an opportunity for redemption. Social scientists argue that experience always contributes to the temperament and demeanor of a child.

Certainly if Rhoda had responded positively to her loving parents and to the healthy rearing practices they afforded her, evil would have seemed hard-pressed to combat love's smothering presence. Predisposition, in this line of thought, does not mean destiny.

How utterly frightening for prospects of wickedness. If potential delinquents must devoutly contend with goodness for a crumb of evil encouragement, even at birth, imagine the many opportunities for conflicting behavior. No self-respecting evildoer can work well, much less elegantly, harnessed to that kind of mind lock. Evil needs considerable help to withstand the inertia of aging, the intervention of busybody do-gooders, and the bountiful cheer given to altruistic endeavors.

Evil, frankly, requires a little assistance from the inner self. For a real conundrum of good and evil, consider the case of Travis Bickle, the Robert De Niro character in *Taxi Driver* (1976). Travis, a misfit and loner, decides to assassinate a presidential candidate, for reasons that have nothing to do with politics and everything to do with his convoluted thinking about sex and power. He arms his anatomy in every way necessary, but aborts the assassination attempt only because agents spot him in the crowd as a suspicious figure.

Comparable to the strategy of real assassins, if one target proves unavailable, then shift to the next most desirable figure. Subsequently, Travis performs his own rite of emancipation by killing a pimp and others who control Iris, a child prostitute played by Jodie Foster. Iris does not ask for this freedom, but Travis reaches a point in his lurid view of life that he must act on what is right and what is wrong. His simpleminded morality, ticking on the brink of emotional chaos, compels him to return her to her parents. And from her parents he later receives a letter labeling him a hero.

Is Travis Bickle a hero? No, not as Shane carries the title. A villain? Again, no, not in the sense of a Wilson, a George Brougham, or a Graham Marshall. Honestly, we remain uncertain about the axis of good and evil for Travis. A man of deteriorating mental faculties proposes an assumed "good deed" by removing a young girl from prostitution, yet he does so by pursuing an unorthodox and illegal solution of violence. We suspect, in time, the taxi driver shall ultimately make a disastrous move that will cost him his freedom, and possibly his life.

EVIL'S SAFEGUARDS

Fortunately for the dark kingdom, evil wayfarers possess one black ace in the hole that goodness finds difficult to match: **Evil commands fascination.** We do not cluster at gruesome murder scenes just to express sympathy for the victims. We do not indulge in gossip solely to hear and convey good tidings. We do not attend movies to root for the hero and heroine alone. Evil bewitches our conscience through its absolute contempt for what most of us hold dear.

Sometimes connoisseurs of wickedness undermine our sense of control, although jeopardizing that sense can prove invigorating as entertainment. We feel close to Captain John Miller (Tom Hanks) and his squad in *Saving Private Ryan* (1998), even though we see the squad kill Germans willing to surrender. This breach of morality proves acceptable, in part, because of the relentless peril that Miller and his men face, day to day, minute to minute: a sniper's bullet, a land mine, or a tactical decision, such as Miller's arguable choice to risk his men and his leadership in taking out a machine-gun nest that they have the option to avoid.

Customarily, **sacrifice** designates one safeguard to keep evil's perverse fascination flourishing. Former Governor Edmund Brown (1989, p. 153) argues that the power to put people to death serves "as a kind of talisman against the dark forces that surround and threaten us all." Put another way, the murderer depicts "society's permanent scapegoat" (Symons, 1985, p. 19). Absolute evil must suffer absolute damnation. Goodness demands nothing less. When unrelenting evil enters the picture, we prefer not to accept lukewarm retribution. The wicked should die wickedly. No other recourse seems equitable or sufficient.

Our entrancement with evil, therefore, contains a safety net. We balance an attraction to dark forces by exacting a lethal price for this attraction. Evil must perish, regardless of its power and beauty. The sacrifice will happen, if not through the sword of legal justice, then by some fate as yet unforeseen. For Wilson, it arises through the arrogance of one gunfight too many. For Rhoda, it becomes nature's intervention. For George Brougham, it materializes as an underestimation of the enemy, a mistake that leads to his being impaled upon the needles of a reaping machine. For Graham Marshall, who knows? Suffice to say that some ironic twist shall occur to bring his ego down. Given the man's imperious inspirations, he must suffer a cinematic death commensurate with his free-wheeling spirit of vengeance.

The problem with evil in *Saving Private Ryan*, however, concerns the almighty price paid by the allied forces of goodness to repel and conquer the scurrilous Nazis and their evil aspirations. Ryan loses three brothers, but many men also die to save Private Ryan. Evil in this film exacts an up-front, bloodthirsty toll that makes viewers look more than once to assure themselves that their safety net is, indeed, in place.

Accordingly, a second safeguard against evil concerns **psychological distance**. Any raw exposure to evil's filth--such as the pervasive terror of dying in *Saving Private Ryan*-- makes the witnessing of its handiwork distressing to behold. The April 19, 1995 bombing of the Alfred P. Murrah Federal Building in Oklahoma City left human beings, young and younger, in rubble. No grounds existed for romanticizing this disaster. The mourning of the survivors and the days taken to remove the victims, instead, marked a record of cautious excavation as rescuers searched for bodies at the hazardous site. Whatever "beauty" attended the Oklahoma City saga dwelt in the heroic and tireless efforts of the living to honor the dead, and in the willingness of strangers to comfort other strangers in anguish.

Cinematic distancing, in particular, provides a wholly different venue of evil compared to the blasphemous disregard for life that occurred on April 19, 1995. The carnage in Oklahoma City erases any safety net for those individuals who found themselves personally affected by the blast's aftereffects. Psychological distancing proves problematic for the many Oklahomans who made that day an integral part of their lives. The distancing for those individuals who lost loved ones must come, if ever, through a passage of time.

By contrast, evil that assumes mythic proportions, as in the Holocaust, weaves its spellbinding imagery within the lustrous fabric of dramatization (Hare, 1993, p. 80; Staub, 1989, p. xii; Lanzmann, 1985, p. x). Time and the eventual demise of Holocaust survivors will leave this evil to the museum keepers, historians, filmmakers, and other recorders of the past.

The harsh intimacies of *Saving Private Ryan* and the dark satire of *Dr. Strangelove* each prove provocative, although the two films differ markedly in the viewers' inclination to embrace psychological distancing. Expressions of evil appear more diffused and diverted amid the colorful characters of *Strangelove*, whereas no comparable frivolity accompanies the somber encounters in *Ryan*. Too, *Strangelove* portrays an evil yet to happen, playfully fabricating a "What if" scenario. But *Ryan* portrays a monstrous evil of record, and encourages a personal reassessment of personal combat.

Another distinction between *Ryan* and *Strangelove* lies in the viewer's **sense of control**. *Dr. Strangelove* and its dark humor permits a more comfortable viewing experience than does the literal brutality of death and dying in *Saving Private Ryan*. The safeguards against evil in *Ryan* do not function well, and the outcome impairs our sense of control, our sense of security as a passive observer. Consequently, if we feel too threatened, the alternative remains to turn away. Evil entertains and plays its morbid song, but we enjoy the freedom to decide how long, how much, and to what effect.

True evil does not adhere to these rules of constraint. True evil remains pinched by goodness, yet occasionally manages a stark release with terrifying unpredictability. Evil's ugly aftermath, only occasionally examined on film as in *Schindler's List* (1993) and *Judgment At Nuremberg* (1961), proves staggering and differs from cinematic treatments because it appears beyond the grasp of any humane message.

A PERVERSE BEAUTY

There exists no beauty in the reality of a Wilson, a George Brougham, a Rhoda, or a Graham Marshall. Beauty arises through the subjective proposition of "What if": What if Wilson imagines himself as a legend, as the greatest, most frightening gunfighter ever? What if George Brougham becomes so obsessed with the prestige of claiming Gleneyre that he willingly expends 107 innocent souls to gain his precious title? What if 8-year-old Rhoda genetically tunes herself to evil, and possesses the imagination to do that evil justice? What if Graham Marshall brings competition to new heights in a world of cigar-strutting executives as he gleefully sanctions his rivals? Artistry accounts for these absurd personalities, beginning with script, characterization, locale, and all the other elements that cater to orchestrating evil as a perverse beauty.

Surely we find no beauty in the flesh-and-blood Adolf Hitler or in the daily desecrations of the Holocaust that he engineered. Viewing both subjects in retrospect permits hindsight, and sometimes hindsight encourages insight: an insight that attains graceful prose and imagery, and that transcends evil's recurring degradation. But the beauty comes in the artistry of telling a story, not in the actual experiences of skeletal humans who lived a sub-human nightmare.

Evil's most precious safeguard to keep the wicked wicked, and to keep us mesmerized as observers, concerns the **beauty of perversion**. Cinematically (and in reality), evil proves as addictive as any drug, any amount of wealth, any passionate love. If Satan can not capture his own kingdom, he can, at least, send his subjects to the pinnacle of abject malevolence where the slightest imperfection means oblivion.

And what of this magical experience? What kind of beauty invigorates the evildoer so that he will risk his existence? Leonard Wolf (1980, p. 2), attempting to capture the thoughts of Gilles de Rais (Bluebeard) who performed atrocious acts of wickedness, speaks of "The Rage":

> The Rage, though it may come as a seizure, is not madness. There is no letting go of the sense of right or wrong. It is only that when the Rage happens one is filled with a terrible lucidity in which one sees all the known seams of the creation ripping apart, and is flooded with joy at the sight. It is as if one were standing like God in the midst of chaos, in the gorgeous moment *before* the creation, watching the interplay of possibility. At the center of that excitement, there is only one age: youth. Only one mood: power. Only one person: self.

Evil's sheen of beauty unfurls at a terrible cost. Purveyors of wickedness balance precariously on the lip of the precipice. Poised for destruction, they incur the ultimate risk to glimpse the splendor of an exquisite darkness. Does any personality, in reality, possess the cognitive and emotional skills to weather the all-consuming demands of pure evil? Can a personality hold together and defy goodness with a self-centeredness that propels him, or her, past virtue's rarified pronouncements?

Yes, such a character does exist. Cognitively, he (she) shows proficiency at secrecy, misdirection, and surely in abdicating responsibility. Emotionally, a shallowness in caring for others exists, but the capacity also arises to reach triumphant heights when scoring a selfish victory. The personality is not perfect, however. If less committed to the dark side, this figure becomes embroiled in moral conflicts that waste time and deter him from his appointed mission.

The personality must believe in himself to persevere, regardless of the obstacles and distractions that goodness throws his way. He must prevail for as long as he can, and, often enough, does, even to the degree of receiving a label that acknowledges his unwavering signature of evil in film: We call him, and her, the Psychopath.

Lesson 4

The Cinematic Psychopath

Psychopath. The very expression delivers a mishmash of images, from a silent figure of stealth to an odious person hellbent on cannibalism and chaos. Cynical professionals criticize the definition of a psychopath as too expansive to apply precisely. The target magically acquires all the qualities that an observer decides a psychopath ought to possess. These apparent traits are neither uniform nor suitably pronounced to prevent a bevy of slap-dash accusations. Anyone who appears self-centered and unfeeling toward others, certifiably crazy or not, can wear the label.

A working profile must show a streak of vulnerability. Theorizing about a psychopathic personality, cinematically or scientifically, should include limitations concerning who appears psychopathic...and who does not. If the psychopathic label becomes so lax as to fit any suspect of convenience, the concept and the target are in trouble.

Theorizing about psychopaths requires definitive boundaries to remain productive. Two distinctions include a differentiation (1) between psychopaths and those personalities who behave selfishly at times, yet are not psychopathic; and (2) between psychopaths and those individuals who are not responsible for their actions because of mental illness. These comparisons do not receive quick and easy recognition in the real world, much less in the celluloid universe of dark figures.

DEFINING PERVERSITY

Using **labels** to define perversity offers a measure of **order**, whether real or imagined. For example, the brutality of H. H. Holmes that appears to have begun over money, escalated to an even more senseless incentive: the enjoyment of killing (Mactire, 1995, p. 20). Holmes, as a serial murderer during the late 19th century, required a designation befitting his morally degenerate nature. Since "psychopath" was not readily available, titles such as "archfiend," "monster," and "demon" had to suffice (Schechter, 1994, p. 4). These labels allowed Chicago's inhabitants of the 1880s to profess a sense of outrage, if not a comprehension of H. H. Holmes's parlor atrocities.

Labels, therefore, function beyond mere acts of classification. To call a murderous individual an "archfiend" or a "degenerate" or a "devil" does not explain the disorder, but it keeps the offender at bay--keeps him from intruding too closely on the sanctity of normal behavior. The murderous individual seems less unruly and less ill-defined when placed under the identifying umbrella of a label.

Trolling for this antisocial creature denotes a two-way game of designation: We wish to identify the psychopath's deviance, yet we also desire to differentiate ourselves from such a personality (Tucker, 1985, p. 57). Maintaining a healthy psychological distance between normality and perversity reassures the "normals" that they are, truly, normal.

But overplay the game and our creature becomes a creature for all seasons. If a murder or rape occurs, a psychopath probably did the deed. It seems more comforting to assume that a cruel act demands a cruel person--preferably someone who differs markedly from ourselves (Revitch & Schlesinger, 1981, p. 97). Portrayals of psychopaths in film, for instance, frequently emphasize the difference between "them" and "us" as a staple of entertainment.

After years of conceptual fermentation, a German psychiatrist introduced the term **psychopathy** in 1891 (Hickey, 1997, p. 64). A central problem with psychopathy then, as now, concerns the capacity of an offender to engage in deranged acts without exhibiting the delusions (false beliefs) and emotional instability associated with psychotic behavior. Thus, psychopathy displays deviance in action, but fails to complement this activity with the kind of cognitive and emotional turmoil that warns psychiatrists of a mental disorder. Crazy performances are not followed by demonstrably crazy beliefs and feelings.

So, what kind of social malady does the psychopath possess? The answer, at least for some researchers, points to a **character disorder**. This compromise keeps psychopathy on the diagnostic books as an undesirable individual who shows thinking errors and emotional flatness when dealing with social relationships. Attempts to elaborate on what is meant by "thinking errors" and "emotional flatness" have taken the concept of psychopathy into slippery channels. Slippery enough, according to Eric Hickey (1997, p. 65) and his study of serial murderers, to acknowledge that "...the psychopath often has turned out to be exactly what we want him or her to be."

DOES THE PSYCHOPATH EXIST?

Psychopathy describes one category under **psychopathology**, a broad system of disorders that includes anxiety reactions, phobias, major depression, obsessive-compulsive behavior, and substance abuse. But amid this company of disorders, the boundaries and limitations mentioned earlier remain too relaxed to permit psychopathy the distinction of a valid, reliable, working concept. The question then becomes, "Does psychopathy constitute a legitimate disorder?"

Verifying psychopathy depends on the concept's credibility to occupy a prominent niche apart from other diagnostic classifications. If the psychopath characterizes symptoms that frequently "bleed" into other disorders (or vice versa), the scientific question arises, "Does the psychopath really exist?" Can professionals reach a consensus on who is psychopathic and who is not (Holmes & Holmes, 1996, p. 29; Radzinowicz & King, 1977, p. 90)?

Diagnostically, psychopathy should offer a singular set of traits that accentuates its mental disorder from other mental disorders. This profile, to prove effective, ought to capture the eccentricities of its subject matter and exclude other psychopathological disorders from consideration. Instead, certain social connections surface to keep psychopathy in disarray. The disorder becomes less a sharply-etched classification of predictive characteristics and more a free-floating ephemeral agent.

Conceptually, for instance, it does not help to have a kissing cousin. Psychopathy has one in **sociopathy**, the latter term a social connection that seems in many ways comparable and even preferable to psychopathy. A preference arises because the "socio" of "sociopath" gives emphasis to the offender's social background, and because this emphasis seems less likely to be confused with psychotic behavior (Holmes & De Burger, 1988, p. 66; Kunen, 1983, p. 217).

Both concepts cater to roughly the same territory of deviance, with "psychopath" favored by professionals intent on the psychological, biological, and genetic contributions to deviant behavior; and "sociopath" fancied by professionals who focus on early experiences (Hare, 1993, p. 23).

David Lykken (1995, p. 6) seeks to clarify this distinction by placing the less common psychopath at one end of a continuum (maximizing temperament) and the more common sociopath at the "socio" end (maximizing inadequate parenting). The ambiguous social connection between both creations, unfortunately, continues to bedevil the diagnostic scene for everyone. And in the realm of popular culture-- certainly in film--labeling the villain a psychopath or sociopath has absolutely no bearing on the "psycho" or "socio" distinction just observed.

Another social connection that psychopathy can do without concerns the presence of comorbidity. In a review of the classification problems associated with psychopathology, one team of researchers defines **comorbidity** as "the co-occurrence of two or more disorders in the same individual..." (Clark, Watson, & Reynolds, 1995, p. 127).

Suppose we find that a person classified as a psychopath

also admits to alcohol addiction (substance abuse in the psychopathological system). Do we simply assume that psychopaths crave excitement and therefore will drink when they become bored or depressed? And do we further assume that when psychopaths experience severe boredom or depression, they will drink a lot? Given this rationale, the social connection linking psychopathy with alcohol abuse appears natural, and seems to offer no real threat against the integrity of the psychopathic profile.

Well, not so fast. What if we possess information that allows us to articulate the concept of psychopathy into interpersonal and deviant behaviors. We recognize that the interpersonal domain includes behaviors like callousness, and that the deviance domain includes criminality. Then, lo and behold, we discover that alcohol addiction correlates more strongly with criminality than with callousness (Clark, Watson, & Reynolds, 1995, p. 134). Moreover, the question not asked earlier, must be asked now: How clearly can we surmise the criminal version of the psychopathic personality when that personality also must cope with an addiction to alcohol, perhaps a lifelong addiction? Does the individual's criminality stem more from alcoholism...or from his psychopathic orientation?

The question may have an answer, but it is not an answer that soars forth with bells ringing and flags waving. The task of psychopathy to exclude entangling maladies and assume a straightforward, homogeneous classification works better in the world of popular culture than in the fog banks and muddy waters of real life.

DISPARAGING THE PSYCHOPATH

Labels command a sterling simplicity that, at face value, help and hinder their application. To this end, two camps of thought--the cynical and the cautious--come to mind when wrestling with the vagaries of defining the psychopath.

The **cynical camp** considers psychopathy as so much hokum. Janet Malcolm (1990, p. 75), in her examination of the Jeffrey MacDonald case, argues that "The concept of the psychopath is, in fact, an admission of failure to solve the mystery of evil--it is merely a restatement of the mystery-- and only offers an escape valve for the frustration felt by psychiatrists, social workers, and police officers, who daily encounter its force."

Psychopathy, in other words, lets people like Jeffrey MacDonald (convicted of murdering his family) evade moral responsibility--and still fails to provide any substantive explanation of the man's actions. Even worse, the label of psychopath does not capture the true depravity and uniqueness regarding that most celebrated of criminals, the serial killer.

Brian Masters (1993, pp. 279-280), in his portrait of the British serial murderer, Dennis Nilsen, speaks to the weaknesses of attempting to stereotype a complex killer like Nilsen:

> For these reasons, I have avoided using the word *psychopath*, which seems to me to be a passe-partout noun dragged in to apply to any criminal whose motives are inaccessible. Its connotation is so wide as to be useless. Doctors admit that it is employed too freely, and furthermore point out that it is virtually undiagnosable. So-called psychopaths can be to the expert as well as to the casual observer perfectly normal people who are so adept at concealing their disturbance that they can live among us undetected for years. A man has to be called a psychopath before the symptoms of his condition stand out in relief or slot into place; the label usually precedes the diagnosis. By this yardstick, we are all potential psychopaths, yet it is only those of us who do something vicious and inexplicable who earn the label. In other words, the term applies to the deed, not to the condition. Before his arrest, no one would have thought of calling Dennis Nilsen a psychopath...

Clearly, Malcolm and Masters show little regard for the concept. Psychopathy, they conclude, is vague, bloated with surplus possibilities, and useless as a vehicle for providing insight into deviant behavior. The beleaguered concept also assumes a bias inherent to all labels that bear on psychopathology: Namely, a belief that the figure so designated--the alleged offender--truly reflects all that such a label encompasses. To call a serial murderer like Dennis

Nilsen a psychopath may prove innocuous. But to apply this label to someone less notorious, someone whose innocence may be genuine, results in a bias hardly favorable to that desperate individual (Winslade & Ross, 1983, p. 10).

Note, moreover, one possible consequence of such labeling: How do we imagine an innocent person will respond to being labeled a psychopath, especially if he happens to harbor suicidal inclinations (Hare, 1993, p. 183)? Suicide may appear improbable, but if we have one very stressed individual who finds his reputation in tatters, a tragic resolution is not beyond question. Labels depict more than cosmetic nomenclature: Labels can be taken quite personally, particularly if untrue.

The **cautious camp**, while not embracing the cynicism of banishing psychopathy evermore, does pursue the concept with prudence. Stanton Samenow (1989, pp. 26-27), in his practice with troubled children, avoids labels like **antisocial personality** when reporting on a child's mental state. Yet he finds value in using this label, not to predict or diagnose such behavior, but as a guide for clustering related behaviors. Antisocial personality denotes another kissing cousin to psychopathy, although this classification offers broader coverage that includes psychopaths, sociopaths, and other habitual criminal offenders (see Lyyken, 1995, p. 32).

A psychiatrist, Hervey Cleckley, provided the first extensive list of symptoms on psychopathy, gathered from his patients' case histories and published in 1941 (Hare, 1993, p. 27; Nettler, 1982, pp. 174-175). The title of Cleckley's book, *The Mask Of Sanity*, reflected his belief that these psychopaths appeared civil, sane, and functional, wearing the appropriate masks to blend into society. The masks hid their true personality characteristics--the very same characteristics that Cleckley attempted to divine via his descriptive items.

Robert Hare, an experimental psychologist, has perhaps been most industrious in continuing Cleckley's legacy. Hare's (1993, Chapter 3) **Psychopathy Checklist** includes Emotional/Interpersonal characteristics as well as traits related to Social Deviance. Symptoms expressive of the Emotional/Interpersonal category involve an individual who is glib, egocentric, lacks remorse and empathy, is deceitful, manipulative, and displays only shallow emotions.

Should the individual receive a classification of Social Deviance, this diagnostic category indicates impulsiveness, poor behavior controls, a need for excitement, a lack of responsibility, the likelihood of early behavior problems, and the manifestation of adult antisocial behavior.

Still, given the constraints exercised by advocates of the cautious camp to apply the label carefully, Hare (p. 34) adds that "...people who are *not* psychopaths may have *some* of the symptoms described here. Many people are impulsive, or glib, or cold and unfeeling, or antisocial, but this does not mean they are psychopaths. Psychopathy is a *syndrome*--a cluster of related symptoms."

The impression arises that even if a troubled person exhibits most of the related behaviors just described, a cautious professional like Robert Hare may still wish to know more of the individual's social history. This history will include the offender's work and family relations, chemical addictions, and any prison record.

Career criminals, for example, become more likely to wear the psychopath label, compared to offenders who impulsively court trouble during their adolescent years before settling into citizenship. Unlike the rise and fall of such adolescent deviancy, the psychopath maintains a steady conduct of risk taking. He also attempts to control his surroundings, and, sometimes, behaves dangerously with little regard for others (Hickey, 1997, p. 67).

The bottom line suggests that to diagnose psychopathy is to walk on egg shells. The process proves delicate, tentative, and frustrating. But the cynical camp's declaration to vanquish psychopathy as a scientific spook seems unlikely to happen. Why? Because popular culture will not allow it. Because the exquisite characterization of a psychopath can lift a drab drama from the doldrums. And, most importantly, because the presence of a conniving, wicked personality in film can boost that drama's commercial prospects. Commerce and art fuel the cinematic psychopath's longevity, quite apart from the scientific creed of holding the psychopath accountable as an effective diagnostic category.

A PARALLEL LIFE

A **parallel life** refers to psychopathy's independent usage, apart from its role in science, as an image of popular culture. Customarily, **popular culture** goes its merry way, projecting the psychopath autonomously through news items, magazine articles, book exposés, television features...and movies. Popular culture, to wit, offers fictional portrayals of psychopaths based on "fact," and fictional portrayals based on fiction.

Scientifically, no professional can say with certainty how an individual falls into the characterization that we designate "Psychopath." The drive that compels a person, male or female, to engage in psychopathic behaviors may stem from a predisposition toward certain traits (genetic); from neural damage or chemical irregularities in the brain (physiological); from abuse as a child (environmental); or from a conglomerate of causes too intricate and obtuse to unravel (a genetic/physiological/experiential triad). But it is this obscurity, this mystery, that makes a concept like psychopathy so inviting to popular culture.

When does the wickedness begin, and why? Lional Dahmer (1994, p. 11), the father of Jeffrey Dahmer, contends that no one can solve the mystery of why a human being becomes a serial murderer, including the murderer:

> So who was Jeffrey Dahmer? We must admit immediately that no one will ever know, that Jeffrey Dahmer is a mystery even to himself. Because the darkest of crimes proceed from the darkest of hearts, no book can claim to have discovered the ultimate solution to the enigma either of the criminal or his deeds.

Put aside for the moment how well Jeffrey Dahmer meets the specifications of Robert Hare's Psychopathy Checklist. Instead, note that the **intangibles** of thinking dark thoughts and of committing dark deeds will not appear on any scientist's checklist. The researcher's concern is verification, and verification proves a rigorous taskmaster.

A literary or cinematic characterization of the psychopath takes scientific researchers beyond their tools of analysis.

Indeed, a literary or cinematic depiction of the psychopath may permit greater eloquence about this creature than any scientific report with its priorities of validity and reliability. Conversely, literary and cinematic sources also must acknowledge the creation of numerous bone-crunching monsters who wear the label, "Psychopath," because one size fits all.

Popular culture gives psychopathy a parallel life, a different life, the kind of life that takes advantage of the concept's elasticity. Psychopathy's vagaries stoke the scientist's ire, and yet this same semantic haze inspires the artist's imagination. Artistically, the psychopath transforms to a chameleon, bringing along his or her pedigree of ugliness, and making the ugliness acceptably diverse as entertainment.

Practitioners of popular culture enjoy using a concoction like the psychopath because the characterization draws attention and requires no lengthy explanation. The stereotype kicks in, and the psychopath becomes whatever the viewer wants the figure to be: a sadist, a seductress, a charming cad, an opportunist, or a plain-vanilla serial killer. But, as researchers of the concept will testify, these cultural stereotypes often stray far from psychopathy's scientific jurisdiction.

Consider just how psychopathy can differ under the influence of popular culture from psychopathy under the regimen of **scientific conservatism**. We learn in the course of the film *Psycho* (1960) that Norman Bates (Anthony Perkins) spends more time as Mother than as Norman. When Mother kills Marion Crane (Janet Leigh) and ultimately finds herself/himself committed to an asylum, we are not surprised. Norman's crazy as a loon and an asylum is where she/he belongs.

Occasionally, however, popular references to *Psycho* address Norman Bates as a "psychopathic killer." Now, does she/he fit the Psychopathic Checklist? Norman seems guided more by the false beliefs of a psychotic--someone who exhibits delusions of persecution and sexual identity--than as someone driven by the cold, calculating manipulations of a psychopath.

Recall that one reason for inventing the concept of psychopathy involved the idea of accounting for deviant behavior by individuals who did **not** appear to display psychotic symptoms. Psychopaths deliberately perform crazy, wicked, atrocious acts, yet their shallow affect and sometimes charming conduct do not betray such actions (Kirwin, 1997, p. 23).

Therefore, how different are science and popular culture in pursuing the elusive psychopath? Two concepts, supposedly one and the same, pass in the night. The scientific version travels sluggishly ahead, fractured through disagreements over the concept's diagnostic worth. The media version, more buoyant and skittish, flits over the water in whatever direction the wind carries it. Each version of psychopathy has its advantages and disadvantages, although the adherents of popular culture open themselves more freely to careless interpretations.

The credentials of popular culture are not those of social science. Dramatizations of psychopathy occur with an eye for commercial gain, giving less concern to the story's educational value. As long as "Psychopath" delivers chills and awe, as long as the idea remains entrenched in the vocabulary of popular culture, it does not matter what scientists think of the concept's rash applications. It does not matter because the psychopath holds favor as a marketable idea.

FROM THE BOOK TO THE MOVIE

Clearly, the psychopath of film differs from the psychopath construed scientifically. The cinematic psychopath responds to what the commercial market will bear, and the market bears quite a load. Indeed, not only can the actor transform into whatever "psychopath" the filmmaker desires, the medium of film demands a more succinct interpretation than occurs with the written word.

Time and circumstance are precious in movieland. A book can wander adrift for hundreds of pages, allotting considerable space to the characters' innermost thoughts. Readers may return to and reflect on a novel's narration at their leisure. The pace, the purpose, and the enjoyment all can differ substantially from a book to a movie. Whereas one medium at times favors the tortoise, the other medium leans toward the hare. Imagine, for instance, translating this narrator's stream of consciousness into a movie scene (Wilson, 1994, p. 26):

> I took the call on a day when a light breeze would white-face your eyebrows and glaze your lips for posterity. But I must admit that my eyebrows and lips felt better than Calvin's. He lay coiled by the hearth next to a fire that only the dead could ignore. He had my card, so they called. The card baffled me. What I remember of Calvin would have encouraged me to kick him in the groin, not leave a card. Calvin the creep. Calvin the monster. Calvin the bully. He bullied me. Guys don't forget those primal tokens of terror. The bully may be gone, but the bullying stays with you. I could kick him in the groin now, but it's too late. Even if Calvin were alive, it would be too late.

Read as a passage, the intent seems clear and straightforward. Calvin provokes some unpleasant memories of youth, suppressed until now. Cinematically, the trappings of winter and of Calvin's hearth pose no problem. A production designer can supply wintry cues and stage the hearth and fire appropriately. No, it is not Calvin or the setting that causes difficulty. It is the narrator...**he's** the problem.

Narration in a novel poses no concern. A central character can relate events in the "first-person" and thereby become the reader's frame of reference for the entire story. But in a movie, narration proves awkward. Either the audience hears a voice explaining someone's thoughts, or, on rare occasions, viewers actually see an actor speaking directly to them.

Perhaps the trickiest feat of narration for filmmaking involves breaking down the **fourth wall**. This expression concerns the "wall" that exists between performers and viewers. Michael Caine (1990, p. 96) comments that his role as the sexual wayfarer in *Alfie* (1966) required him to speak to the camera. Conversing with the audience allows the amoral Alfie to become more likable because Caine learns to covet the camera and pretend to speak with one person rather than to a large, unseen audience.

Alfie shares intimacies with the viewer, thinking of the viewer as an old friend. Caine's character puzzles over his inability to bring himself to marriage, given the fact that he has had numerous opportunities. Nor can he bring himself to worry much about another fact, namely, that he has left so many wenches in sexual disarray. Note, however, that without Alfie's shared confidences, his unflattering lifestyle as a sexual con artist leaves the audience with less reason to generate any affection for him.

What films do best involves an **intensity of experience through the immediacy of vision and sound**. The intensity usually surpasses any comparable experience of reading a book. Movies seldom realize the depth of sensitivity that books can attain when exploring characters and plots. But movies possess a mastery to lock viewers into spellbinding moments of lust and fear and awe. Who will readily forget the bom-bom-bom-bom beat that accompanies the great white shark's arrival in *Jaws* (1975); or the creature's "birth" from a crew member's stomach in *Alien* (1979); or the emaciated and demonic young Regan in *The Exorcist* (1973)? These happenings evoke gut-wrenching reactions that go beyond a novel's description of the same terrifying moments.

The finer points of cinematic finessing even suggest a magic peculiar to the movies: What images do we conjure up for what we **do not see**? At the close of *Rosemary's Baby* (1968), Rosemary (Mia Farrow) expresses shock and repulsion when she first sees her "son"--a son presumably sired by Lucifer. The mother initially displays horror, then recovers with a softer gaze, a mother's gaze, and, finally, she sings a lullaby to her new life.

We see Rosemary's face but we do not see the baby--and we should not. *Rosemary's Baby* allows something to happen that the movies ought to attempt more often: the opportunity for us--as moviegoers--to fantasize, to provide closure, to interject our personal idea of what we do not see. Regarding Rosemary's offspring, we must imagine the baby's appearance...and the evil that constitutes that newborn's legacy.

A LURKING INTELLIGENCE

If a movie is to finesse, it must warm our expectations and heighten our moods. A film's theme becomes the place to start because the theme presumes a basic or native intelligence. Our delayed awareness of the film's **lurking intelligence** surfaces only when the cumulative effects of well-played emotional scenes shock or nudge us into realizing what we perceive as the film's true message.

So, what lurks exactly? The filmmaker's scheme, actually. A scheme designed to entertain by creating anticipation, humor, tragedy, passion, but most of all, by cultivating **deception**. The filmmaker does not want us bored, mouthing the character's next lines before the character reacts. The story--a good story--delivers its truth gently yet invincibly, articulating the characters and plots with sufficient mystique to entertain, enlighten, and seduce us into wanting more.

Characters and the plots that comprise a story prove less flexible as they progress. Surprises are easier to introduce early in a film when the performers and their purpose remain ambiguous. Later, surprises with established characters demand more careful thought. Entertainment relies on deception to maintain at least a hint of unpredictability, but entertainment also depends on the film's cohesiveness to clarify and consolidate storylines. A sexually repressed wimp does not soar forth as a suave, calculating psychopath--not in any logical sense--unless the filmmaker legitimately prepares the audience for this revelation.

The movie's **emotional truth** reminds us--indeed, primes us--to consider ideas for explaining the characters' actions. A movie that addresses its theme well emotionally can serve as a conduit for intellectual ideas (Schank & Childers, 1988, p. 91). Specifically, a film that arouses our feelings for reasons other than vacuous thrills, becomes a film capable of using emotion to inspire intellectual considerations.

Thus, if the filmmaker proffers a worthy theme, and executes this theme well, the film's lurking intelligence will slowly manifest a truth or truths not fully realized earlier. Easy to say, of course, but very trying to accomplish. The "if" in question denotes a lofty aim that most movies do not attain.

When film as a collaborative project succeeds, as did *One Flew Over The Cuckoo's Nest* (1975), the payoff goes beyond profit at the box office. Collaboration included director Milos Forman drawing on a screenplay by Lawrence Hauben and Bo Goldman, based on the novel by Ken Kesey and the play by Dale Wasserman. McMurphy (Jack Nicholson), the classic anti-hero, squares off against the mental health establishment, coldly personified by Nurse Mildred Ratched (Louise Fletcher). McMurphy pretends abnormal behavior to escape detail at a prison work farm, only to find himself confined in a pill-popping mental ward, complete with muzak, sterile interiors, mindless schedules, aimless group therapy sessions, and, naturally, Nurse Ratched.

McMurphy gains the edge for a time, circumventing the ward's bland regime. He excites the other patients over his demands to see the World Series; he shows them how to play slam-dunk basketball and beat the male nurses; and he arranges an "unauthorized" boat charter so they can learn to fish (while he enjoys some sack time with his girl). These incidents dramatize the movie's apparent theme: that of a hell-raising free spirit who rebels against institutional constraints and wins the loyalty of his fellow inmates.

But no, these events strike a mere prelude to more substantial matters. *One Flew Over The Cuckoo's Nest* only appears to play as a raucous comedy. The principles are really tragic figures bearing a somber message, although this message does not surface until the movie's climactic moments--as befits the idea of a film's lurking intelligence. McMurphy, preparatory to escaping from the ward and heading for Canada, throws a midnight party for the inmates by smuggling in two women and enough booze to make everyone forget their troubles. It is at this juncture that the movie's theme assumes a more complex revelation.

McMurphy pairs off one woman with Billy (Brad Dourif), a lad possessed of an inferiority complex, exhibited through his stuttering attempts at speech. McMurphy, in his wily ways, knows that Billy's chance to experience his first sexual intercourse will do far more for the boy's confidence than an infinite number of group therapy encounters.

During this midnight fling, McMurphy has the means to escape. He even mumbles to his closest ally, a massive Indian called Chief Bromden (Will Sampson), about the good times "When we get to Canada." But as the camera closes in on McMurphy, we see a face of changing moods: A grin of anticipation fades to wistfulness, then to woeful contemplation, then, slowly, we witness a quiet smile of reality.

A man, amid drink and celebration, catches a hard glimpse of himself. McMurphy knows he is going nowhere. He discloses a moroseness over the splinters of his life that no amount of hell-raising, free-spirited hilarity will chase away. McMurphy, beneath that veneer of "running with the wind," traps himself in a prison of his past.

Two "murders" follow. First, Nurse Ratched arrives at her accustomed time to confront the antithesis of all she holds dear. HER ward is a mess, and HER patients are collapsed in ungainly positions, sleeping off their merriment. Ratched finds Billy in bed with his paramour, and all pretense at gaiety goes south.

Billy, full of pleasure at his sexual fulfillment, finds his now unimpeded speech and his gratification short-lived. Mildred Ratched, the silky psychopath at her venomous best, threatens to tell Billy's mother of his immoral behavior. Billy's self-confidence evaporates quickly, and, in a subsequent state of self-loathing, he slashes his throat with broken glass to commit a bloody suicide.

McMurphy, realizing that Billy's suicide translates to Nurse Ratched's vindictiveness, launches himself upon her. She's Nurse Ratched, she's the unholy authoritarian, she's the civilized instrument of oppression who murders Billy. Put bluntly, she's the nemesis of them all--and he must commit the inmate's Cardinal Sin and choke the life from her.

McMurphy does not prevail in his righteousness, because he can not prevail. Nurse Ratched's sanctimonious authority remains inviolate, even to the point of authorizing a second murder: Portraying the victim, she influences the system to perform a lobotomy on McMurphy, reducing this robust character to a vegetative state. He is no longer McMurphy, or even a fair semblance thereof. He is just another warm body who has yet to expire.

Does Nurse Ratched truly become a murderess? No, not in the sense of poisoning, or stabbing, or shooting the victim. She may not even have wished Billy to die, but, then, his death seems unlikely to cause her remorse. And McMurphy's "death", for her, proves a fitting triumph. You must not contest the system--and Nurse Ratched **is** the system.

She regains her controlled environment, ushers her flock of inmates back to their old haunts, and restores the ward to its status quo as if McMurphy never existed. The patients shall not forget him, but will they recall that one breath of life when he led them to defy the pills, the rules, the antiseptic environment? They appear unable to mount the necessary opposition in his absence...with one exception.

Chief Bromden cushions the tragedy by responding to the vital McMurphy he remembers. He locates his friend, pained at what the establishment has condemned McMurphy to be. The Chief performs two acts of freedom. First, he embraces McMurphy and mutters softly, "Let's go"; then he smothers him with a pillow, knowing that the rebel would prefer death to a comatose state. And second, the Chief frees himself by escaping the institution, choosing--via McMurphy's inspiration--to tackle the world outside rather than remain in a timeless ward.

What theme do we discover now? The earlier notion of a hellbent rebel rousing other inmates to oppose the system does not really capture the ultimate nature of *One Flew Over The Cuckoo's Nest*. McMurphy **makes** a difference, although not for himself, not in changing his own unfocused life. But he reaches one individual who finds the world outside frightening, and who would never have ventured into that world except for McMurphy. (Previously, in a nice touch of irony, the huge Chief explains to McMurphy the difference between them as he admires McMurphy's desire to escape: "For you maybe, you're a lot bigger than me.")

Now what is the film's theme? A lurking intelligence envelops us to consider how the mental health system can function as an oxymoron. The system betrays the very people that, on paper, it was established to help. Nurse Ratched, the truly dangerous personality, shows that she can do irreparable harm to the human spirit when she has "goodness" in her corner. This supercilious psychopath believes herself an angel of mercy. And, in keeping with that high-minded image, she convinces institutional authority to place McMurphy in her cross hairs, not for elimination (that would be murder), but for "alteration."

The concluding theme comes to us in layers. The World Series incident, the boating escapade, the adversarial thrusts and parries between McMurphy and Nurse Ratched--these scenes build emotionally to tell us that previous conceptions about characters and story need revision. Instead of a "good-old-boy" romp, we witness the sad paradox of an environment that dupes its inhabitants into feeling "good" about themselves. The system does so, however, by subordinating individuality, and by medicating the inmates to accommodate a lifestyle of inertia.

Nurse Ratched only **looks** like an easy target to ridicule. Gradually, we learn the "beauty" of her evil. She presents herself as the quiet, formidable figure who wreaks a personal brand of vengeance. We learn, too, that McMurphy recognizes her dangerousness, yet he achieves only one solid victory: the escape of Chief Bromden. McMurphy manages this one stroke for humanity against the loss of a tormented Billy, and the sacrifice of his own haphazard dreams.

But how does Nurse Mildred Ratched fare regarding our 3/2 model of evil? Frankly, her access to **authority** alters the cognitive and emotional practices of this model. The more power a psychopath retains, the less she or he need cater to deception. Note that Nurse Ratched entertains no worry of secrecy, misdirection, or the abdication of responsibility. She can withhold information from her inmates, leaving them to speculate, for example, on McMurphy's fate. Or she can reveal all, since nothing will change in her insular world of pills and platitudes. Nor does misdirection and abdication of responsibility prove crucial, since both practices are vested in the institutional "welfare" of the ward's inhabitants: The system reflects the psychopath's desires.

Emotionally, any patentable concerns about her people are encompassed in Nurse Ratched's modulated demeanor of a low-hum philosophy. She cares professionally, although her "caring" reflects a shallow concern that fails to touch genuine feelings of sympathy or remorse.

Nurse Ratched's low-hum philosophy of maintaining a quiet existence for staff and inmates prohibits the kind of outward joy expressed by McMurphy. She does not think of herself as wicked, but as a guardian of compassion. Exuberance of evil, therefore, does not square with her agenda. A measure of authority, consequently, can compensate for deficits in a psychopath's aptitude for wickedness. Nurse Ratched becomes more imposing than she might individually because the system bolsters her banal oppressiveness.

THE CINEMATIC PSYCHOPATH

Nurse Ratched quietly embodies a cinematic psychopath who harbors the potential to emerge as a subtle creature of perverse thought and feeling. But the price paid for this occasional eloquence includes the acknowledgement that other movies-- lesser movies--dilute the psychopath into many figures, with no identifiable center or core of characteristics.

Robert Hare's Checklist (1993, p. 34), though formalized for scientific pursuits, at least suggests how psychopaths tend to behave: They care more for themselves than others; they show little responsibility for their actions; they lie and manipulate; they command the ability to charm victims for underhanded purposes; they overstate their accomplishments and understate their failures; they crave excitement, sometimes the wrong kind...and so the list continues, a litany of self-absorbed declarations.

Secrecy, misdirection, the abdication of responsibility, and the emotional considerations of lack of remorse and exuberance for evil appear essential to honor Hare's Checklist of Psychopathy. Argumentatively, some experts may demand a greater number of fundamentals to explore, although, likely, not fewer. And yet the three cognitive and two emotional practices described seem most imperative for appraising the cinematic psychopath's aptitude to inflict harm. Evaluating this aptitude from the muted tenacity of a Nurse Ratched in *One Flew Over The Cuckoo's Nest*, to the cannibalism of a Hannibal Lecter in *The Silence Of The Lambs* (1991), to the grandiose verve of a Graham Marshall in *A Shock To The System* (1990) calls for a diverse frame of reference.

Scientifically, the task may prove questionable, but, cinematically, there is no argument. To capture the psychopath on film requires a provision for strikingly different characterizations. When we speak of Absolute Evil, we speak of a cinematic character who truly adores himself, and who glories in his criminality. As we shall discover, it is this exuberance for evil that most vividly defines the cinematic psychopath.

Part 2

The Busy Psychopath

Lesson 5

Character

Aldrich Ames pursued the role of a CIA double agent from 1985 until his arrest in 1994. During those years the Soviets paid Ames a total of 2.7 million dollars for secrets that, among other disclosures, led to the betrayals and executions of 10 CIA operatives. In a CNN interview on December 27, 1994, Ames commented that "His decision to do this...was like the leap into the dark" (Wise, 1995, p. 119).

Money became the prime reason to explain Ames's treason. Certainly no spy in the history of cloak-and-daggerism rivals his output to pass along so much information for such a lucrative return. Ames's continued success as a spy, including his indulgence to buy Jaguars and pay $540,000 cash for a two-story home, may have insulated him from the lethal treachery he instigated. After all, Ames did not personally murder the exposed agents. He preferred to think of their demise as the risks that spies take in becoming spies.

Whether Ames believed this rationalization or not, his "leap into the dark" placed him at a point of no return. If he worried about the course taken, it likely concerned his capture rather than any compassion over the lost souls that he betrayed. Possibly, too, Ames viewed his perverse dance with evil as an adventure. Working for the CIA and stealing classified documents under the agency's nose must have excited him. A hoot? An ego-stroking exercise in gamesmanship? A cavalier belief that he would never be caught? Something!

So, why does a man betray his country? If money becomes the ultimate reason, what can we know of Aldrich Ames that explains his greed? No striking circumstances present themselves in Ames's background: no evidence of sexual abuse, no witnessing of chronic family violence, no impoverished upbringing. We see a young Rick Ames in his 1959 high-school yearbook, voted "wittiest" by the senior class. But, later, we also meet Aldrich Ames, the heavy drinker, and, finally, Aldrich Ames, the traitor.

All was not well within the Ames family, but the drinking of Ames's father and other stresses do not muster the severity to explain Ames, the counterspy. The CIA had recruited the father as a spy, and, subsequently, the agency also attracted the son. The tandem of father and son appeared to find the spy business fascinating. If so, part of the answer governing Aldrich Ames's tragic behavior involves the thought of taking chances, of living deceptively, of using his wits to play the game. The remainder of the answer, it seems, rests with the notion that Ames never possessed the wealth he desired. And the yearning for money can erase any number of moral thou-shalt-nots.

A NECESSARY EVIL

Aldrich Ames does not fit the familiar profile of a serial killer. He did not stalk his victims or dispatch them by any of the gruesome means usually associated with these covert murderers. And yet, before Ames's detection, CIA officials thought of the mole within their agency as a "serial killer" (Weiner, 1994).

Upon discovery, Ames earned other titles of notoriety, such as "murdering traitor" and "malignant betrayer"; titles that in some way attempted to capture the monumental depravity of his actions (Weiner, 1994). But aside from greed as his primary motive, Ames maintained a detachment between the agents executed and his responsibility for those executions.

The lives lost were distant to his life, lives made less meaningful by the machinations of Washington and Moscow that included risk as a part of the bureaucratic game.

Thus, what kind of evil does Aldrich Ames represent? Consider this appraisal of evil's "psychology" by Vernon Geberth, a forensic professional (1996, p. 786):

> A psychology of evil provides the serial murderer with a unique ability to withstand ordinary investigative interview techniques which focus on guilt, admission, and disclosure. Remember, in a psychology of evil, the fundamental machinery of conscience, responsibility, and feeling or empathy for other human beings is totally lacking. For instance, attempting to invoke sympathy for the victims or surviving families or appealing to the subject's conscience will probably be a waste of time. An offender who evinces a psychology of evil doesn't care about anyone except himself because he is evil. An evil person is clever, devious, selfish, and extremely narcissistic.

Clever, devious, selfish, and extremely narcissistic...like a psychopath. Geberth describes characteristics vested in our cognitive and emotional model of evil. Ames confessed his duplicity, but the mole realized little choice given the mounting evidence against him. Had he found himself in a more tenable position to mislead and implicate a scapegoat, it seems likely he would have done so.

Aldrich Ames, nonetheless, demonstrates an aptitude for the cognitive practices of secrecy, misdirection, and the abdication of responsibility in his role as counterspy. Emotionally, he shows little remorse for the lives lost through his betrayals. Conversely, the emotional "beauty" he envisions from such treachery appears centered on his statement, "...the leap into the dark" (Wise, 1995, p. 119).

What mad excitement does this statement entail? The exhilaration of passing off wads of sensitive material to the Russians? The secret amusement of doing so under the nose of his colleagues who pride themselves as "experts" on espionage? The ardor in secretly knowing of the repercussions--and deaths--caused by him, and him alone? If these speculations proximate the truth, then "deviancy" and "maladjustment" fail to provide the connotations necessary to address Ames's conduct.

Scientifically, professionals appear reluctant to regard "good and evil" as legitimate ideas for study (Tavris, 1982, p. 23). Recalling our conclusions from Lessons 1 to 3, evil becomes a critical concept, not to explain the malevolence of people like Ames, but to strike the exclamation point that suggests the extent of their depravity. Aldrich Ames managed to ride the crest of his sinfulness for nine years before the luxuriousness of "fickle beauty" deserted him.

The characters encountered in the remainder of this lesson are fictional, although we should remember that evil assumes many masks of deceit and manipulation. Therefore, keep Aldrich Ames in mind as a frame of reference. Fictional psychopaths can perform outlandish feats as amoral characters, but look beyond these performances to the cognitive and emotional features that assess such personalities and their proficiency for wickedness.

In the name of evil, does fiction really outdistance reality?

CHARACTER

If we should package the saga of Aldrich Ames for entertainment, our first hurdle would be the vexing question of motivation. Yes, he liked money, and, yes, he liked taking chances, but how did Ames, the high-school wit, develop into Ames, the traitor? Cinematically, any attempt to explain Aldrich Ames as a psychopathic character must begin with the right actor.

Character, as an abstraction, refers to a person's conduct or personality. Character reflects the essence of what the individual **is**, and what the individual **does**. By contrast, **out-of-character** indicates someone who does not behave according to his or her customary disposition.

Once we leave these simple thoughts, an encroaching jungle of qualifiers creeps into the fray. If one person tells another, "She *has* character," the intent seems positive, indicating integrity, honesty, someone who stays the course. Yet if one person tells another, "She's *a* character," the meaning becomes more questionable. She's a lot of fun? She's eccentric? She's argumentative? Or, if one individual judges the other as having the character of a "surly, snot-nosed shithead," we suspect that someone's reputation needs retooling.

And then we have the character in a drama. We will not gain the necessary perspective on psychopaths as characters if we ignore the performers who create these creatures. **Acting is pretending**, and a small number of performers receive exorbitant sums of money to pretend to their heart's content. Not all actors seek the celebrity of fame and fortune, but, richly paid or not, they ply their profession nobly (Detmer, 1995). Actors usually perform industriously to do their best with the talent at hand.

Performers work hard, if for no other reason than to weather the boldface demands of their art: Actors must parade themselves for all to see, and all to judge. Director Sidney Lumet (1995, p. 59), regarding his analysis of what goes into making a movie, believes that actors are brave:

> The *talent* of acting is one in which the actor's thoughts and feelings are instantly communicated to the audience. In other words, the "instrument" that an actor is using is himself. It is *his* feelings, *his* physiognomy, *his* sexuality, *his* tears, *his* laughter, *his* anger, *his* romanticism, *his* tenderness, *his* viciousness, that are up there on the screen for all to see. That's not easy. In fact, quite often it's painful.

Lumet notes that the art of painful self-revelation applies to men and women, although women assume the added burden of finding themselves treated as "sexual commodities" (Lumet, p. 61). The aging process in movies not only proves more graceful for men than women, but the passing years seem inescapably entwined with a female's "character." Unlike the male, she witnesses her potential for sex appeal slipping away after...how long? Forty years of age? Fifty? Whatever the time frame for a particular actress, her sensual staying power appears in greater jeopardy than the male's tenure as a commercial asset.

Image becomes the actor's currency. The image may be contrived or natural, may depend on lust or virtue or fanaticism, may lean toward heroism or villainy, or may involve an exceptional ability to convey one kind of character at the expense of other prospects. Whatever its nature, image allows the performer to become someone of interest to movie audiences. Heroes offer the possibility of awesome attractiveness and justice for all. But villains, especially compleat villains, command their own rooting section. A "good" villain to moviegoers means that it is so nice to become acquainted with someone so bad.

Image can differ even when two actors portray the "same" character. Robert Mitchum and Robert De Niro inhabit the beastliness of Max Cady, a brutal psychopath, but do so almost 30 years apart in two versions of *Cape Fear* (1962 & 1991). Mitchum's screen persona gives viewers a rough-hewn Cady, lacking in polish and civility, though loaded with animal cunning and a physical arrogance that signals what he is, and what he wants. De Niro's Cady comes forth as a "clever, tattooed gospelmonger who speaks in tongues" (Wilson, 1994, p. 273). De Niro, slighter in build than Mitchum, compensates by making his character more beguiling and rapturous. He is capable, for example, of sweet-talking and seducing a young girl, whereas Mitchum's Cady possesses none of these skills.

A more sensitive comparison indicates that the two performers do not really play the same character. Each actor projects his image onto the role of Max Cady. The natural strengths and weaknesses of a performer's physiognomy, apart from other psychological considerations, dictates an important consideration of what moviegoers will accept from the actor's characterization. Tattoos, for instance, become more crucial to De Niro's evangelical version of Cady than to Mitchum's Cady of brute strength. Later we shall examine Mitchum's role in detail, because his character comes closer to illustrating the classic psychopath.

INTENT AND MOTIVE

A character's motivation differs from a character's intention. **Intent** signals the personality's inclination to prefer a certain course of action. The psychopath, therefore, gravitates toward self-glorification and taking advantage of others. **Motive**, however, asks the question, Why? Why does someone become a psychopath? What reasons exist to explain the psychopath's nefarious pursuits? "Intent" doesn't ask why; "motive" does.

The movies, when delving into a villain's motivation, frequently offer an extraordinary happening to "explain" the evil personality's ultimate behavior. *Halloween* (1978) begins, for instance, with an apparently deranged six-year-old boy who murders his sister. Obviously **something** is amuck with this kid and authorities ship him off to a mental institution. He returns as an adult on the anniversary of his violence-- Halloween--to inflict more devastation. We do not know what is wrong with him, except that his mental problems started early and, yes, they are serious.

Thus, the child in *Halloween* evidences deliberate behavior that culminates in violence (intent). But killing his sister does not explain why he instigated her death (motive). To decipher the boy's motivation, we must speculate, for instance, whether he behaves more as a psychopath, or primarily as a mentally deranged personality who can not account for his actions. The "why" of his behavior--the motivation--remains elusive.

The question of motivation, of how an individual becomes a compleat psychopath, varies in importance to filmmakers. Movies typically travel the **low road** to fashion a cinematic portrait of the psychopath's origins. Filmmakers either blithely ignore the villain's past, or they profile his alteration through a singular incident of prior violence--as in *Halloween*--to "explain" the evil figure. The low road usually gives motivation perfunctory attention while emphasizing the film's other qualities, such as action, humor, and broad characterizations as selling points.

UNDERCONTROLLED PSYCHOPATHS

Recall that our cognitive definition of a compleat psychopath involves the villain's use of secrecy, misdirection, and a willingness to abdicate moral responsibility. But how well does the psychopath utilize his cognitive skills?   How disciplined is he--or she--in guarding against impulsive decisions that lead to murder?   The answer in most cases offers little encouragement.   Leonard Berkowitz (1993, p. 284), surveying issues on aggression, suggests that psychopaths as murderers readily exhibit "extreme antisocial tendencies and weak inhibitions against aggression."

The psychopath, in other words, commonly characterizes an **undercontrolled personality**. This type of personality, once aroused, finds difficulty in managing his criminal impulses. Gathering momentum, the energized psychopath gives little thought to the consequences of his destructive actions. Emotionally, the excitement that wickedness generates serves to cloud his cognitive acumen.

The undercontrolled psychopath conveys two patterns in the movies: First, we seldom receive an adequate understanding of the villain's motivation, nor does this inadequacy seem too important; and, second, we anticipate that the undercontrolled personality will prove rousing and unpredictable. The undercontrolled villain, candidly, provides good entertainment fare.

One favorite strategy of the low-road moviemakers includes a suggestive sketch of the murderer's younger days. This sketch often amounts to a lame shot in the dark, especially when applied to cinematic psychopaths who flaunt themselves recklessly. These suggestions seldom possess the sophistication to explain the villain's carnival antics. Filmmakers suspect, and probably suspect correctly, that viewers who cheer the psychopath's wild shenanigans, will care less about the catalyst that sets this evil into motion.

Speed (1994) demonstrates the quintessential elements for a thriller, directed by Jan De Bont with the screenplay by Graham Yost. The good guys marshal all sorts of help and technology in the film, although the basic conflict pairs off one hero and one villain. Jack Traven (Keanu Reeves) and Howard Payne (Dennis Hopper) fulfill these roles, and, frankly, neither character amounts to warm spit without the other. Howard is a nut, but a smart nut. He has worked diligently for two years to plan and rig an elevator job, only to see his handiwork go awry because of Jack's resourcefulness. Howard reflects on his disaster by noting ruefully, "This day has been real disappointing, I don't mind saying."

Howard's wit, tenacity, and sheer malevolence resurface to equip a city bus with an explosive device. A speed of 50 mph arms the device, but if the bus slows to below 50 mph, well, goodbye cruel world. Viewers sit back and know that, for most of *Speed*, Howard Payne will enjoy himself immensely. He loves giving orders, making outrageous demands, and strutting his superiority over the peasants who scramble hither and yon, bewitched, bothered, and bewildered.

Dennis Hopper has a lock on this kind of madness, as demonstrated in *Blue Velvet* (1986). He commands the actor's physiognomy, temperament, and style to play the undercontrolled psychopath: someone who needs the wild ride of emotional evil, someone who places himself in danger to make the game worthwhile. Howard invokes secrecy and misdirection as tools to buy time and further his schemes, but he evidences less interest in using these tools for the sake of anonymity.

Undercontrolled psychopaths in film do not care to maintain a low profile; instead, they crave attention and desire recognition for their monumental egos. (Think of the Joker, Penguin, Catwoman, and Riddler of the *Batman* series; think of egomaniacs like Goldfinger in the *James Bond* adventures; think of Hans Gruber, the haughty ringmaster of *Die Hard* (1988), who gave John McClane a few close calls; think of James Cagney in *White Heat* (1949): "Made it, Ma. Top of the world!")

The question of motivation in *Speed*--of why Howard Payne feels the need to engage in attempted mass murder-- prompts little concern. He portrays an ex-cop with a minor injury in the line of duty, and all Howard has to show for his plight is a cheap watch and a miserly pension. He wants more, say, three million dollars more: "I want money, Jack. I wish that I had some loftier purpose, but I'm afraid in the end it's just the money, Jack."

Actually, Howard's not completely honest here. Money

constitutes his material motive, but, psychologically, he entertains delusions of grandeur, which, of course, can make him paranoid as well as pathological. The indecision occurs because Howard depicts an evildoer who enjoys killing, yet he has not lost touch with reality. Indeed, he becomes an individual capable of expressing the height of his emotional evil. Howard harbors godlike thoughts of superiority, although his thoughts appear grounded in the real world. Whether he has crossed the line into a fantasy world and left reality behind becomes an issue that the moviegoer must decide.

A final confrontation with Jack does lead Howard off into a mental wilderness when he contemplates the "beauty" of a bomb: "You still don't get it, do you Jack, huh? The beauty of it. A bomb is made to explode. That's its meaning, its purpose. Your life is empty because you spend it trying to stop the bomb from becoming..."

Given Howard's existential philosophy about explosions, it seems time for him to make his dramatic exit. And to no one's surprise, he does so in grand, mind-boggling fashion. The point, however, is that *Speed* does not bother with Howard's reason for being. Any explanation will do since Howard Payne's paramount calling involves his parody as a psychopathic bomber. He entertains us with a stylistic exposition of undercontrolled villainy. *Speed* does not concern itself with anything less than an acceleration of the senses, an unsettling thrust forward that accords prime value to psychopathic traits like impulsiveness and arrogance. Emotionally, Howard's an evil hoot.

But Howard, for all his skills and grandiose ideas, pales in comparison to Mona Demarkov (Lena Olin) of *Romeo Is Bleeding* (1994). The film, directed by Peter Medak and written by Hilary Henkin, exemplifies Demarkov as the undercontrolled psychopath, unfettered and unconcerned for even her own safety: a woman who boasts enough sexual sadism to launch a line of leatherwear, enough street smarts to bury a mob boss alive (which she does), enough deadly charm to scare the hell out of everyone who is near her, and enough moxie to cut off her left arm if it serves a selfish purpose (again, which she does). Like Howard, Mona relies on secrecy and misdirection to keep the opposition off balance, but she is too much the exhibitionist to go incognito for long.

Jack Grimaldi (Gary Oldman) is not too reassuring as the "good guy." He represents a flawed police officer who informs a mob boss, Don Falcone (Roy Scheider), on the location of hostile witnesses before they testify. Jack rhapsodizes, not about his wife or his mistress, but about the money he puts away as an informer...and about Mona.

He meets Mona after her capture by federal agents. She has sprayed the room with bullets and left several corpses behind, but agents and police want Mona in protective custody to testify against her old flame, Don Falcone. Jack, transporting Mona to her hideaway, observes, "So you're the big hoodlum. Personally, I don't see it." Mona's reply is, "Keep looking." Naturally, Jack fails to take her advice, and, predictably, Mona proceeds to make his life an even worse torment than he can imagine.

Before *Romeo Is Bleeding* winds down, Mona, peeling forth her raucous laugh of elation, attempts to strangle Jack, first with a wire, and later with her legs wrapped around his throat. The latter effort results in a car accident from which she escapes. She then frames him for murder by finessing Jack into killing his mistress whom he mistakes for Mona. She further dulls his senses by tempting him into sexual intercourse, offering the befuddled "hero" an option: sex with or without her artificial arm. (Mona severs her left arm at the elbow and leaves it at a crime scene to convince Don Falcone and the authorities that she is dead.)

Mona is a work of grotesque art, a beautiful creature hiding untold layers of ugliness and deceit. What possible motivation transforms her into this snarling wolverine with heels? Frankly, she is too undercontrolled a psychopath, too bigger-than-life a femme fatale to permit any serviceable explanation of her behavior. Mona concocts a low-road "explanation" when she recounts her first sexual experience-- an incident at age 16 with a lifeguard on a beach. She reminiscences with "I guess you never forget the first time," but what Mona means is that the guy became her first lover...and her first victim.

The climactic scene occurs when Jack, in custody, encounters Mona, "back from the dead" and about to walk free after finagling the justice system with her indescribable charms. Indeed, Mona **would** have gone free except for her arrogance, the psychopath's Waterloo as we learned in Lessons 1 to 4. She taunts Jack, telling him she never liked him--even when they were screwing. Then Mona crosses the line, not realizing that Jack would harbor any moral scruples for such a line to exist. She mentions his wife (who Jack has sent away with the money) and issues a warning: "Too bad, Jack, because you're never going to get a chance to do it to her again. She's a dead woman, just like you're a dead man."

Mona underscores her prophecy by slipping a hand in her blouse as if to pull a gun, then, reveling in Jack's look, she removes her hand to give him a gesture of contempt. Jack, knowing that Mona will search for his wife and fulfill the threat, manages to grab a detective's gun and gives Mona the fitting termination she deserves. Plastered with bullet wounds, her face contorted in pain and surprise, she turns full view to the camera, and gasps a final breath: Mona, paying evil's price for her almighty ego.

OVERCONTROLLED PSYCHOPATHS

Overcontrolled personalities prove less amenable to the psychopathic label. They constitute self-contained individuals who keep a low profile, hold their own counsel, and maintain a tight rein over impulsive behaviors. The suppression is not perfect however, because on infrequent occasions overcontrolled psychopaths punctuate their low-profile demeanor with some high-profile violence.

The overcontrolled personality fails to blend as naturally with the dynamics of psychopathy compared to the undercontrolled individual. Psychopaths characteristically find patience a burden, and prefer to possess what they want as soon as possible--if not sooner. But filmmakers do not concern themselves with such disparities. They enjoy presenting a personality as a shadowy, menacing force, who becomes all the more evil for his ghostly presence. Thus, this overcontrolled cinematic psychopath shares the key quality of abdicating moral responsibility with the undercontrolled type, yet differs in other respects.

The overcontrolled psychopath behaves softly and circumspectly, although not for reasons of low self-esteem or feelings of guilt. This evil figure conjures up an inner world of superiority and anticipation. He possesses the discipline to bide his time, and, unobtrusively, to gain gratification in surprising our hero by entering through the back door. Secrecy and misdirection, used casually by the undercontrolled psychopath, prove more indispensable to the overcontrolled psychopath's true image.

Women who portray overcontrolled psychopaths assume **omega roles** in the movies (Wilson, 1994, p. 150). Omega characters reflect women who use their considerable sex appeal to quietly go about the business of deluding men, manipulating men, and, sometimes, murdering men. We speak--not of undercontrolled personalities, like Mona Demarkov, who adore their notoriety--but of cold, calculating minimalists like Phyllis Dietrichson (Barbara Stanwyck) of *Double Indemnity* (1944); Catherine (Theresa Russell) of *Black Widow* (1987); and Margaret Ford (Lindsay Crouse) of *House Of Games* (1987). These femme fatales work in the best film noir tradition of playing the overcontrolled psychopath. Boisterous demands do not suit their character; instead, they portray smart, sexy, reclusive...and deadly predators.

Omega characters flash glacially on the screen, presenting themselves as captivating, bewitching, tantalizing, and unattainable. Certainly Matty Walker epitomizes such qualities, and more. Ned (William Hurt) and Matty (Kathleen Turner) find themselves drawn to each other in *Body Heat* (1981): he, a lawyer of dubious skills, and she, a femme fatale of dubious reputation. She is married and affluent; he is neither, but these differences seem to enhance their torrid affair.

Directed and written by Lawrence Kasdan, the deception begins when Ned "pursues" Matty at an outdoor concert, searching for an introduction. He conveniently makes himself available as she walks away from the concert for a breath of air, not realizing that Matty engineers his pursuit to spin her own entanglements of deceit. She even tells him, "You're not very smart. I like that in a man."

The lovers acquaint themselves in a rush of lustful passion: on the floor, across the bed, in a hot tub. These recreational activities depict the plot's nicer moments. Murder and deception follow. Ned and Matty conspire to kill Matty's husband, who is not a nice guy anyway. The conspiracy leads Ned to club the husband to death and transport his body elsewhere for arson. The lawyer in him tries to be careful but he is doomed because of Matty. Matty, with her surreptitious scheme, dupes him. She dupes him when she selects Ned as a lover; she dupes him into killing her husband; and she dupes him away from her embrace and into the arms of the law. Justly, Ned goes to prison. Unjustly, Matty goes to Hawaii. She stays free of Ned, of the police, and of any remorse over her duplicity.

Ned harbors a premonition that fate will work against him, but he is no match for Matty's skullduggery. Ned's experience occurs as he seeks to establish an alibi for himself before he murders Matty's husband. He sees a car very similar to his vehicle, driven by a man dressed as a clown. A fool. Ned's eyes open wide to show his awareness that the fool and the car strike a personal chord. The foreboding remains too fleeting to afford Ned much insight or to deter him, but the uneasy thought lodges in place. Something will go wrong, very wrong, and Ned senses that he does not possess the foresight to free himself. And...he is right. Matty's subterranean skills doom him and give her everything she wants. If you have an omega female for a friend, you do not need an enemy.

Characteristic of the overcontrolled psychopath is the mystique of Matty's feelings about her duplicity. She appears genuinely attracted to Ned as a sexual partner, and to sex in general. But does the attraction reflect true passion on Matty's part, or is she playing another role? Recall that part of evil's perfection involves the enjoyment of one's devilish success. Matty represents more than a cognitive match for her opposition. Emotionally, however, she remains a cipher.

The overcontrolled psychopath also denotes a different kind of man from the undercontrolled antics of a Howard Payne in *Speed*. Since every hero needs a nemesis, what better adversary than to fashion a strong, silent male who almost rivals the hero in his capabilities. The operative word is "almost." The difference between the two opponents centers on the nemesis's dark soul, and, in particular, his belief in a quiet superiority that places him above the also-rans.

Henry Fonda plays this type of stark, overcontrolled villain in *Once Upon A Time In The West* (1968), as does Jack Palance in *Shane* (1953). Neither character has much use for secrecy and misdirection since the gunfighter's mere presence creates a sense of dread. The shootist does not need to hide his evil, and, truth be told, makes use of his victims' fear to gain a psychological edge in life-or-death contests. This version of the overcontrolled psychopath says little and does little, except that his opponents know he can erupt into violence at any time.

On the other hand, Thomas Boyette (Tommy Lee Jones) of *The Package* (1989) can hardly afford such an open, ruthless reputation. Directed by Andrew Davis and written by John Bishop, based on a story by Bishop and Dennis Haggerty, *The Package* presents Boyette as a soldier, a good combat veteran, though a veteran gone bad. A few rebel leaders within the military know that he is an assassin and desire his services. This group wishes to give the military/industrial complex succorance by halting a nuclear disarmament treaty in order to spruce up the cold war. Boyette's responsibility involves terminating the President of the United States. His willingness to undertake the team's assignment tells us that Thomas Boyette carries a deep respect for money, and that he boasts all the arrogance viewers can ask of the compleat psychopath.

Boyette, however, realizes the need for secrecy and misdirection. He covers his true purpose by presenting himself as a hothead who gets into trouble with authority. Even so, Boyette finds it difficult to hide his disdain for the mechanics of deceit and for the military brass who need his skills. He travels back to the states, ostensibly a prisoner (with a false name: Walter Henke) in the custody of a sergeant, Johnny Gallagher (Gene Hackman). The two military men exchange comments that prove more telling than Gallagher comprehends at the time: Boyette tells Gallagher, "You think I'm full of shit, don't you John?" Gallagher replies, "I think you're going to prison, Walter." But, ominously, Boyette only says, "You don't know where I'm going."

And, of course, Gallagher does not. Later, when the military team captures Gallagher and plans to leave the sergeant in a burning house, Boyette brings the beleaguered veteran milk and cookies--not to ridicule him but as an ironic last meal before Gallagher's execution. The assassin respects Gallagher as an adversary more than he respects the military fanatics who require his expertise. Indeed, the arrogant loner rebuffs his co-conspirators at every turn, and maintains a detached air during the period of preparation. Thomas Boyette knows he can do what others can not: Wait for that perfect moment to place the cross hairs on the President's head, and, with a marksman's skill, squeeze the trigger.

We do not expect Boyette to succeed, and he does not. But we do admire the man's self-possessiveness and utter lack of remorse as he moves with an expert's quiet grace to fulfill his mission. If the word "admire" seems too generous a descriptor, then choose another expression. Remember, however, that evil conveys an illicit appeal as entertainment: the more captivating the psychopath, the more fulsome the evil. Compared to the rigid, humorless mind-sets of the rebel military force, Thomas Boyette's wry contempt for their philosophy makes his character more intriguing--despite the man's underlying malevolence. (Consequently, Boyette's irreverent demeanor plays a notch better than do the solemn portrayals of assassins who stalk their prey in *The Manchurian Candidate* (1962) and *The Day Of The Jackal*, 1973.)

The beauty that Boyette finds in evil appears to rest with his exceptional skills as a strategist and marksman. He sets himself, not apart, but above those lesser individuals who need his services. He does so, moreover, as a philosopher who considers his "take" on human relations superior to that of the powermongers and their conscriptional ideas for a more militant world.

Still, mustering the proper motivation to understand overcontrolled psychopaths in film fares no better than do the low-road interpretations to understand undercontrolled personalities. Beyond the immediate idea that psychopaths do what they do because of their sheer delight in manipulating victims, these evil types may as well have no past.

Matty Walker's background remains vague, prompting the assumption that she has been playing the game to her advantage for a long time. And combat may have changed Thomas Boyette's priorities, but more likely war offers him the catalyst he needs to perfect his lethal skills. Again, why Matty and Thomas become psychopaths proves less prepossessing than to consider how these characters hone themselves into "serene" figures who dispatch human obstacles with a minimum of fuss and bother.

CLASSIC PSYCHOPATHS

Filmmakers favor undercontrolled and overcontrolled psychopaths because, with only a few cinematic brush strokes, the characters are quickly identifiable to viewers. First impressions of these caricatured personalities do not change much as the story progresses. The extreme characters we see in the movie's opening action generally continue unabated and unaltered until the movie's finale.

Undercontrolled and overcontrolled psychopaths represent cinematic bookends. Do you desire a predator who claims virtually no past, who never does anything in moderation, and who appears exquisitely endowed to give mere mortals a harrowing taste of evil? Fine, then savor the likes of a Howard Payne or Mona Demarkov if you wish a loose cannon; and swing towards Matty Walker or Thomas Boyette if you crave a muted instrument of violence.

The problem is that extreme psychopaths denote rather austere personalities. Extremes are fascinating but they hardly do justice to the psychopathic character. What about those psychopaths who realize a more complete individuality? What about those amoral personalities whose conduct appears more believable than the fanaticism of an undercontrolled or overcontrolled psychopath?   What about the dynamics of taking the **high road** in exploring character?

The challenge of examining the **classic psychopath** arises because psychopaths do not characteristically improve themselves to please their families or society.   Robert Hare (1993, p. 98) offers a bleak assessment regarding the psychopath's likelihood of enhancing his or her maturity over time: "The difference is that they have learned to satisfy their needs in ways that are not as grossly antisocial as before. However, this does not mean that their behavior is now moral and ethical."

Character development for the psychopath does not mean becoming more benevolent and loving with age.   Quite the contrary, it **can** mean that the evil personality assumes greater sophistication in learning how to tweak the opposition.   The psychopath's selfish gratifications do not change, merely the process by which he or she gains these gratifications.

So, how does a filmmaker conquer the daunting task of presenting the classic psychopath as a believable, developmental character?   To wit, how does the filmmaker make the classic psychopath more credible than the undercontrolled and overcontrolled figures who slam home their far-fetched schemes of celebrity and greed?

One answer--a high-road answer--concerns evaluating a movie like *Hud* (1963), based on a Larry McMurtry novel *Horseman, Pass By*, with direction by Martin Ritt and screenplay by Irving Ravetch and Harriet Frank, Jr.   Our appraisal involves giving Hud (Paul Newman) a bit of life history, and judging the effects of his longevity on those individuals close to him.   Thus, we first make Hud's acquaintance, not face to face, but via the artifacts of his rabble-rousing aftermath on the town: broken glass from a fight in a bar, and a married woman's shoe. Hud's nephew, Lon (Brandon de Wilde), arrives to retrieve his uncle from the lady's house, just as her husband returns. Hud, thinking fast, leads the husband to believe that it was Lon with the man's wife, and then manages to drive away before the husband can act.

Homer Bannon (Melvyn Douglas), Hud's father, long ago surrendered any hope for his son. Homer holds strong affection for Lon, for Alma (Patricia Neal) his housekeeper, for his cattle (especially his two longhorn steers), and even for the desolate Texas landscape. But he draws the line at Hud. On one occasion, Lon asks his grandfather, "You don't carry a picture of Hud around with you, do you?" And Homer replies, "No, I don't."

The characterizations and their relationships become painfully clear, painfully early. Hud cares for himself, and money, and rowdy times, and available women, and some women not so available, like Alma. Hud does not care for the ranch, and he particularly does not care for Homer's interfering presence. Homer tells him, "You're an unprincipled man, Hud." Hud knows, and hates Homer for reminding him.

Alma, wise and weary about men, understands that Hud represents trouble. She can match him retort for retort, but Alma flashes a worried look when she realizes that Hud is closing in. Hud says to her, "Honey, the only question I ever ask any woman is what time is your husband coming home." Alma replies, "No thanks. I've done my time with one cold-blooded bastard. I'm not looking for another." But Hud tells her, "It's too late, honey. You already found him." This final statement proves prophetic, justifying Alma's concern and resulting in another Hud-inspired tragedy.

Homer strikes an imposing figure as Hud's adversary. The one person who knows Hud best, the one force who harnesses the kind of goodness that his son and his amoral ways fail to overcome. When Hud asks his father why he has never cared for him, Homer goes through chapter and verse, citing Hud's lack of values, shallow charms, and oversized sexual appetites, summing up his son's sad credo on life with this denouncement: "You live just for yourself, and that makes you not fit to live with."

A series of misfortunes bring the relationships to a boil. The cattle, diseased, must be destroyed, a catastrophe that saps Homer's already weakened physical condition. Hud wants to end all cattle operations and use the land for drilling oil, a conversion that Homer finds totally unacceptable. The land is the land, it is meant for cattle, not oil. Hud, rebuffed again, then commits three sins that Lon, his nephew, cannot forgive.

First, in a drunken state, Hud attempts to rape Alma, but Lon intervenes. Despite Lon's pleas, Alma knows she must not stay. Waiting at the bus stop with her tattered suitcase, she accidentally meets a now sober Hud. A heartfelt apology is not in him, although he does admit that things got out of hand. Then, as Alma boards her bus, he ventures a more Hud-like, parting thought: "I'll remember you honey. You're the one that got away."

The second sin concerns Hud's revelation to Lon that he plans to declare Homer incompetent and gain control of the ranch. Hud has not changed his amoral philosophy, but he has devised a different strategy for getting what he wants. He wants the ranch, he wants to drill for oil, and he wants Homer out of sight and out of mind, pronto.

Before Hud can begin his legal tactics, Homer falls from his horse on an evening ride and suffers a heart attack. Lon and Hud find him crawling across the road. A dispirited Homer, looking at Hud, tells Lon, "Hud there's waiting on me, and he ain't a patient man." Homer knows what Hud wants, and what he wants is not necessarily for Homer to stay alive.

Lon knows, too. Sin number Three: He recognizes that, besides the financial setbacks and Alma leaving, Hud has simply worn Homer down through the years, engaging in one unloving episode after another. Hud has given his father no reason to live, a transgression of selfishness that Lon finds unforgivable.

The final scene shows Lon carrying his gear and leaving the ranch. Hud protests that it is a crappy world out there, but he can say nothing that will redeem himself to Lon. Sin number Three fosters an irreparable rift between Lon and Hud. Hud moves to the icebox for a beer, and watches Lon disappear from view. He pauses for a moment as the unsettling cloak of loneliness engulfs him...though only for a moment. Then, with the familiar smirk in place, he gestures good riddance and closes the door.

Hud depicts the classic psychopath. He is not a hot-blooded assassin or a cold-blooded, calculating killer, but he is clearly an individual who cares little for moral responsibility. Whatever humanity lurks in his iniquitous heart finds itself smothered by a mantle of self-centeredness and greed. Hud seems to have always been Hud, apparently unable to conform to basic decency. In this regard, we attain no greater insight into psychopathy's origins with Hud than we do with our other figures.

Hud's conduct, however, does not easily fit the pronounced behaviors of an undercontrolled or overcontrolled psychopath. Indeed, one complexity of the classic psychopath concerns the experience of learning more about someone like Hud from the personalities around him than from Hud himself. Hud's self-examination provides little insight, other than to contend that the world is no damn good and we may as well take what we can get. Paul Newman's sterling portrayal crackles and pops with vivacity as we glimpse the psychopath's shallow core, but it is his relationships with Homer and Lon and Alma that paint the harsher portrait: the portrait of how an amoral character can exert such a debilitating presence on others through the years.

Robert Mitchum's Max Cady of *Cape Fear* (1962) presents us with a classic psychopath more dangerous than Hud. Drawn from John D. MacDonald's *The Executioners*, and directed by J. Lee Thompson with the screenplay by James R. Webb, the film projects Cady as a primitive being, a bull of a man who sports a Panama hat and a big cigar to signal his signatures of self-esteem. Mitchum's physique and swaggering walk give Max Cady's body language just the right composition of insolence toward authority and his lust for female flesh. Entering the courthouse of a small southern community, Cady strolls past a woman who has dropped a book without helping her, and refers to a black janitor as "Daddy" when asking directions. We know quickly that this character stands a breed apart.

Max Cady does not conceal his degeneracy, indeed, the man thrives on glorifying sub-human appetites as a badge of distinction. More importantly, he possesses a native cunning;

an intellectual asset that makes all the difference in executing his decadent mission. Cady, consequently, begins to think differently about revenge while he is serving a prison sentence for assault and rape. Eight years, four months, and thirteen days later, the caged animal emerges from his lair to seek a different kind of retribution.

Max Cady's vendetta occupies our attention, but the lurking intelligence in *Cape Fear* concerns a more substantial message. The movie's theme details how the law seems to unravel when needed the most--to help innocent victims. And, yet, the movie also dramatizes how a reprobate like Cady can make the law work for him. Cady denigrates the ideal of legal rights by subverting these rights to accommodate his evil needs.

The psychopath demonstrates his predatory focus when he tells Diane Taylor (Barrie Chase), a bar girl, that she has one hour to get rid of her friends because he plans to pick her up. Diane, reading her "date" with marvelous accuracy, gives Cady an unmerciful assessment of himself: "Max Cady, what I like about you is you're rock bottom. I wouldn't expect you to understand this, but it's a great comfort for a girl to know she could not possibly sink any lower."

The question of why Diane wishes to tumble in bed with such an animal may have something to do with that animal's physical attractions, and with Diane's low appraisal of her self-worth. Whatever, it is a decision she dearly regrets. Cady stands and stares at her from the foot of the bed, stalking her with his eyes, sending a silent yet shrill warning that an experienced woman like Diane understands all too well: He needs to vent his rage, and she is the convenient victim.

Diane Taylor embodies the immediate target, but Max Cady's rage has more desirable prey in mind--a lawyer, Sam Bowden (Gregory Peck), his wife, Peggy (Polly Bergen), and 12-year-old daughter, Nancy (Lori Martin). Years before, while on business in Baltimore, Sam happened upon a severe beating. The victim, a woman; her attacker, Max Cady. Sam's testimony delivered Max to prison, and, naturally, Max found himself with ample time to remember, and remember, and remember. Later, when Sam tries to buy him off, Cady ventures the question: "What do you reckon eight lost years is worth? You reckon a court could fix a value on that?"

Max informs Sam that for seven years he simply wanted to strangle him for revenge. But the eighth year led Cady to a different philosophy--the "Chinese death of a 1000 cuts." The sadist instigates a little fear here, a little fear there, administering small doses that amount to a vexing fear of unpredictability.

This slow torture proves supremely taxing over the long haul, and Max Cady claims the time and the intellect to enact his leisurely program. He is going nowhere anyway, and, most importantly, he now marshals a knowledge of the law to complement his vengeance. The value that Cady places on those lost years is not to murder, but to sexually humiliate and savage Bowden's wife and daughter--especially the daughter.

Max reassures the police that he will cooperate with them when he must, and defy them legally when he can, even to the point of hiring a lawyer to protect himself from undue harassment. Cady, clear of police intervention, makes brief appearances at a bowling alley, Nancy's school, a boating dock--all locales that the Bowdens frequent. His Chinese war of nerves does not take long to fray the family's good spirits.

The implicit message of Cady's stalking, moreover, becomes the classic psychopath's cruelest psychological weapon: the foreknowledge and dread that Max Cady desires one Bowden, in particular. Sam informs Peggy, "It's Nancy he's after." Again, the law: Cady knows that the Bowdens will not put Nancy through the shame of a rape trial. The predator will find a way to savage the child, no problem; but, aside from the gratification, his cunning and arrogance tell him that he shall not suffer legal punishment.

The law figures at every turn of the hunt, surfacing more as an instrument of evil than protection for the innocent. Max Cady assures the authorities that he has money in the bank (not a vagrant), agrees to a strip search (cooperative), and refuses to fight with Sam at the boating dock (nonviolent). When Max does break the law, by poisoning the Bowden's dog and assaulting Diane, he does so with impunity. A dead dog is a dead dog; and Diane refuses to help the police, so

paralyzed is she by Cady's threat of harm. We last see Diane
heading for the bus station.

Sam Bowden then commits an almost fatal mistake. He
allows himself to be drawn into Cady's foul-smelling world by
authorizing thugs to attack the animal in hopes of scaring him
away. Bad move. Max fights off his enemies, and makes a
jubilant phone call to Sam: "You just put the law in my hands,
and I'm going to break your heart with it." Sam, facing
disbarment and the loss of any legal protection, desperately
calls on personal favors to try one final plan in bringing Cady
to justice.

The plan involves a scheme to lure Max to the Bowden's
houseboat on the lonely waters of Cape Fear, an opportunity
too inviting for the wily monster to dismiss. Even with the
trap set, Cady almost succeeds. He strips off his shirt as a
ground-level camera captures him poised, just for a moment,
fixated on his prey across the water. Then, silently, he slips
into the dark swamp, a 'gator in human form. The bodyguard,
helping to ambush Cady, carelessly slaps his face to ward off
an insect. The sound alerts Cady and he murders the man
using a head lock, murmuring, "You going to die without a
mark on you. You just got too big for your pants." After this
brief eulogy, Max gently pats the bodyguard's lifeless form, a
perverse gesture of pleasure at his own prowess.

Max confronts Peggy, feigning an attack on her, again
reciting the law by telling her that if she "consents," it is not
rape. His true target from the beginning, however, is little
Nancy. He forces the girl outside, but Sam intervenes and the
two adversaries--as distant morally as one can imagine--
commence their death struggle. Cady's muscular build gives
Sam Bowden little chance, although heroes in movies have that
undeniable resourcefulness to shatter the odds. For Sam, it
involves playing dead and, by chance, finding a large rock to
slam against Cady's head. It also involves discovering a lost
revolver and using it to shoot Max a split second before the
murderer can swing a club at Sam.

Given the odds, Cady should have realized victory, a
triumph of evil over good. But by the cinema's code of
conduct, Max Cady never has a chance. Goodness, though

apparently enfeebled and seemingly crushed beyond hope, bends but does not break. The wounded predator, in fact, urges Sam to kill him. Sam, however, brandishing his own form of Chinese torture, informs Cady that "We're going to take good care of you. We're going to nurse you back to health. You're strong, Cady. You're going to live a long life...in a cage!" For Max Cady, that denouement comprises the animal's darkest conception of a living Hell.

Comparing the two classic psychopaths, we find that Hud Bannon appears less threatening in character than Max Cady. Faint praise, of course, but the nuances of personality found in classic psychopaths permit such comparisons. Frankly, the more believable Max Cady becomes in an otherwise conventional southern town, the more frightening his presence.

Contrary to the absurdities of undercontrolled and overcontrolled individuals, the credibility of a classic psychopath allows us to contemplate the reality of his fear campaign. The belief that a Max Cady need not be wholly fictional adds another dimension of anxiety. And, unlike those personalities verging on the absurd, the complex presence of a classic psychopath institutes the greater likelihood that our movie experience will linger. A lurking intelligence persists that will not go away: What if you had a Max Cady in your life?

LECTER & ANTONY: A PAIR OF PREDATORS

Dr. Frederick Chilton (Anthony Heald), the eminently narcissistic psychiatrist of *The Silence Of The Lambs* (1991), speaks his pompous mind on Hannibal Lecter: "Oh, he's a monster. A pure psychopath...It's so rare to capture one alive. From a research point of view, Lecter is our most prized asset..." (Tally, 1995, p. 149). From a psychiatric point of view, however, Chilton's diagnosis consists of "pure blarney."

Hannibal Lecter (Anthony Hopkins) symbolizes a contrivance of personality traits: psychopathic, yes; delusional, definitely; poised, even likeable, certainly. But add to these contradictory traits a jarring penchant for cannibalism and we find ourselves perplexed over the man's true nature. Lecter's core, his center of being, remains a mystery. The serenity and coarseness that incongruously issue forth suggests an inner character of warring tendencies, waiting for the right moment to become whomever he must to feed his ego, both literally and figuratively.

Surely, such a creature consists of sheer literary and Hollywood hokum. The truth, however, proves more unnerving. A psychiatrist, Martin Lubin (Lubin & Coe, 1982, pp. 35-36), recalls his encounter with an inmate at Bellevue Hospital in New York:

> This was no tattooed, growling brute, but an unremarkable, middle-sized man whose unusual light green eyes looked through yours. He could slowly recite the details of his known killings--he mentioned others too--with smiling calm. He often smiled, though of course he hadn't the slightest sense of humor. That smile and a certain way of cocking his head quizzically and staring meant that he was concentrating on you, bringing you into his personal focus of interest. And it wasn't for effect....The tough black militant Five Percenters and so-called Muslims who threatened judges and assaulted Corrections guards left this soft-spoken loner to himself. He had all the space he wanted. They knew he was made of some alien stuff.

Sound uncomfortably familiar? The inmate of note appears to resemble Lecter in ways that set our teeth on edge, but no one seems likely to own all the faculties attributed to Hannibal the Cannibal. Lecter, bluntly stated, does not fit easily into our study of cinematic psychopaths. He is amoral concerning society's values, although his bizarre behavior in staging a crucifixion of one policeman indicates a deranged mind that connects with reality only when the rewards make it worthwhile. In this instance, Lecter impersonates the other wounded police officer, and uses the ghastly crucifixion scene as an "art piece" to divert attention from himself (Lippy, 1995a, p. 203).

Yet when an officer asks the FBI trainee, Clarice Starling (Jodie Foster), about Lecter, Clarice--unlike Chilton--proposes a more honest diagnosis: "They don't have a name for what he is." Hannibal Lecter is too cosmopolitan, too obtuse, too depraved, too overwhelming in character to be anything other than a cinematic wonder cut from literary whole cloth (we first meet Lecter in Thomas Harris's novel *Red Dragon*, 1981). Anthony Hopkins's achievement with Lecter is to make the man "good company," so that viewers momentarily forget the murderer's beastly innards. Hannibal Lecter constitutes a perverse beauty, a truly inviting, frightful, watershed creation of a villain. He is just not a pure psychopath.

Argumentatively, Bruno Antony (Robert Walker) personifies the best classic psychopath that movie history has to offer in a screenplay by Raymond Chandler, Czenzi Ormonde, and Whitfield Cook, based on the novel by Patricia Highsmith. We meet him in Alfred Hitchcock's *Strangers On A Train* (1951) as a well-dressed, urbane, and knowledgeable chap full of interesting stories and seeming good will. These qualities, of course, merely exhibit the classic psychopath's kindly veneer. Beneath the bonhomie, Bruno's desire to "do everything before you die" includes committing murder, free of any recrimination.

An accidental encounter on a train leads Bruno to initiate a conversation with Guy Haines (Farley Granger), a tennis player harboring political ambitions. Bruno, in his lighthearted way, suggests that they "trade" murders to avoid suspicion. Bruno will murder Guy's estranged wife so that Guy can pursue his new sweetheart and a political career, and Guy will dispatch Bruno's father who, for Bruno, keeps too tight a check on him. Guy thinks that Bruno is talking hypothetically...but Guy is wrong.

Bruno proceeds to keep his end of the "agreement" by following Miriam (Laura Elliott), Guy's wife, and her two male companions for an evening of fun at an amusement park. Bruno hangs back and makes eye contact with Miriam. Miriam is curious. She sizes up this stranger with knowing glances that pass as sexual foreplay, but Miriam has too much ego wrapped up in her bespectacled attractiveness to imagine the lethal game Bruno intends.

He waits until she goes through a tunnel of love and arrives at the park's "Magic Isle." Once she separates from her boyfriends, Bruno approaches Miriam and intrigues her by asking, "Is your name Miriam?" When she answers yes, he quietly strangles her (Brill, 1988, p. 81). Strangling, a sexually intimate form of execution, occurs here via a distortion viewed through the lens of Miriam's eyeglasses that have fallen to the ground. Bruno's large hands appear larger still in the lens. Unwittingly, Guy is now committed to Bruno's secret and the psychopath's persistent reminders to complete the "trade."

Unlike Hannibal Lecter, who appears invulnerable, the distinguishing human quality of Bruno Antony's character concerns a susceptibility to his own indulgences, of which murder is the most majestic. He attends a formal party and approaches two older women, charming them with a hypothetical game of the best way to murder someone. Enthralled with his attentiveness and the idea, one lady allows him to use her as a pretend victim for strangling. Bruno, however, sees a senator's daughter who resembles Miriam, complete with glasses, and, transfixed on her image, he loses control and begins to strangle the "victim" in earnest.

Fortunately, he passes out from the deliciousness of the thought before the older lady succumbs to his large hands. Later, when Guy has Bruno taken to the den and revives him, an odd scene of "character suspension" occurs, an interlude that could never happen with Hannibal Lecter. Guy berates Bruno for coming to the party uninvited, and for scaring the lady in question. Guy, enraged at his own entanglement with Bruno, punches him. But then, feeling guilty for losing control, he straightens Bruno's tie and makes him presentable enough to leave the party without undue commotion. Bruno, dazed and taken aback at the strength of his fainting experience, allows Guy to tidy him up as if he has become big brother.

This scene highlights the sole moment whereby Bruno relinquishes control of who and what he is, whereby he permits any kind of helping hand to touch him. The moment will not last, and Bruno does not last, but his characterization reaches the kind of apogee that only transpires in a classic psychopath of impeccable credentials.

CHARACTER AND THE 3/2 MODEL

Aldrich Ames shares with his cinematic counterparts the same cognitive and emotional properties that lead into avarice, sexual lust, and duplicity. But he shares with them the Great Fall, as well. The counterspy played his enchanting game too long and too carelessly to escape the punishment that goodness brings to bear on evil's imperfections.

Abdicating responsibility and displaying no remorse, as always, denote the cognitive and emotional keys that differentiate psychopaths from those who care. Villains vary, however, in how they choose to employ secrecy and misdirection. Overcontrolled psychopaths usually find maintaining a low profile essential to executing a prescribed scheme. Undercontrolled psychopaths use these resources as they must to avoid detection, but prefer to exhibit themselves and flaunt their evil.

Classic psychopaths, less pronounced in conduct than the undercontrolled and overcontrolled personalities, also prove less conclusive regarding the importance of secrecy and misdirection to their mission. Because psychopaths characteristically do not dupe anyone very successfully over an extended time, their ultimate transparency as self-absorbed characters reflects a shallow disguise as well. Most psychopaths are not killers, and most are not so sophisticated that they can accomplish the trickery and deceit of a Hannibal Lecter--a feat quite natural to the world of movies.

Emotionally, the zest for wickedness appears quite evident with the rabid behavior of undercontrolled psychopaths like Howard Payne and Mona Demarkov, whereas this zest proves more subtle and complex with classic and overcontrolled personalities like Hud Bannon and Matty Walker. Such vitality reflects the beauty of evil and permits filmmakers to invest a certain magic into the psychopath's character. Hence, Hannibal Lecter's disposition remains more a mystique of "psychopath plus something" than does Bruno Antony's personality. This magic, after all, constitutes the artist's touch--a finessing of reality.

But the god-like delusions of grandeur experienced by

genuine cinematic psychopaths, whether expressed atrociously or veiled in superiority, do not indicate a psychotic's delusions. Psychotics create their own world of triumphs and persecutions, usually lacking the perceptiveness to negotiate adroitly with the world at large. The true cinematic psychopath, however, no matter how frenzied or guarded in character, continues to acknowledge and manipulate reality.

Lesson 6

Breach Of Character

$\mathbf{T}$*he Wolf Man* (1941) sounds a special chord because the film capitalizes on how its hero can become both **predator** and **prey**. Larry Talbot (Lon Chaney, Jr.), bitten by a werewolf, finds himself with a new, nocturnal avocation: prowling the foggy woods of rural England for human prey.

But Talbot also finds himself in torment. He is a nice guy who is transformed into a "bad guy" by default. Through no sin of his, and, indeed, because he attempts to save a victim from a werewolf, Talbot suffers a bite that sends his life spiraling downward. (Technically, the metamorphosis viewed briefly on screen required 20 hours of stop-and-go filming, as the makeup artist added yak hair, fangs, claws, and other assorted wolfish paraphernalia to Chaney; see Nash & Ross, 1987, p. 3893.)

The finished product, although exhibiting a respectfully fearsome appearance, still seems more man than beast. Nor do we witness untrammelled evil in the Wolf Man. Recall, as we discussed in Lessons 1 to 3, the usual limitations on malevolent monsters: The Wolf Man must restrict his carnivorous cavorting to an isolated wooded area during full-moon nights of the lunar cycle.

Worse, he is vulnerable to a silver bullet, a silver knife, or, in the case of Chaney's character, a cane crowned with the silver head of a wolf. Given that the Wolf Man depends on his habitat for secrecy, he must relinquish all hope of misdirection since no one who encounters this creature on a foggy evening will mistake him for a gentleman.

And, as if to ensure that Larry Talbot will not remain stress-free for long, three characters on separate occasions offer him the same swatch of werewolf verse: "Even a man who is pure in heart/And says his prayers by night/May become a wolf when the wolfbane blooms/And the autumn moon is bright" (Skal, 1993, p. 215). Notice that this verse fails to mention the need of a specific curse or a werewolf's bite to accomplish the metamorphosis.

The Wolf Man abdicates responsibility and commands the instinctual cunning and vitality of a lupine predator. Certainly we have a case of lycanthropy here, but do we have psychopathy? The Wolf Man does what werewolves normally do, staying true to its nature. Upon doing so, however, we could argue that the werewolf's natural inclinations just happen to resemble psychopathic behavior.

Larry Talbot constitutes the weak link to evil's success, which, in reverse, means that his decency works to curtail the werewolf's chances for longevity. (Indeed, Talbot's transformation to beastly form proves more modest and less vicious compared to later special effects that permitted a werewolf to look more like a wolf, as in *An American Werewolf In London*, 1981; see Paul, 1994, p. 384.)

Physically, good and evil appear in sharp contrast with regard to man and monster. Talbot agonizes over the blood spilled, whereas the Wolf Man mindlessly attacks whomever materializes in the woods, including Gwen (Evelyn Ankers), a young woman attracted to Talbot. The human abhors his beastly trappings, and, in retrospect, the two creatures personify the chasm between civility and chaos.

But psychologically, good and evil prove more complicated. Goodness, once again, presents itself as a pervasive force. The Wolf Man, on one sojourn, steps into a steel trap set for him. Writhing in pain, he passes out and is discovered by a gypsy woman, Maleva (Maria Ouspenskaya). She observes the fallen predator, his lower lip quivering from the evil energy that both shackles yet gives him life.

Maleva speaks quietly to the now passive beast: "Find peace for a moment, my son." The gypsy, more than anyone, understands the werewolf's curse and inevitable destiny. The Wolf Man, not wholly man or wolf, will die because the beast lives as an outcast. Larry Talbot, before his final transformation, asks his father (Claude Rains) to take the cane with the wolf's head, knowing that the father will be among those hunting for him that night.

The father agrees, not fully grasping his son's fatalistic gesture. The son can not protect his father from the Wolf Man, but, as Larry Talbot, he can try by making an unselfish decision: Talbot stacks the odds against his lupine counterpart and the evil that the werewolf legacy empowers.

THE SHADOW CONCEPT

Carl Jung's concept of the "**shadow**" involves a vital darker self we harbor, yet also a self that reflects the distasteful, more unfavorable qualities of our personality (Henderson, 1964, p. 118). A first impression suggests that the shadow simply belies another expression for acknowledging a "beast within," such as the Wolf Man (Sanford, 1982, p. 49):

> The term "the Shadow," as a psychological concept, refers to the dark, feared, unwanted side of our personality. In developing a conscious personality we all seek to embody in ourselves a certain image of what we want to be like. Those qualities that could have become part of this conscious personality, but are not in accord with the person we want to be, are rejected and constitute the shadow personality.

Good and evil, however, do not represent exact opposites, and neither does the shadow denote a one-dimensional cloak of malevolence (Rushing & Frentz, 1995, p. 39; Watson, 1995, p. 247). Rather, this archetype possesses the beneficial potential to deliver vigor and intensity, as through healthy anger or humor. The shadow contributes to humor, for instance, by provoking hearty laughter that designates an unguarded moment: laughter derived from the shadow's wellspring of emotions as opposed to polite laughter modified through social constraints.

But the ego, our cauldron of consciousness ("I did this" and "I did that"), wages its war to keep the repressed world of the shadow mostly repressed. The ego strives to submerge that unseemly part of our personality--the life not lived (Sanford, 1982, p. 51). This conflict normally favors the ego, which works consciously to maintain an acceptable self-image.

Regardless, the shadow personality's darker side **does** slip into awareness, fostering rage, harsh ridicule, and other ugly expressions. More pertinent to our aims, the shadow can become an integral part of the conscious personality. Such a maladjustment arises when the child fails to bond with his or her parents: The child does not learn how to love or to follow the civilities of society. As John Sanford (p. 55) states in his study of the shadow, "This can lead to the development of criminal or sociopathic personalities, that is, to an identification of the ego with the shadow."

Considering the prosperous ways in which the ego can develop, identifying with the shadow is not a good sign. Such an afflicted partnership gives secrecy, honesty, and responsibility a perverse twist. The shadow/ego "dualism" not only utilizes these cognitive functions for self-glorification, but it does so with verve. Emotionally, the shadow/ego personality truly enjoys utilizing what most of us would perceive as undesirable traits, best kept under lock and key.

METAMORPHOSIS

The shadow/ego "dualism," however, fails to provide us with a pure adversarial relationship. Sometimes the shadow and the ego join forces, and, when they do, we have trouble. The psychoanalytical language of "shadow" and "ego" does not muster much scientific support, but these concepts permit us to sketch a few complexities that attend good and evil.

One value of this language is to show that dualisms tend to fray at the edges. The straightforward idea of a **dualism** involves two independent principles, or entities, or divine beings, or anything that resolves itself into two mutually irreducible parts. Positive versus negative ions will do the trick, as will a binary system, or the opposing points on a compass. The nature of a dualism is that if we are one, we can not be the other.

The **metamorphosis** of certain creatures, at first glance, appears to encompass a dualism in transformation. The profound change from caterpillar to butterfly appears dualistic in function because of the organisms' striking dissimilarities. But both life forms share a transformation state, the pupa, that shows a continuum in change between the first stage and the last. Metamorphosis, therefore, constitutes a **continuum of development**, despite the striking transmutational contrasts of maggot to fly or tadpole to frog.

TRANSFORMATIONS OF GOOD AND EVIL

Imagine the werewolf legend in a more urban setting. Will Randall (Jack Nicholson), a book editor, inadvertently hits a wolf with his car as he travels through Vermont on a snowy evening, returning to New York. He is tired, he is stressed, he is apprehensive about losing his job because of a corporate takeover...and he hits a wolf in a locale where no wolves exist.

Will is also a nice guy, someone with "taste and individuality" who finds himself eased out the door because, frankly, he is not ruthless enough for the publishing business. When Will attempts to move the animal off the road, he is bitten--and what transpires afterward may or may not be a most fortuitous experience for this passive character.

Directed by Mike Nichols and written by Jim Harrison and Wesley Strict, *Wolf* (1994) begins as did *The Wolf Man* with an accidental bite, and a changed life. But unlike Larry Talbot, Will Randall thrives on his new, though as yet unexplained vitality (courtesy of the shadow personality). He feels good, occasionally punctuating savored moments with soft growls of appreciation: He sniffs a co-worker's breath and knows the man had a tequila for breakfast; he edits a manuscript without his glasses; and he extends his hearing threshold to detect snippets of conversation from distant offices.

Will is no dummy. He realizes that feeling so good comes at a price. One price he pays, upon sniffing an executive's scent on his wife's clothing, is the wolf's instant awareness of carnal pleasures behind his back. He arrives to confront his wife, Charlotte (Kate Nelligan), and the executive, Stewart Swinton (James Spader). Stewart tries to restrain him, but Will, in a canine rage, bites the executive and literally leaps up the stairs to find Charlotte in Stewart's bedroom.

The man's basic decency keeps him from harming his wife, but the marriage crumbles...as does Will's heretofore passive nature. He shifts from defense to offense by threatening to take a line of top authors and set up business elsewhere. The corporate boss, Raymond Alden (Christopher Plummer), knows a smart bastard when he sees one, and acquiesces to Will's demands of reinstatement. Will, sensing triumph, gives Alden a wolfish smile and adds the *coup de grâce* to his conquest: "But I still have those two big drawbacks, taste and individuality."

He clearly has more taste and individuality than the resident psychopath, Stewart Swinton. Stewart's overworked tactic of misdirection involves proclaiming loyalty to Will, no matter what. But Stewart's private agenda, aside from his sexual indiscretions with Will's wife, reveals a deceitful swine who ardently pursues the job that Will desires.

Even when exposed on both counts, Stewart, encountering Will in the restroom, continues his lame entreaties to save face: "I'm glad in a way...I couldn't have given it up and I didn't like the way I got it. I hope we can work together without rancor." The old Will may have indulged Stewart, but the new Will simply lets him run out his spill. Then, in a act of canine inspiration, Will pees on Stewart's expensive shoes, informing the duplicitous executive that he is "Just marking my territory and you got in the way."

Visiting Dr. Alezias (Om Puri), a scholar on the werewolf, Will seeks a sense of what will happen next. The doctor gives him a charm to help defy the next metamorphosis. Speaking of the transformation, Alezias explains, "Sometimes one doesn't even need to be bitten--only the passion of the wolf is enough."

Recall this same wisdom conveyed to Larry Talbot: Namely, that the wolf's spirit of cunning and freedom can capture a man's passion--even a man pure in heart--and make him susceptible to the werewolf's devilish haunts. The prophecy carried foreboding and finally death for Talbot, but the wolf's sensual zest harbors a more optimistic choice for Will Randall. Dr. Alezias buttresses this optimism when he adds, "The demon wolf is not evil, unless the man he's bitten is evil."

Ahhh, yes, well...let us not forget Stewart Swinton. The psychopath tumbles, and later murders, Will's wife; the psychopath surreptitiously covets and temporarily gains the position that Will deserves; and the psychopath engages in these covert activities, while overtly professing his allegiance and support to Will. Stewart possesses the requisite mechanisms, cognitively and emotionally, to foster his evil.

But he falters in his ability to show cleverness through misdirection. Stewart shackles himself with a one-track motive called ambition, and fails to behave as adroitly as he might in feathering his nest. The outcome of this failure results in Stewart receiving his comeuppance by suffering a bite from Will, and by losing his job.

The bite, of course, unleashes Stewart the werewolf. His viciousness as a prowling beast sets him apart from Will, and confirms the continuity of evil from one life form to the other. Indeed, the dualism proves less noticeable between Stewart the slouching sycophant, and Stewart the callous beast. Gaze either way and we discover an amoral creature.

The central figure in the werewolves' final duel concerns Laura Alden (Michelle Pfieffer), Raymond Alden's daughter. The dislike Laura feels for her father instills in her a maverick spirit. She is attracted to Will and his dilemma, and Will is attracted to her. Stewart, lamentably, makes three.

He sexually assaults Laura, as Will, wearing the amulet given him by Dr. Alezias, watches helplessly. Then, making his fateful choice, Will chucks the charm, regains his lupine strength and attacks Stewart. Two werewolves fighting for survival, one purely evil and one a complexity of compassion and ferocity.

Thinking he has won, Will turns away from a prostrate Stewart. But Stewart, as villains have done for many a moon, rises from the ashes. He launches himself in a wolfish leap to stab Will in the back with a pair of garden shears. Laura, however, surprises Stewart in mid-leap by emptying her pistol at him, leaving us with one less werewolf, and one less psychopath in the world.

Will, nonetheless, now finds his options simplified. Choosing to save Laura, he delivers himself to the wolf's kingdom. Will leaves behind one life for a different existence as he progressively becomes more wolf than man. And Laura, bitten in the struggle with Stewart, subsequently makes her choice. She, too, transforms, tracking Will's scent to join him. Her eyes gleam with a predator's glow, changing from blue to yellow, changing to a hunter's eyes...a wolf's eyes.

BREACH OF CHARACTER

Stepping back from the sheer dynamics of metamorphosis, we encounter one of the purer cinematic tools for character alteration. **Breach of character** refers to an infraction, a violation, a transgression of conduct contrary to the individual's accepted personality.

A key consideration in assessing the good and evil associated with breach of character concerns the idea of **personal control**. Does the personality assume command of the change in character? Clearly, Larry Talbot finds himself at the mercy of the werewolf's curse. He represents a victim, someone whose lack of control over the transformation and the creature leaves him with two options: (1) Continue to suffer the metamorphoses and agonize over the Wolf Man's prey during those full-moon excursions; or (2) manipulate the odds, which Talbot does, and engineer the Wolf Man's next venture into a suicide mission.

Commanding the least personal control over his fate, Larry Talbot bears less moral responsibility for the deaths caused in wolf form. A dualism of character becomes most evident in his plight, although the underlying continuum and complexity of relating good to evil remain in place. Talbot does not mask his conflicted state well, prompting the prejudices of certain townspeople to surface. They suspect him of wrongdoing, but do not comprehend the full scope of Talbot's anguish.

Will Randall, however, possesses greater personal control. Frightened by the metamorphosis and his predatory behavior, he nonetheless thrives on a heightened sensitivity to the sights, sounds, and smells around him. He enjoys becoming more savage toward those who wrong him--both as man and wolf--but he exercises discretion against his adversaries and in his search for food. Unlike Talbot, Will realizes an opportunity to slip away from the curse, but forgoes that option when he dispenses with the amulet to save Laura.

Stewart Swinton provides us with the most promising prospect for evil, evidencing, at best, slightly less restraint as wolf than as man. Stewart nurtures all the malevolent yearnings we associate with a werewolf. Had he not been summarily terminated, the psychopath would have reveled in his metamorphoses and the atrocities thereafter. Just the celebrity of knowing that **he** was the nocturnal serial beast, slashing throats and littering bodies, would have tickled his pathetic heart.

The bleak outlook for metamorphic characters begins most notably with Robert Louis Stevenson's (1983) *Dr. Jekyll And Mr. Hyde*. Naïve regarding the intricacies of good and evil, Dr. Jekyll initiates an experiment to separate the two forces: The evil Mr. Hyde will go his way, and the saintly Dr. Jekyll his. Sadly, Jekyll never understands the foolishness of this belief (Saposnik, 1983, p. 113).

The dualism of Jekyll and Hyde, as with most literary and cinematic personalities, is not absolute (Wilson, 1996, p. 116). Indeed, Jekyll voluntarily begins the metamorphosis by drinking his "potion," although as the transformations continue, he loses personal control and Hyde becomes dominant. They differ in appearance, but, psychologically, each is harnessed to the other. The release of Jekyll's shadow figure simply means that the evil in Jekyll manifests itself more outwardly in Edward Hyde.

Here, **physical mutation** is deceiving. Because movies lock viewers into the sensations of vision and sound, what moviegoers see and hear monopolize their attention. Filmmakers can be very cinematic when they "split" a character, especially if they do so through metamorphosis. The intense experience of observing a dramatic change, namely, the physics and biology of transforming one character into a contrasting character, precludes other considerations.

The **psychology of dual characters**, however, represents another matter. Cognitive and emotional changes occur, yet the supposedly disparate characters can not rupture their psychological bond. Even Larry Talbot shelters a shadow personality, and it is this personality that gains release as the Wolf Man. Whenever evil finds manifestation and intensity in the metamorphic creature, that evil realizes its origin in the more humane host (think of Stewart Swinton as a prime example).

Likewise, evil suffers diminished power as the creature reverts to human form. The link between dual characters varies according to the host's personal control in managing the transformation, and by the evil already vested in the host character. But whatever the degree of control and the evil present, the two personalities--psychologically--find themselves in a peculiar state of symbiosis.

Forbidden Planet (1956), for example, conjures up a sampling of Freudian fare to dramatize the psychological limitations that plague metamorphic evil. Directed by Fred Wilcox and written by Cyril Hume, the story begins when a space crew travels to a distant planet, Altair-4, to monitor the planet's colonization, initiated by a party of scientists 20 years earlier. What Commander Adams (Leslie Nielson) and his crew discover instead, is Dr. Morbius (Walter Pidgeon) and his daughter, Altaira (Anne Francis), as the sole human dwellers.

A reluctant Morbius explains away the mystery by noting that a dark force killed the other colonizers, except for Morbius's wife, who died of natural causes (an important exception to solving the puzzle). But other mysteries remain, including a profoundly intelligent robot who serves Morbius and Altaira as a benign guardian and master of many trades and languages.

How did Morbius, though possessed of a high intellect, construct such a robot and other marvelous inventions? The answer, peeled off layer by layer, is the Krell. The Krell denote a prodigiously bright civilization, long since extinct. Their legacy of intellectual accomplishments remains, however, symbolized by massive power stations that continue to function and to provide self-maintenance.

One auxiliary of Krell power concerns the "brain booster," a knowledge accelerator that Morbius learns to use, despite the physiological toll this device exerts on his brain. The increase in brain power allows Morbius to survive in luxury, and to protect himself and his daughter from the invisible monster that lurks outside the Morbius domain.

Murder and destruction follow, leading to the nihilistic conclusion that the evil monster exists, not in substance, but as part and parcel of the subconscious. In Freudian terms, the creature derives from the id (Twitchell, 1985, p. 80):

> "The id--what's that?" queries the Commander, and Morbius, ever the patient instructor, explains. The id, he says, is an "obsolete term once used to describe the elementary structure of the subconscious." So it seems that the Krell were destroyed, not by Faustian overreaching, but by neglecting to care for the "mindless beast" of their subconscious.

The Krell, in other words, allowed their intellect to overlook the dark forces residing in their subconscious. Magnified by the "brain booster," the evil creature becomes more than an apparition. The "id" monster, or as Carl Jung might prefer, the "shadow" monster, wantonly murders in a display of pure evil. The problem is that the demon belongs, not to the Krell...but to Morbius.

The music of *Forbidden Planet*, instead of relying on synthesizers, uses electronic impulses to give the spaceship, the robot, and especially the id-monster a special other-worldliness, a kind of "futuricity" (Brown, 1994, p. 183). This "futuricity" shadows the monster with an eerie presence, particularly when viewers have almost no visual reference to use in imagining the beast.

The creature represents a protective measure by Morbius to apply when he feels threatened. Morbius's protectiveness, exaggerated manyfold courtesy of the Krell intellect, dampens interference from Morbius's conscience and soars out of control. Thus, the monster eliminates the colonizers and, later, members of the space crew who, Morbius believes, jeopardizes his safety...and his ideas. Morbius's wife, therefore, dies a natural death, never in danger since she falls within his protective sphere.

Physically, we view the creature briefly when it contacts an electronic barrier: The demon appears huge, beastly, and unrelenting in its ferocity. Psychologically, however, the demon **is** Morbius; or at least the subconscious Morbius, enhanced via the brain booster to become a frightening and devastating creation. But a creation that Morbius can stop only by stopping himself. To wit, Dr. Morbius must die so that others may live--a costly tradeoff for putting his id (or shadow personality) to rest.

Breach of character by metamorphosis does not bode well for evildoers. Judged against our model of cognitive and emotional evil, these metamorphic characters must depend too heavily on their host and habitat to survive. Frankly, it becomes difficult to keep a secret or engage in misdirection when a man or woman transforms to a wolf...or whatever.

The beast may abdicate responsibility--no problem, at least it was not for Stewart Swinton. The beast can even exalt in the thrill of being a beast, and doing what beasts do best. But the creature derives, usually, from a different personality; a personality that has the power to impede the beast's natural inclinations toward unrestrained evil. Thus, the creature's human counterpart can pull the evilmonger away from absolute perversity.

BREACH OF CHARACTER IN REVERSE

The parameters associated with breach of character include not only the emergence of evil, as through metamorphosis, but also the **subversion of evil**. What happens if we shift gears and decide to "brainwash" the evil away? We speak not of killing the "other character," which amounts to executing both personalities, but of creating--or recreating--a more loving character from the evil figure in force.

Two problems arise with this rationale of backward logic. First, the pain and agony of dispensing with evil will not come cheap. Recall in *The Exorcist* (1973) that to remove the demon possessing young Regan (Linda Blair), Father Karras (Jason Miller) must reclaim his faith and believe that he **can** accomplish this remarkable feat. Then, he must struggle with the demon physically, wrestling it away from Regan and into himself. This selfless act frees the girl of her tenacious incubus, but costs Father Karras his life. The message seems to say, **evil does not relinquish its captive without a parting sting**.

Second, the filmmaker does not serve logic well in attempting to reverse a breach of character. Imagine a man who becomes an alcoholic, as opposed to an alcoholic who reforms. We can accept both changes in character, although the impression lingers that an alcoholic who reforms faces the more precarious task of staying sober.

Suppose, further, we hear of a youth who evolves to the level of a reckless murderer, versus this same youth who later claims to have discovered religion, or at least the error of his ways. The youth now wishes to tread the straight and narrow. Do we believe him? Logic enjoys greater credibility when the individual moves toward rather than away from evil. **Indulging in a familiar evil proves more reasonable and believable than rejecting a familiar evil to assume a more positive lifestyle**.

This difficulty certainly holds true for the psychopath. Realistically, these calloused souls do not abandon their foul habits over time. Satisfied with themselves and their assumed superiority, psychopaths realize no urgency to change or to make themselves susceptible to therapy. Therefore, if the goal involves instilling a sense of conscience and remorse in the psychopath, forget it.

Robert Hare (1993, p. 204), challenged to develop a treatment program that **might** work, took advantage of his years in studying the psychopath to suggest a different approach:

This means that the program for psychopaths will be less concerned with attempts to develop empathy or conscience than with intensive efforts to convince them that their current attitudes and behavior are not in their own self-interest, and that they alone must bear responsibility for their behavior. At the same time, we will attempt to show them how to use their strengths and abilities to satisfy their needs in ways that society can tolerate.

Psychologically, Hare concocts a back-door strategy, using **self-interest** to encourage the psychopath's motivation for change. Give the evildoer a bona fide reason for altering behavior, preferably a reason that will divert the troublemaker's behavior to more constructive goals. This ambitious task poses a tall order for realizing success, although the realization becomes more attainable in film than in reality.

Cinematically, the self-interest strategy opens up some intriguing dramatic possibilities. Recall the first axiom that **evil does not relinquish its captive without a parting sting**, a lesson that bears on the French film *La Femme Nikita* (1991). Directed and written by Luc Besson, the film opens when a young woman, Nikita (Anne Parillaud), joins three doped companions to vandalize a drug store, searching for more of the same. Roger Ebert (1996, p. 417) describes Nikita as "projecting a feral hostility," and, indeed, she appears lost in a twilight zone of indifference except for her next fix. While in this netherworld of amorality, Nikita places a gun beneath a policeman's chin, and, with a foggy half-smile of anticipation, she pulls the trigger.

Instead of execution, however, government agents secret Nikita away for a "second chance" at life. Their plan? They see killer potential in her feral hostility, and wish to reshape Nikita's destitute character into a stronger, more resourceful personality. Because we know so little of her early life, and how she came to descend into a drug-induced stupor, the new Nikita does not appear as a polarized transformation.

She rebels at first and shows a "street toughness" to survive on her own terms. But the odds work against her. The organization plants a fake item detailing Nikita's "suicide" in prison and, subsequently, her burial. If she continues to defy the rules, well, the "suicide" conveniently becomes fact.

Recalling Robert Hare's treatment strategy with psychopaths, Nikita finds it in her self-interest to play along.

"Self-interest," in Nikita's case, means more than feeling narcissistic about herself. Agents train her on computers, firearms, martial arts, and the feminine graces of beauty and etiquette. But they also set her up. Nikita, truly touched upon receiving a birthday present from her trainer, Bob (Tcheky Karyo), opens the gift to see a gun. Bob then dispassionately gives her an assassination assignment, and leaves.

Nikita executes her assignment, only to find that the agency has deliberately blocked her escape route as a final test. She barely evades her pursuers, and, in a rage, returns to the organization. For a battered woman who has painfully pulled herself up by the proverbial bootstraps, Nikita learns a harsh lesson about "self-interest": Follow orders, but look out for yourself and trust no one.

Given a hiatus before her next assignment, Nikita meets and falls in love with Marc (Jean-Hugues Anglade), a kindly grocery checker. The fact that she possesses a reservoir of genuine affection indicates that we see Nikita, less as the fully-blossoming psychopath and more as the tortured soul searching for honesty and intimacy.

She finds the honesty and the intimacy with Marc, yet she must continue her dual role of the cold-hearted assassin. This tug-of-war on the windmills of her mind reaches a literal stress point in Venice, Italy. Delighted by another gift from Bob--tickets to Venice for herself and Marc--Nikita then discovers that the agency planned her trip as a working vacation.

Receiving surprise instructions to execute a target in the next few minutes, Nikita leaves Marc in the bedroom and enters the bathroom to find her equipment and prepare for the murder. Marc, disturbed by her change in behavior, chooses that critical time to talk to Nikita about their relationship. Nikita, with only the bathroom door between them, assembles the rifle and lines up the cross-hairs on her target, crying softly.

Her future (Marc) is on one side of the door, and her past (Nikita, the trained killer) on the other. The distance between the two worlds proves insurmountable. Nikita can not bear the thought of sustaining such double jeopardy. A compleat psychopath using her feminine wiles could manage the duplicity. But the psychopath, of course, would not feel the kind of genuine affection that Nikita feels for Marc.

Other events follow to underscore her dilemma. Earlier in training, Amande (Jeanne Moreau) grooms Nikita to improve her appearance, and sees in her a "faint fragility." This fragility surfaces as we gaze one last time at a forlorn figure. She sits in a darkened room, gazing into nowhere, making the inevitable decision.

Nikita finds her double existence at tether's end: (1) She has just survived a botched mission; (2) Marc now knows of her double life and still loves her, although the knowing places him in danger; and (3) the organization forever presses upon her, an ogre designed to intrude and fetch her at its beck and call. The one solution for Nikita, though imperfect, involves flight and anonymity. This alternative means looking over her shoulder, means striving to put her shadow self away, and means losing Marc as her one true love.

The true evil in *La Femme Nikita* rests with the heartless government that manipulates her life. The agency's head aptly sets the psychopathic credo for success: Agents are usable and expendable. Nikita's shadow/ego self reflects this cold, impersonal void of the agency's philosophy.

But Nikita does not lose herself in the harsh confines of the compleat psychopath. Earlier, believing she faces execution, Nikita calls for her mother, and expresses great despair at her mother's absence. Genuine feelings are there; and, despite the hardened core of past tribulations, those feelings finally emerge when she meets Marc. This affectionate relationship awakens dormant emotions of joy and closeness.

How does Nikita fare in her "reversal" of character? Recall, again, that one problem in subverting evil concerns the **price**. Nikita does not die--the ultimate price--yet she sacrifices a warm attachment with Marc to ensure his safety and maintain her freedom from the agency. Evil's sting, nevertheless, goes beyond these penalties. What lies ahead for a woman on the run? Nikita's conflict with two disparate characters will haunt her as she seeks to stay alive...and searches for a reason **to** stay alive.

Now consider the second problem of subverting evil, namely, the **credibility of moving away from a familiar evil, as opposed to embracing that evil**. Remember that originally we encounter an in-the-gutter addict who murders, yet later "rehabilitates" herself to becomes a resourceful killer through training. Can Nikita subvert this evil and rise above it?

The logic of becoming such a split personality, and of still retaining a sense of compassion in mind and behavior, stretches even the cinematic imagination. A woman--and a rebel--learns to follow orders and kill more effectively; yet, somehow, she manages to divorce this talent from her desire to lead a conventional life. Does this breach of character compute?

Nikita the assassin seems "better" than Nikita the drug addict. But "better" is relative here, and we must remind ourselves that her breach of character entails a fragile compartmentalization. We are asked to accept a personality who realizes her potentiality for killing, yet who spontaneously spawns another character anchored in optimism and the joys of everyday living. If goodness can spring from such a cavity, then Nikita illustrates just how trying it must be to behave cognitively and emotionally as a fully functioning psychopath.

Alex, on the other hand, gives evil soothsayers reason to hope. Alex (Malcolm McDowell) of *A Clockwork Orange* (1971) lives in a futuristic environment of chic decadence, bawdy young toughs, and a work ethic that flew south. He and his three fellow droogs embark on an evening's agenda: They kick a helpless old drunk; they incite a confrontation with another gang; and they invade the home of a writer and his wife, raping the wife and kicking the writer into an invalid--all to the sprightly tune of "Singing In The Rain."

Alex, let us say, carries all the credentials of a well-oiled psychopath, who, when he commits rape and other misdeeds, appears to do so as an aesthetic adventure (Haskell, 1987, p. 362). But he also sports a truckload of arrogance, and we know that arrogance unchecked can disable the psychopath's best-laid plans. Alex indulges himself with a superiority complex that includes the "bliss and heaven" of listening to Ludwig Van Beethoven, especially the composer's Ninth Symphony. John Anderson (1995, p. 180) notes in his review that Stanley Kubrick, the film's writer and director, gives kitsch a kind of berserk stature:

> ...Alex may practice evil, but on the other hand, he's sent into rapture by Beethoven; he's not untouchable, just largely untouched. When Kubrick goes inside his head, we see beauty--twisted, malevolent beauty, perhaps, but beauty all the same...

The youth, in other words, fits seamlessly into a hedonistic market of wayfaring evil, blown hither and yon by the prevailing winds of opportunism. One officious friend of the family asks him: "You've got a good home here, good loving parents, you've got not too bad of a brain, is it some kind of a devil that crawls inside of you?" It is an old puzzle--how evil can derive from apparent goodness--and the puzzle never has a satisfactory answer.

However Alex came to be, evil appears situated firmly in his nature...or so we believe. The youth belittles his cronies, too self-absorbed to realize the repercussions of his contemptuous attitude. The repercussions arrive when Alex breaks into a health club, containing one irate woman and a family of cats. The cats know when to leave, but the woman finds herself in a morbid dance with Alex, who totes a large penis sculpture. He sees the merriment of it, she does not, and it all goes wrong when he smashes the sculpture on her prostrate figure.

Alex seeks to escape the police, but the other droogs turn nasty and betray him, leading to his capture and imprisonment. Always adaptable, he adopts a veneer of godly serenity, with the old, perverse Alex lurking in the shadows. No intriguing breach of character here, however, merely a facade of convenience until a better opportunity comes along.

And, of course, it does. Alex learns of an experimental program for curing violence and desires entry to shorten his prison stay. A clergyman explains the program's risks as a form of aversive therapy, but Alex replies, "I don't care about the dangers, Father. I just want to be good. I want for the rest of my life to be one act of goodness." Alex naturally has no intention of pursuing such a noble venture.

Unfortunately, he misjudges the treatment's potency, which consists of a drug that makes him physically sick upon viewing films of violence. But what really tears Alex apart concerns the experimenters' use of Beethoven's Ninth Symphony. The youth relied on the symphony to celebrate his exploits of rape and aggression. Now, alas, he experiences a polarized reaction: Hearing Beethoven makes Alex physically ill and, psychologically, uproots his sense of values. How can the "bliss and heaven" of Beethoven be transformed into such a mind-shrieking torture?

The breach of character that manifests itself represents Alex the vulnerable youth, currently a victim, no longer a predator. His final test causes him to gag when he attempts an aggressive reaction, first, to a performer who deliberately insults and strikes him; and, second, to an almost nude woman who stands provocatively, waiting for Alex to assault her. He wants to have a bit of "in-and-out" with her, but finds himself unable to perform.

The Minister of the Interior, who has placed his political support behind the program, sums up the government's philosophy about Alex's cure: "Our subject is impelled toward the good by, paradoxically, being impelled towards evil." Put another way, the closer the youth draws to his old ways, the sicker he will become.

What neither the government nor Alex anticipate, however, occurs rather quickly: The former victims of Alex the predator, now become the predators of Alex the victim. The old bum that Alex kicked earlier recognizes and turns on him, enlisting other bums to give the youth a beating; two of his fellow droogs, now policemen, take him out in the country for a walloping; and, staggering to the nearest home, he meets-- yes--the writer he had turned into an invalid.

The writer does not recognize Alex at first, but when the youth begins to croon "Singing In The Rain," the writer flashes back to his agony and sees a sweet chance for revenge. He locks Alex in a top-floor bedroom and pipes through a piece of music--Beethoven's Ninth--that predictably drives the youth to attempt suicide.

Alex leaps from the top floor intending to die, but only succeeds in breaking a number of bones. We next see him cocooned in a hospital bed, visited by the Minister of the Interior. The Minister is hurting politically and needs Alex to salvage an experiment gone bad. Alex likes to be needed, because being needed means he has leverage: a chance to shoehorn himself away from his enemies and toward more favorable circumstances.

Throughout his trials, Alex the psychopath seeks to assert himself, but the treatment interferes. He moves about in limbo, puzzled by his quasi-state of being. Clearly, he does not cope well as a nonaggressive chap, handicapped as he is by his inability to fuel some fire and brimstone into the old Alex. Thus this breach of character offers an odd impression of seeing the psychopathic Alex transparently veiled--he is not hidden--yet the psychopath in him seems unable to surface and resume his familiar evil.

Finally, with the Minister's cushion of comfort and protection, the old Alex revives and flourishes. The breach repaired, we last view our durable "hero" having a bit of the in-and-out, and enjoying himself immensely. Evil, after some tittering moments of near-extinction, perseveres to show that its instrument was down...but never out.

Alex's reformation fails because his psychopathic tendencies stay suppressed rather than extinguished. They are there...waiting, waiting, waiting, and then bingo! Alex is back in business. The price of suffering goodness may or may not bring a lesson to bear. Psychopaths do not learn lessons well, and, if such happens with Alex, he must hope that the Minister stays in power.

A BREACH OF TIME

Imagine, as another twist of character, how we might feel encountering our younger self, say, from 10 or 20 years ago. A younger, more idealized character, not yet pummeled by the rigors of broken promises, empty marriages, monetary travails, and...possibly murder. If we could tinker with the past and thereby influence the present to our advantage--would we take the chance?

A tempting proposition born and bred for the movies. The logic of such a fantasy transcends reality's rules of conduct. Morality takes a bruising, for instance, if we use past and future information to assemble a super portfolio of stocks. Nor does the idea of killing Hitler prove a simple, humanitarian effort, since the ramifications of that change in history--good and bad--become difficult to project.

Morality does not stop the villain, however, and, occasionally, not even the hero. *Timecop* (1994), directed by Peter Hyams and written by Mark Verheiden, slops these notions to and fro, sometimes using questionable tactics in how characters play with past and present logic to break the time dimension. But lapses in the mechanics of negotiating past and present time are not our concern here. Our problem rests with the breach of character that places the film's psychopath, presidential candidate McComb (Ron Silver), in the year 2004. Two scenes in the story permit the evilly seasoned McComb a backward visit to meet his younger self, Senator McComb of 1994. The meeting allows the older, more reptilian McComb to parade his psychopathy around with such lines as "Never interrupt me when I'm talking to myself."

Most fascinating, but underdeveloped, is the disparity in malevolence between the two characters. The younger McComb's naïveté causes him to react with shock upon hearing the older McComb's amoral suggestions. These suggestions entail greed and corruption, and focus on arrangements to make the presidential campaign easier for both of them in 2004.

The continuity between the two McCombs is evident, but the Senator has not yet honed his selfish political skills to rival those of the older McComb. And, who knows, the Senator may even possess a wee sprig of positive values, although that optimism asks a lot of the compleat psychopath. More likely, we can assume that 10 years seems ample time for a clever psychopath to learn what he needs to know about political secrecy and misdirection.

Someone must stop the more evil McComb from monopolizing time travel for his own selfish designs, and that job falls to Max Walker (Jean-Claude Van Damme). Max has a few priorities of concern too, including the erasure of his wife's murder in 1994, and the termination of McComb so that the ruthless presidential candidate has no future.

The key to these shenanigans involves remembering that when the same young and old character happen to meet--hero or villain--consequences differ sharply, depending on which counterpart bites the dust. Killing the older personality means nothing in time travel since the younger version in 1994 may remain alive for 2004. Kill the younger personality, however, and that is all she wrote. No "future" (2004) exists for either character.

The older McComb credits Walker with the status of a gnat and seeks to treat him accordingly. The villain, whose arrogance seeps out of control, offers this parting observation to our hero: "You're at a disadvantage in this from the beginning. You see I'm an ambitious, Harvard-educated visionary, who deserves to be the most powerful man in the world."

Spoken like a true megalomaniac. But McComb, for all his education, appears oblivious to how easily **he** can be negated. Walker pushes McComb's younger self into his older self, and, since the same matter can not occupy the same space at the same time, the two McCombs find themselves imploding, inextricably yet incompatibly intertwined. The year 2004 will now have one less presidential candidate.

The breach of character in *Timecop* constitutes a continuum of time and experience. Had the more evil McComb died alone, and had efforts been made to reform the younger McComb before he slipped into a truly malevolent mode, then the idea of reversing his character from "evil" to "good" would have applied.

But psychopaths being psychopaths, what we see here pertains to a **delay in character development** of McComb's evil skills. He is not likely to reverse his core traits. Instead, McComb becomes more likely, over time, to intensify the ambition, greed, and deceit that feed his self-centeredness.

THE MOST PROLIFIC BREACH OF CHARACTER

Just as with Brer Rabbit's briar patch, the psychopaths' sanctuary constitutes any turf on which they can strut their stuff with verve. Transformations, brainwashings, and time traveling denote problems for the evildoer through a loss of control. By contrast, the model of cognitive and emotional evil realizes its finest chance of fulfillment when the psychopath knowingly carries an olive branch in one hand, and a dagger in the other.

Consider the number of films in which the villain pretends to friendliness and loyalty, while shielding a heart of the darkest magnitude. Yes, it is a long list. Think of the Alfred Hitchcock movies alone that include charming psychopaths who beguile: among them the villains in *The Thirty-Nine Steps* (1935), *Shadow Of A Doubt* (1943), *Dial M For Murder* (1954), *Vertigo* (1958), and *Frenzy* (1972). The villain may surprise us with his or her identity, or we may find ourselves in the know all along. The main thrust of these characterizations, however, points to **duplicity and cunning as prime instruments of secrecy and misdirection**. The breach of character is pseudo, not genuine.

Low-profile psychopaths lose themselves in a crowd. Their breach of character blends harmoniously with more innocent personalities, providing the evildoers with a convenient mask of misdirection to further their aims. The ensemble cast of a murder mystery denotes the purest form of this misdirection. Viewers (the **viewer ignorance** mentioned in Lesson 1) must search for clues and juggle several suspects, trying to pinpoint the culprit.

The Last Of Sheila (1973), directed by Herbert Ross with the screenplay by Anthony Perkins and Stephen Sondheim, presents such a mystery. The cast consists of Clinton (James Coburn), a producer and instigator of parlor games, and his disreputable, show business cronies: Tom (Richard Benjamin), a writer in need of work; Lee (Joan Hackett), his wealthy and supportive wife; Philip (James Mason), a director who now directs commercials; Alice (Raquel Welch), an actress, and her opportunistic husband, Anthony (Ian McShane); and Christine

(Dyan Cannon), a hyperactive agent who needs to cut back on men and caffeine.

Clinton's egomania, more than his compassion, brings these members together for games and booze on the producer's yacht. Months earlier, at a party that his "friends" attended (except for Lee), Clinton's wife, Sheila, had a tiff with her husband and stalked away. Walking angrily down the road, she turned to face the glare of weaving headlights, and...swat! Sheila became the victim of a hit-and-run driver. Or, as Christine describes the incident in her show business parlance: "...the night Sheila got bounced through the hedges."

Clinton suspects that one of the six drove the car, and plans through secrecy and game playing to divine the hit-and-run killer. Each suspect harbors a dirty little secret, known only to Clinton, that the other suspects must discover: a (S)hoplifter, a (H)omosexual, an (E)x-convict, an (I)nformer, a (L)ittle child molester, and an (A)lcoholic--the initials spelling out "Sheila."

Secrets seem to carry their own momentum. The six suspects, under their host's mocking scrutiny, cast uneasy glances at one another and wonder about exposure. Alice supplies a glimmer of insight on these dynamics when she comments, "That's the thing about secrets. We all know stuff about each other, we just don't know the same stuff."

Clinton, however, does not survive beyond the second secret. Setting up the game in the confession box of an old monastery, Clinton receives an ice pick in the neck. The murderer then mimics the producer's voice from the darkened box to make others believe that their host is still alive.

Once his death becomes a reality, differing reactions follow. No one cared for Clinton, but all needed him. Knowing their needs, the producer frequently chided them with salty reminders, such as "You don't deserve a good king like me." These remembrances prompt Philip, learning of Clinton's demise, to offer his own epithet: "Apparently, there is a god."

And, a murderer. Philip and Tom, the better puzzle players, attempt to piece together the convoluted events that led to Clinton's death. Tom reconstructs the crime scene, and asks each member to put his or her "secret" card on the table. A tense session ensues as the suspects, in turn, reveal their true secret, culminating with Lee who admits to her drunken driving and to hitting Sheila by accident that fateful night. Drinking heavily and shaken by her disclosure, Lee adds that she wants to make a "clean exit."

Later, she is discovered in Clinton's tub with her wrists slashed, apparently a victim of suicide. But no, her death becomes one murder too many. The real killer of Clinton and Lee plays the contrite husband, the dry wit, the skillful mimic. He mimics Clinton's voice to Lee and Philip earlier, stating prophetically, "The harder you try to keep a secret in, the more it wants to get out."

Thus, for Tom, the secret finds release because Philip will not let the puzzle go, a characteristic of puzzle devotees. The director finally comprehends the vicious scenario: Tom murders Clinton with the ice pick, knowing of Lee's accidental killing of Sheila. He implicates Lee in Clinton's murder to drive her back to the bottle, but all the while acts out his breach of character as a concerned, helpful husband.

The flashback scene in which he carries an alcohol-drowsy Lee to Clinton's tub, lowers her in the water, and begins meticulously to cut her wrists, shows a busy psychopath at work. During the cold-blooded sequence, Tom's countenance bears no expression at all--underscored by his smoking a cigarette that dangles carelessly from his lips throughout the grisly proceedings. The cigarette symbolizes far better Tom's lack of remorse than any verbal declaration of callousness. His workmanlike behavior reveals Tom as quite capable of dispatching Lee for her wealth, which she **would have given him**, but which he desires on his own terms.

Ironically, the two most compassionate characters--Philip and Lee--serve pivotal roles. Lee proves one victim too many for Tom to explain, and Philip alone has the intelligence and concern to flush Tom from his pseudo-conduct. Philip realizes, among other mistakes, that Tom removed the "Alcoholic" card and substituted a "Hit-and-Run" card to apply more pressure on Lee. But with the "Alcoholic" card out, and the "Hit-and-Run" card in, Tom misplays his hand because the initials of each secret no longer add to "Sheila."

Help arrives for Philip as Tom almost strangles him. Show business savvy takes over when Philip and others imagine how "The Last Of Sheila" will play as a commercial vehicle. The inside joke becomes a movie within a movie, since the actual film had puzzle enthusiasts Stephen Sondheim and Anthony Perkins as its writers.

Tom shrewdly practices misdirection by helping to "solve" the murder, and by doling out "comfort and care" for Lee. But he fails because Philip proves a more astute observer of details. Consequently, we last see Tom collapsed on a couch looking dour, deflated, and defeated. The music swells and Bette Midler comes on track singing "Friends," which means if you have friends like the "friends" in *Sheila*, you had best watch your back.

High-profile psychopaths make their duplicitous presence known to viewers from the beginning. The victims, unfortunately, have no clue regarding the punishment that awaits them. Contrary to an ensemble of suspects, high-profile evildoers can quietly or loudly become the film's centerpiece: They set their insidious plan in motion, maintain the tempo, and, if they possess the requisites of cinematic charisma, will command fascination from the audience.

The beguiling Tony Wendice (Ray Milland) of Alfred Hitchcock's *Dial M For Murder* (1954) fits our high-profile psychopath nicely. Just as Tom wishes to implicate Lee for murder to obtain her money, so does Tony ultimately plan to blame his wealthy wife, Margot (Grace Kelly), for a murder. The difference between these scenarios occurs when we, as viewers, become privy to all the fine details of Tony's cold-hearted scheme.

Formerly a stage play, Frederick Knott's screenplay provides *Dial M For Murder* with a faithful cinematic adaptation, keeping and maneuvering its characters within the confines of the Wendice apartment (Spoto, 1992, p. 208; Leitch, 1991, p. 163). Plan A for Tony involves the conning of a second psychopath, Swann (Anthony Dawson), into helping him murder Margot. Tony's original intention places Swann as an intruder in the Wendice household. When Tony calls at midnight, Margot enters the living room from the bedroom to answer the phone. Swann steps from behind the curtains and strangles her. The intruder receives his 1000 pounds, Tony inherits Margot's wealth, and Margot, well...Margot becomes a statistic.

The film offers a 22-minute segment of how deftly Wendice manipulates Swann to accept his role as the "hands-on" murderer: (1) Tony fakes an injury and uses a cane as his prop to bring Swann to the apartment, purportedly to buy a car from him; (2) Tony then pretends to share a confidence by admitting Margot's affection for a previous boyfriend, Mark Halliday (Robert Cummings), a writer of crime mysteries; (3) Tony "accidentally" drops an incriminating letter from Mark to Margot, which Margot had always carried with her before it was stolen, causing Swann to unwittingly retrieve the letter, now containing his prints; (4) Tony then abandons his cane and all pretense when he cites Swann's criminal past, including an unsolved murder, and concludes by stating smugly: "In fact, there were times when I felt that you almost belonged to me."

And Swann does. He probes Tony's plan for weaknesses, all of which Wendice anticipates. Swann at one point asks about the detailed preparation, "For a murder?" Tony then replies in the psychopath's fashion of making even murder appear ordinary: "For a few minutes work."

Note that Tony need not murder Margot to keep her or her money. Margot, choosing to remain true, ends her affair with Mark, a temporary indiscretion known to Tony. But as a compleat psychopath, Tony already schemes to eliminate Margot. Her one lapse of infidelity simply makes his strategy easier to execute.

Tony tells Swann of following Margot to Mark's apartment and watching them through an open window: "It's funny how you can tell when people are in love." An interesting observation, spoken derisively by Tony as the psychopath's dismissal of genuine affection. He recognizes the state, yet fails to imagine how two lovers can make themselves so vulnerable. Such affection will never become a problem for Tony (Brill, 1988, p. 25).

Plan A, in Hitchcockian fashion, crumbles when Margot kills Swann in self-defense. Gasping for breath, she gropes frantically for something--anything--to survive against a stronger adversary. Margot's hand discovers and clutches a pair of scissors. Then, with a ferocity borne of primal rage, she slams the scissors into Swann's back. He stiffens upright and falls on his back, causing the scissors to impale him further. Given the quiet civility in which *Dial M For Murder* conducts its lethal proceedings, Donald Spoto (1992, p. 212) comments on Swann's stabbing as "one of the few viscerally shocking moments in the entire Hitchcock filmography."

Tony must now show his psychopathic worth by improvising Plan B, namely, to incriminate Margot by giving her a surreptitious reason for "murdering" Swann. The suave deceiver almost succeeds, except for careless mistakes about money and a telltale key, plus the dogged pursuit of a policeman, Chief Inspector Hubbard (John Williams). As Hubbard remarks on the "perfect crime," referring both to Mark's effort to solve the crime as a writer and save Margot, and Tony's attempts to send her to the gallows, "They talk about flatfooted policeman. May the saints protect us from the gifted amateur."

Tony's only hint of compassion occurs when he sets the stage for Plan A, calls Margot, and silently listens as Swann attempts to strangle her. Tony reveals a stricken expression when he hears Margot's cries, but quickly recovers once he realizes that she has somehow killed Swann. Otherwise, Tony Wendice meets all the cognitive and emotional requirements of a devoted evildoer. Thinking that the investigation has ceased as Margot's gallows date nears, he overlooks Chief Inspector Hubbard's penchant for details and loose ends, a dedication quite as persistent as Tony's own preparation.

Hence, as viewers, we enjoy the satisfaction of anticipation, of monitoring a high-profile psychopath's seemingly foolproof scheme, detail by detail. The evildoer's breach of character proves all the more chilling because we **know** that he lies effortlessly, suavely masking the raw sewage of his true personality. This insight for viewers harks back to Lesson 1 and our reference to the **performer's ignorance**: We know of the psychopath's treachery, but other performers about him do not.

Then, against the odds, goodness intervenes: The true mastermind realizes exposure as the duplicitous perpetrator of a brutal and altogether senseless act. Tony Wendice, like Tom in *The Last Of Sheila*, might have gained his wealth without resorting to murder. But the psychopath always wants more, and he wants it his way--to personally control victims and events as a puppeteer, coercing lesser mortals to perform the chosen scenario according to his script and direction.

PLAYING THE LIE

The cinematic psychopath, whether low profile or high profile, **plays the lie**. We lie occasionally with half-truths, sometimes total fabrications. We lie for purposes of embellishment, to spare someone's feelings, or, truthfully, to spare our feelings and malign another person. Indeed, if we become adept at telling untruths, this skill seems unlikely to denote an isolated habit. More probably, learning to easily voice lies indicates an opportunistic personality, someone who finds it gratifying to dupe others.

The psychopath characterizes an individual whose traits go beyond merely a person who lies well, although misdirection depicts a cornerstone of the psychopath's armament. Consider, therefore, an individual who lies convincingly, in a profession where participants lie with impunity...and are paid for their performance. Consider, in other words, a psychopath who acts for a living, and who practices this artistry with no distinction between onstage and offstage behavior.

Imagine Eve (Anne Baxter) of *All About Eve* (1950), written and directed by Joseph Mankiewicz (1997, p. 56). Karen Richards (Celeste Holm), wife of playwright Lloyd Richards (Hugh Marlowe), encounters Eve in an alley outside the theatre where Margo Channing (Bette Davis) performs in Lloyd's play. Eve has seen every performance, prompting Karen to unknowingly offer a prophetic remark: "There isn't another like you. There couldn't be--" She is right.

Karen brings Eve into the theatre to meet Margo, but once inside, Eve moves to the stage, transfixed by the moment. She looks at Karen and says, "You can breathe it--can't you? Like some magic perfume..." Little does Karen realize that Eve's adoration of the stage, and the applause that it nurtures, reaches monstrous proportions.

Eve tells her forlorn tale to Margo and others, a tale of hard times in Wisconsin, of working in a brewery, of marrying Eddie, of losing Eddie in the war, of discovering Margo Channing on the stage in San Francisco, of becoming enraptured with Margo and all that she represents. Eve's yarn of woe causes Birdie (Thelma Ritter), a friend and helper to Margo, to comment caustically, "What a story. Everything but the bloodhounds snappin' at her rear end..." Margo reacts angrily to Birdie's assessment, but later, both women recognize the truth in Birdie's statement. Acting is acting, and Eve harbors the talent to mesmerize an audience--even an audience as cynical and self-centered as other actors.

Eve moves to curry favor with Margo, making herself useful to the actress, becoming intoxicated by the applause that Margo receives night after night. Margo's initial impression involves protecting Eve, viewing the young woman with the sad past as "...a lamb loose in our big stone jungle..." Thinking of Wisconsin, however, a badger would better symbolize the truth.

Eve's breach of character proves almost seamless. She acts the ingratiating ingénue with passion, all the while drawing a bead on those figures who can help her climb that stairway to the stars. Still, "almost seamless" does not indicate perfection. Actors, being astute judges of other actors, know a climber when they see one. Margo and Birdie (the latter formerly in vaudeville) are the first to detect the ambition in Eve's overly gracious attitude. The look that passes between the two friends says far more than any line of dialogue. Eve has been made.

Margo, concerned about playing characters younger than her age of 40, sees the youthful Eve as a professional threat, and as a personal rival because of Margo's love for a director, Bill Sampson (Gary Merrill). Margo's low point segues into

Eve's high point when the climber elicits a favor from Karen to become Margo's understudy. Karen, with the best of intentions, decides to chastise Margo for her temperamental behavior by arranging to keep Margo from the theatre so that Eve, as the understudy, can have her evening of glory.

Eve's evening of glory turns into a smashing performance, including a pitch for Bill's affections, which he declines. Ever adaptable, Eve forms a pact with Addison DeWitt (George Sanders), theatre critic, columnist, and sage observer, *extraordinaire*. Addison, already knowing more about Eve than Eve's selfishness allows her to comprehend, tells the "modest" actress, "It is just as false not to blow your horn at all as it is to blow it too loudly..." Eve, who turns her humility on and off at will, suggests to him, "You take charge." Whereupon Addison replies, "I believe I will." Unknown to Eve, one psychopath has just assumed control over another psychopath--a casual changing of the guard that Eve will live to regret.

Addison gathers Eve under his formidable wing and writes a column extolling her Thespian talent, an interview that includes comments by Eve about...aging actresses. The trashing of Margo reconciles Margo and Bill, and leaves Eve *persona non grata* with friends loyal to Margo.

Karen, at a table with Lloyd, Margo, and Bill, receives a note from Eve, asking for a chat in the ladies room. Urged by her friends to learn of Eve's latest skullduggery, Karen reluctantly meets the now budding actress. Eve at first resorts to her humble-pie character, declaring teary-eyed, "...I want my friends back."

But what Eve truly desires is the part of Cora in Lloyd Richards's new play, a part intended for Margo. Grasping Karen's hand with the dedication of a suckerfish, Eve tells Karen she knows of her tricking Margo to miss that performance--and Eve will tell all, unless Karen agrees to help. Recall that Karen engaged in the trickery to give Eve her chance to perform, a gesture of good will that Eve conveniently forgets.

Fortunately for Karen, she dodges a bullet. Margo and Bill plan to marry, and Margo informs Karen and Lloyd that she has no interest in Lloyd's new play. The quartet watch Eve and Addison depart, with Margo intoning, "There goes Eve. Eve Evil. Little Miss Evil." Eve's breach of character reads as a posturing of false modesty, her duplicity markedly apparent to the four friends.

The theatre sports a short memory, however, and producers, directors, writers, and actors indulge in selective forgetting when genuine talent shines brightly. Eve has the talent to play Cora, no matter how rapaciously she runs the gamut from waif to bitch. Eve gains the part. She also proceeds to engineer, more in fantasy than reality, the luring of Lloyd to leave Karen and marry her. All looks well for Eve, despite the incongruity of transparently maintaining an air of humility in a profession where true humility designates a rare commodity.

Addison DeWitt becomes her Waterloo. She tells Addison of her plans for Lloyd, assuming foolishly that the critic will exit her life gracefully. Instead, Addison provides Eve with a harsh lesson, one "killer" to another. Using his most condescending tone (he has several), DeWitt states, "Is it possible--even conceivable--that you've confused me with that gang of backward children you've been playing tricks on--that you have the same contempt for me that you have for them?"

The masterly sophisticate begins to riddle Eve's tale of woe: Her parents haven't heard from her in three years; she was paid to leave town because of a sex scandal at the brewery; no Eddie, no marriage, no San Francisco, even. All artfully managed to maximum effect, except, now, Addison DeWitt has control. He tells her that she belongs to him, the same kind of possessiveness as that expressed by Tony Wendice when he researched Swann's movements in *Dial M For Murder*.

Addison then explains the **psychopath's lament** to Eve, a perspective on life that the actress can not understand without DeWitt's intellect to clarify her limitations: "You're an improbable person, Eve, and so am I. We have that in common. Also a contempt for humanity, an inability to love and be loved, insatiable ambition--and talent. We deserve each other."

What Eve deserves is the award as the finest stage actress of the year. What she does not receive, despite her self-effacing remarks, is the friendship of those figures instrumental to her success: Margo, Karen, Bill, and Lloyd. Margo reiterates this loss when she tartly offers her congratulations: "...nice speech, Eve. But I wouldn't worry too much about your heart. You can always put that award where you heart ought to be."

Eve, disgruntled, refuses to attend a party in her honor and returns to her apartment. There she finds a young woman who has slipped inside and fallen asleep on her sofa. Prepared to call the police, the young intruder begs Eve's forgiveness. An echo of the past reverberates as the girl seeks to calm the actress's ruffled mood.

Eve deigns to tolerate the girl's presence and moves to another room. The girl, discovering Eve's cape and award, dons the cape and, holding the award gingerly, moves to a multiple mirror. She bows graciously, the music soars, and we eavesdrop on another ambitious figure, waiting not so patiently in the wings.

Joseph Mankiewicz notes that Eve can be found everywhere (Carey, 1997, p. 107): "There are Eves afoot in every competitive stratum of our society, wherever there's a top you can get to from the bottom. Eves are predatory animals; they'll prefer a terrain best suited to their marauding techniques, hopefully abundant with the particular plunder they're after. But in default of that happiest of hunting grounds--they'll work any beat at hand."

Cognitively, however, Eve's breach of character falters in reaching the perfection of a compleat psychopath. She finds it difficult to keep her ambition a secret, and she loses her "humility" too often by pursuing immediate pleasures impulsively, as would an immature psychopath.

Eve's greatest failure, of course, involves Addison DeWitt. His overlord status is never in question. She stands no chance of escaping his aura, until he loses interest in her. The man personifies poise, charm, and wit. He works, moreover, to maintain his social contacts--his lifeline--in the theatre. Even when we despise him, we admire his ability to avoid the stereotype of a ruthless bastard. We know that grace and manners are **his** public persona, though just a mere breath away from his private persona of contempt for those who oppose him. And still, we do not wish to walk away from Addison DeWitt.

Now, **there** is a psychopath to treasure.

Lesson 7

Mood & Circumstance

When the phone rings the first time, Casey has less than 13 minutes to live. The unknown caller, who rings again, and again, seems in a playful mood, wanting to know what she is doing. Casey tells him she is making popcorn and planning to watch a scary movie. He asks what movie, and she says, *Halloween*. Finally, he asks her name, and she replies, "Why do you want to know my name?" Then the caller says, "Because I want to know who I'm looking at" (Williamson, 1997, p. 103).

The mood changes dramatically with that chilling line. Casey whips around, turns on the floodlights and peers outside, but sees...nothing. Her parents have not returned, and she is alone in a remote setting. Casey goes from a bantering exchange with her caller to terror in the blink of an eye. Something is wrong, terribly wrong, and the teenager **knows** that she has more than a crank caller on her hands.

The prologue to *Scream* (1996) sends Casey (Drew Barrymore) through her private little hell, forced to play games with a robed figure wearing a distorted "scream" ghost-face: She witnesses her boyfriend tied to a chair outside, and gutted; she grapples with the evildoer and receives numerous knife wounds; she runs toward her returning parents--only 10 feet away-- but can not speak to gain their attention; finally, the phone still in her hand, ghost-face drags her away, and does what he promises earlier: "TO SEE WHAT YOUR INSIDES LOOK LIKE." Casey's 13 minutes are up, and her parents find their daughter hanging from a tree, savaged like her boyfriend.

The basics of a horror film involve intensifying the victim's fear at the proper time and place, but not to show too much, too soon of evil's presence. *Scream* raises the ante by having its teenage characters exhibit a smart attitude about horror film rules, even as the horror happens to them. Kevin Williamson (Lippy, 1997, p. 140), who wrote the screenplay, notes how one of the psychos and his innocent girlfriend honor these rules:

> I wanted to suggest that the only reason she's not having sex with her boyfriend is because on some subconscious level she realizes that he is the killer. It's only after she's had sex with him that it all becomes clear to her. And then, on the other hand, he's such a psycho--playing by all of these horror movie rules--that he has to take away her virginity before he can kill her.

Virginal heroines, such as Jamie Lee Curtis's character in *Halloween*, apparently can do villains grievous harm, but remain immune from lethal punishment themselves. Succumbing to mad carnal love, therefore, makes the female a loose woman, a slut, a bitch, and certainly a deserving victim in the parlance of Horror Film 101.

To the credit of Kevin Williamson and Wes Craven, the director, *Scream* satirizes these cliches by sometimes following them frivolously, sometimes reversing them, but always by showing how the "pop culture" world of its teenage inhabitants causes these youths to confuse reality and pretense. *Scream* is less a comedy of horrors and more a commentary on how horror film protocol displaces reality to create its own atmosphere of fear and retribution.

Just as with Casey's gamut of feelings during her last few minutes of life, the many moods of *Scream* veer wildly from teasing to eroticism to stark terror. And, for Casey, the terror occurs in an environment long familiar and secure, but now, suddenly, a perverse deathtrap haunted by the unfamiliar. Logic and common sense recede in this "neo-horror" movie about old horror movies, and atmosphere, ambiance, and tone become ascendant. Mood captures the moment, the characters, and the setting to send reality into exile.

THE EVIL LANDSCAPE

Evil plays tricks with the landscape. Darkness makes a familiar path home less familiar. Trees lurch into prominence and spidery fingers reach out, the wind howling, sometimes snarling its discontent. These gnarled appendages and their requisite sound effects foster the sanctuary of gawd knows what. A grove of trees in the failed light transforms to a lair of hobgoblins and hellions.

The evil, however, is our evil, the hobgoblins our hobgoblins. What we see at dawn "out there" unfolds blandly as a stretch of trees. But, at dusk, other mental-sets prevail so that a leafy walkway becomes a forest primeval, a wooded conspiracy of crawling shapes and sounds. We see trees as we see life, conjured up through the sensory and mental registers of a personalized orientation--our self. A bit of night-time sensory deprivation and a dash of overactive imagination remind us of stories we have heard about treacherous trees, dancing shadows, and the ominous figures that lurk therein.

Simon Schama's (1995, pp. 6-7) *Landscape And Memory* emphasizes this intercourse with nature:

> And if a child's vision of nature can already be loaded with complicating memories, myths, and meanings, how much more elaborately wrought is the frame through which our adult eyes survey the landscape. For although we are accustomed to separate nature and human perception into two realms, they are, in fact, indivisible. Before it can ever be a repose for the senses, landscape is the work of the mind. Its scenery is built up as much from strata of memory as from layers of rock.

Landscape, then, marks a distinction between "raw matter" that exists unadorned, and matter embellished through our memories (Schama, p. 10). Cinematically, of course, those hobgoblins and hellions may prove "real" and not the figment of an overworked imagination. A tree launches forth its dormant evil and claws at a frightened child during the early scenes of *Poltergeist* (1982); likewise, Scout and Jem of *To Kill A Mockingbird* (1962) find themselves on a harrowing trek through the dark woods, wondering if the eerie hoots and hollers also include a human predator. And in *Scream* the dancing shadows and treacherous trees become more than fanciful illusions for Casey: They work as evil appendages to abet her demise.

The mood of the piece relates to the characters themselves, but also to the physical environment that envelops these personalities. **Mood** refers to a prevailing emotional tone. A movie's mood concerns the establishment of this emotional tone as a general attitude, a frame of mind. The tone may play campily, as in a horror film like *Scream*; or bleakly, say, in the nihilistic landscape of a film noir production; or the tone can assume a sense of wicked humor to cope with catastrophic events, as in *M*A*S*H* (1970) and *Natural Born Killers* (1994).

Every film conveys a mood, though not always with flair and distinction. The physical locale, the characters' speech patterns and body language, the customs of the period--these features contribute to a story's emotional flavor. Still, even with all such features in place, uninspired dialogue or awkward action sequences will sink a project quickly, no matter how lush the scenery or grammatically correct the regional dialect.

Geography plays a decisive role, sometimes an adversarial role, in dictating the characters' motivation and the story's direction. Indeed, a harsh and unpredictable environment not only ensures hardship for the "good folk," but, on occasion, manages to be protective of the "bad folk."

GEOHAZARDS

A **GeoHazard** reflects the physical environment as dangerous to survival. Literally any locale where humans do not adapt naturally denotes a threatening locale. Movies frequently underscore this danger by highlighting the protective gear needed to cope with a hostile environment. Add to this formula a creature who behaves psychopathically, a creature who adjusts naturally to the landscape...and we have the makings of a suspenseful struggle.

Thus, one of the most elementary conflicts between landscape and character involves a fragile sanctuary amid an unforgiving environment. These elements combine, for example, to temporarily give HAL's electronic machinations the upper hand in *2001* (1968); they invoke the murky waters of *Jaws* (1975) in which a great white shark makes repeated attacks upon a disintegrating fishing boat; and the landscape lays forth an array of shafts and tunnels that shelter the acid-dripping creature in *Alien* (1979) as it searches for human prey.

But the hallmark of claustrophobic settings probably rests with a 1951 science-fiction thriller, *The Thing*. Directed by Christian Nyby and (uncredited) Howard Hawks, and written by Charles Lederer, their portrayal of the film's frozen environment derives from a story "Who Goes There," created by John Wood Campbell, Jr. Certainly, to survive the Arctic, the inhabitants must respect the land and its rigorous demands. So if you were stationed at the North Pole and an alien being crash-landed and imbedded its craft beneath the ice--what would you do?

Well, the first thing the military crew does is to screw up. They attempt to melt the ice using thermite to blow the space ship free, only to blow it up, instead. Oddly, this one-of-a-kind blunder does not faze their equanimity, although knowing the military, the demolition crew should expect a loss of some bars and stripes for such a disaster.

The search party's reaction to the space craft's loss, and to other dire emergencies stays within a tight barometer of "Let's try this, let's try that, and if it doesn't work...so what?" The crew's demeanor, while military at heart, boasts an **irreverence** for their situation and for this "Thing" (James Arness) that they salvage from the ship, frozen in a translucent coffin. What the crew members and scientists do not realize, at first, is that (1) the "Thing" is not dead; (2) it is not like any life form they have ever seen; and (3) the creature really, really does not care for them.

The icy tomb melts by accident, allowing this strange being to fight off dogs and escape into the freezing wilderness, but only after the creature loses its hand in the scuffle. Analysis shows the hand as vegetable matter, yet matter that requires blood to nurture and propagate its seeds. Still, Capt. Pat Hendry (Kenneth Tobey) and his crew face a more pressing concern: Their elusive "super-carrot" appears capable of staying outside indefinitely, whereas the earth's mere mortals, even in parkas and other gear, can tolerate only brief exposure to the Arctic blasts.

But the real friction, aside from bushwhacking the creature before it bushwhacks back, involves Hendry and his military command crossing swords with Dr. Arthur Carrington (Robert Cornthwaite), who represents the scientific team. Carrington wants to preserve the Thing at any cost, noting that "Knowledge is more important than life." Hendry disagrees, and, fortunately for everyone, pulls rank on the doctor (King, 1981, p. 145).

Simple acts of opening doors in the compact research dwelling add a shiver to the viewers' hushed anticipation. We know that the Thing has invaded the greenhouse, before slipping again into the Arctic night. A Geiger counter helps to track the modestly radioactive creature, but even so...guess what happens when crew members open this one particular door? Yesss, it's THERE! And not just deep within the room, but flush in the passageway, losing another hand (which will grow back) as team members slam the door shut.

The geographical surrounds depict a haven for the Thing, yet the creature also lurks inside the research base, compartmentalized as the station is with rooms and narrow corridors. Only the Geiger counter, like the bell collar on a cat, gives the dwellers advanced warning of the Thing's proximity. Bluntly put, the hut's inhabitants will not venture far outside to pursue this being from another world, but they also can not keep the alien from entering their domicile to pursue them.

The film's production occurs on six sets, although the

drama focuses on one locale: the pole camp of corrugated steel. Budgetary reasons prevailed of course, but restricting most of the drama to a single set piece gives the characters' confinement a sense of realism (Sennett, 1994, p. 97):

> ...From the men in the airplane on the way to the North Pole, rattling in their cots while the smooth walls of the plane's skin fold over them like a steel-lined coffin, to the passageways in the pole camp, stuffed with wooden oil drums and packing cases, to the layers of leather, cloth, and fur that the men are endlessly pulling off or on to stay comfortable, *The Thing* is filled with images of men enclosed or trapped. And when the heat fails and the battle against the elements turns into a battle against time, the screws that hold these claustrophobic settings together are turned one notch tighter...

The bantering among crew members extends to Hendry and an old flame, Nikki Nicholson (Margaret Sheridan), who works at the research unit. She is tough and can trade lines with the best of them. At one point, as the crew prepares for a final confrontation with the creature, Nikki glances at Hendry and remarks, "Well, looks as if they have the situation well in hand." A weary Hendry responds, "That's alright with me. I've given all the orders I'm going to give for the rest of my life." Whereupon Nikki retorts: "If I thought that were true, I'd ask you to marry me."

The military team does hold one solid advantage: Their bantering includes a rapid exchange of ideas, and the discipline to improvise these suggestions into reality. The Thing, by contrast, shows sufficient insight to shut off the electricity so that the Arctic outside slowly becomes the Arctic inside, leaving the camp's inhabitants short on time and survival. But the creature underestimates its adversaries, assuming that brute strength will more than match any show of opposition (Nash & Ross, 1987, p. 3372). The consequence? Our Thing from another world, for all its admirable psychopathic intentions, gets fried to a little pile of vegetable powder.

The crew's irreverence for the creature, for blind scientific pursuits, even for the military chain of command, arises as a defining force to set the film's mood. Characters deliver their lines briskly, even "stepping on" a colleague's remarks to create a lively atmosphere of camaraderie: The crew members know one another's likes and dislikes well, and are accustomed to the prickly practice of good-hearted jousting. Thus, their ribbing of the Captain's affections for Nikki derives from a fondness of Hendry, but also a respect for his ability to command. The crew's faith in Hendry's leadership and their abilities to improvise derive from past crises, and give them a fine edge in overcoming the odds to survive the Arctic and defeat this superbly equipped Thing from another galaxy.

GEOHAZARDS RUN AMOK

The North Pole poses a relatively simple formula for survival: Do it my way, or die. *The Thing* epitomizes this fundamental creed because, in the Arctic, the food chain is short and the options to persevere, few. The arrangement of landscape to character bears a simplicity of intercourse: The terrain's overwhelming demands of co-existence force its inhabitants to honor the superior force. We know who rules the roost in this scenario.

Mood, however, enjoys an intangible quality. The emotional flavor of surviving an alien being and the Arctic carries a **surplus meaning** that goes beyond the sum of its tangible parts. Admittedly, claiming a surplus meaning seems tantamount to introducing a weasel factor: We know it is there, we just can not define it. But the impression lingers that as a movie's sense of mood reaches a heightened level of sensory experience, it loses something magical when described or analyzed in concrete terms. The magic dies when dissected, such is the mystical presence of mood and circumstance in telling a story on screen.

But what happens in a more complex society? What happens when a city's dwellers find themselves with greater freedom to challenge their physical environment? Imagine a stack of monolithic buildings, plastered with giant advertisements for an adventurous life in the off-world colonies. Imagine vehicles cruising on cushions of air, soaring in and around this architecture. Imagine a landscape with ample room for everyone to find shelter.

Sifting through this promising prose, we encounter the gritty truth: The monolithic buildings denote monstrosities, bathed in the pollution of a mismanaged environment; the air-cushioned vehicles are police cruisers, needed to maintain vigil over a crime-ridden city; and the ample space for shelter designates domiciles of desolation, offering little warmth and comfort. The landscape signifies a claustrophobic package of decay and decadence. People jam themselves along an aimless corridor of neon and glitter, indulging in the kind of physical pleasures that accord past and future little standing.

Welcome to the early 21st century and the tarnished world of *Blade Runner* (1982). Directed by Ridley Scott from the screenplay by Hampton Fancher and David Peoples, the film draws its bleak world from the novel *Do Androids Dream Of Electric Sheep?* by Philip K. Dick. The brighter folk have left for greener pastures, leaving behind the losers and those cynical citizens who still search for a reason to leave. Deckard (Harrison Ford) falls in the latter category, a blade runner who cares little for a job he does well: to search for and destroy replicants who return to earth illegally. Replicants refer to androids enslaved by the powerful Tyrell Corporation to work as cheap labor on one of those "adventurous" off-world colonies.

The replicants possess human intelligence, but also can behave ferociously and display greater physical strength than humans. Their most frightening quality, however, is that they **appear human**, so a special test must confirm that they are, indeed, still androids. Replicants begin their existence feeling no emotions, although the improved models show indications of developing a range of feelings. The replicants, frankly, come too close to the real thing. Thus, in the interests of egoism and self-preservation, genetic engineers cap off an android's life span at four years.

So, if you were a replicant, how would you feel? A small number, headed by Roy Batty (Rutger Hauer), the most intelligent and dangerous member, escape imprisonment from an off-world colony and return to earth. Batty knows he must

confront Tyrell (Joe Turkel), his genetic creator, to remove the
four-year death knell. Deckard's job, of course, involves
dispatching these unwanted misfits.

He kills one replicant as she attempts to flee, shooting her
in the back. He is almost killed by another android, until an
ally, Rachael (Sean Young), saves his life. Rachael has
received an implant from Tyrell to provide memories of a
childhood, and to deceive her into thinking she is human.
According to Tyrell's rationale, the implant will make Rachael
easier to manage if she thinks and feels as a "human." But
human she is not. She is a replicant, though a very special
replicant to the creator...and to Deckard.

Rachael, however, knows. Commenting on Deckard's
thanking her for saving his life, Rachael notes, "I'm not in the
business. I am the business." She is on earth legally, courtesy
of Tyrell, but she is the kind of individual that Deckard seeks
to eliminate. Not the best beginning for a man and woman to
find affection, unless, by some quirk of fate, Deckard also
harbors a dark secret. Rachael asks if he has ever taken the
test, but the blade runner does not answer. Hmmm.

Two replicants remain, Roy Batty and his beauteous,
lithesome partner, Pris (Daryl Hannah). Roy finagles a visit
to Tyrell, telling him "It's not an easy thing to meet your
maker." The replicant needs a reprieve from the four-year
swan song, but Tyrell tells him that no scientific procedure
can reverse the process. Tyrell eulogizes Roy's turbulent
existence: "The light that burns twice as bright burns half as
long, and you have burned so very, very brightly, Roy. Look
at you, you're the prodigal son. You're quite a prize."

Why smart psychopaths like Tyrell seldom sense imminent
danger must be a testimony to their arrogance. When you
vanquish the replicant's hope for a longer life, what kind of
replicant remains? Answer: a fatalistic one. A figure, whose
last hope lies in Tyrell, must now must find something to
replace this loss. The "something" becomes revenge, and what
better irony than for the "prodigal son" to turn on his "parent":
Why not murder the maker? And Roy does, literally and
symbolically crushing Tyrell's brain.

Pris, elsewhere, assaults Deckard and captures his neck in

a vise-like grip with her legs, almost strangling him. But "almost" is never good enough in the psychopath's world. Deckard frees himself, manages to reach his weapon, and blows Pris into a genetic eternity.

Roy returns, running out of life, to find Pris dead. Gently, he kisses her goodbye, and prepares to meet a very lucky blade runner. Deckard fires and wounds Roy, causing the replicant to taunt him: "I thought you were supposed to be good. Aren't you the good man?" Deckard, at this juncture, is not certain he can answer that question.

The end of a harrowing chase finds Deckard clinging with one crippled hand and one good hand to a steel beam several stories high. Roy looks down at the anguish of his quarry: "Quite an experience to live in fear, isn't it? That's what it is to be a slave." The pouring rain loosens Deckard's grip and in the instant of his release Roy grasps the blade runner's wrist and lifts him to safety.

The adversaries gaze upon one another, Deckard now at Roy's mercy and prepared for a dire end. But Roy has seen all the fear he wishes to see in Deckard's face. Instead, both figures sit quietly in the drenching stink of the city, until Roy reminiscences about the sights he has experienced during his short, volatile life.

"All those moments will be lost in time," he says, "like tears in rain." And then softly he utters a parting declaration, "Time to die." But his death, not Deckard's. Roy Batty, a slight smile of sadness, lowers his head, and dies. A dove flutters from his presence, flying upward, an android soul finding release.

Deckard finally has his reason for leaving the city-- Rachael. He realizes that she was special to Tyrell and had no fixed date to self-destruct, so there is the chance of a life together. How much of a chance, and how long? Deckard does not know, just as we do not know...about him. Is he human, or is he "more human than human," the perfect replicant? (Sammon, 1996, pp. 390-392.)

Unlike the defining line of good and evil in *The Thing*, the personalities of *Blade Runner* strike a chord of puzzlement. Tyrell strides forth, the most familiar characterization of a psychopath, as the overlord who takes undue pride in his genetic and fiscal achievements: "Commerce is our goal here at Tyrell. More human than human is our motto." But at what a cost to human...and android feelings. Tyrell breaks no new ground in psychopathy--making the same mistake of supreme arrogance as other evildoers have made--although he illustrates how a human can be more malevolent at heart than his creations.

Otherwise, who is good and who is evil? We shall hardly confuse Roy or Pris with good Samaritans, since they deceive and threaten others for personal gain. But we wonder, if given extended life and freedom, how these replicants would fare. Roy and Pris demonstrate a conniving affection for each other, the kind of affection that says "Us against the world." And Roy spares Deckard for reasons that Deckard does not fully comprehend.

Nor do we find Deckard's moral posture beyond reproach. He reluctantly accepts the task of a blade runner, yet faces danger from the replicants only because he pursues them so tenaciously, risking life and limb. Blade running is a job Deckard performs well (as a human?), but is it a job he must do? A higher authority acts to ensure his cooperation, although the extent of that authority is never clear. Given the chaos of the city, would this authority attempt to track Deckard and Rachael as they leave to begin another life? We are not sure.

The Thing and *Blade Runner* share a transaction between the landscape and the people. The claustrophobic setting for our Arctic intruders in *The Thing* reduces to an elementary base of corrugated steel, and a generator for light and heat to withstand the enveloping wilderness of snow and ice. But claustrophobia for the city dwellers of *Blade Runner* becomes more problematic: They have desecrated their landscape, and in a fitting denouement, the malignant remnants of metal, mortar, and grime harness them in place. The inhabitants are as ants, inert in purpose, fated to play out the same endless routines. A dying culture mired in a grotesque tomb of concrete and neon, fashioned by the cultural inhabitants' own dark hand.

RAIN, MIST, & SHADOWS

The world of *Blade Runner* pelts its denizens into submission. The dreariness of incessant dampness forces heads to bow and minds to admit subservience. A downpour in the final scenes between Deckard and Roy Batty serves to intensify the conflict between them, but also reminds viewers of where the combatants are and how little they count in a blighted landscape.

Rain fulfills a cinematic function, good and evil. A thunderstorm encourages the childish fantasy of a carefree spirit, so we splash along with Gene Kelly in his whimsical dance from *Singing In The Rain* (1952); or we gad about through gales of laughter and showers with the Trapp children and Maria in *The Sound Of Music* (1965).

Gaiety, however, does not denote rain's fundamental contribution to mood and circumstance. Cinematic rain works to prepare us for more sobering experiences. A steady rain casts forth a solemn mood given over to **reflection**, a melancholy interlude of thoughts and feelings reprised. Perry Smith (Robert Blake) of *In Cold Blood* (1967) contemplates such a moment. He is awaiting execution on a chilly, rainy Kansas night for murdering four members of the Clutter family. Perry gazes from a small window at a dismal scene...and a dismal life.

The moment, however, becomes memorable cinematically because of a visual accident. Conrad Hall in a documentary on cinematography, *Visions Of Light* (1992), recounts how the "accident" transpired. He positioned a hidden fan to blow spray from the rain against the window. He did not anticipate, however, that the light and shadow from the spray would play on Perry's sad countenance, leaving the impression of a rivulet of tears streaming down his face. "Tears" that animated and heightened his forlorn expression of a failed life.

More commonly, filmmakers use rain as a turbulent barometer of unrest. Not a gentle, undulating rain, but gusts of showers; not a tranquil, soaking rain, but trees waving furiously; not the soft patter of drops on a windowpane, but the crack and pop of a storm in heat. Thus, we have Zeus in

Fantasia (1940), who, annoyed with Dionysus's wine-based worship, creates a howling chaos as he hurls lightening bolts with abandon--all accompanied by Ludwig Van Beethoven's "Pastoral Symphony."

These thunderclaps complement characters and story, moving both to a **more pressing direction**. *Eye Of The Needle* (1981), for example, transforms Ken Follett's novel of quiet desperation into a psychological onslaught of brooding weather and suppressed emotions on Storm Island. Directed by Richard Marquand and written by Stanley Mann, the mood and circumstance of Storm Island quicken the pulse in three ways. First, Faber (Donald Sutherland), a Nazi spy, finds himself stranded on the island because a gale has driven his boat onto the rocks. He must radio a submarine off the coast for a rendezvous, but he must do so without exposing his true mission to either Lucy (Kate Nelligan), or her bitter husband, David (Christopher Cazenove). David, a Brit primed to fly combat against the Nazis, loses the use of his legs in a car accident. Now a caustic paraplegic, he and Lucy have retreated to Storm Island to live out the war.

A second outcome of the island's frequent downpours occurs when Lucy and Faber rush to a cave for shelter. As they wait out the cloudburst, Lucy, starved for affection, draws closer to the enigmatic Faber. The Nazi, disenchanted with Hitler's command of the war, opens his psychopathic armor a crack to give Lucy, not feigned affection, but a genuine transfer of passion, long thought dead. The isolated, wet world of Storm Island brings two disparate souls together, masking their dispirited concerns and isolating them from the mainstream business of countries at war.

Alas, their affair of circumstance comes to crashing ruin when Lucy learns of Faber's deception. The weather's third consequence erupts as a harsh, driving rain that underscores Lucy's desperation. She drives to the island's only other shelter, which houses the radio Faber must possess. He chases her, sheets of rain accentuating his dilemma: The spy's first priority is, as always, the mission; but a mission now compromised by his feelings for Lucy.

Lucy is not so compromised. The infidelity she commits

proves apt punishment for a lost marriage, and a husband taken from her through Faber's lethal hand. The searing rain functions as yet another humbling reminder of the debt she must pay, and will pay for years to come. The stark confrontation between two former lovers, as distant now as night and day, goes to Faber. He radios his position and, with information of the allied plan to invade Normandy, prepares a boat to reach his rendezvous.

But Faber, heretofore always the compleat psychopath, does not--can not--kill Lucy. She pursues him to the water's edge, realizing the danger he poses to the war's outcome. Screaming that she will not allow him to leave, Lucy fires wildly with a handgun, and, finally, delivers a life-taking bullet. A bullet that swallows all the amorous passion felt before, shattering their fragile, forbidden intimacy. Faber, never really attempting to protect himself, dies, and with him dies the critical information of troop movements.

The weeping torrents of Storm Island, a brusque testimony to the relentless onslaught of nature's whims, captures in its waves of emotion two fated lovers, destined for tragedy. Imagine accomplishing this same feat on a warm, tropical isle with balmy winds and a turquoise sky. Star-crossed lovers can exist there, too, but not under the same urgency, or the same mood.

Alfred Hitchcock's *Psycho* (1960) also relies on a dense storm, this time to keep Marion Crane (Janet Leigh) from realizing how close she has driven to her destination. Instead, a weary Marion wanders off the highway in search of shelter...and finds the Bates Motel. Subsequently, we recall a series of water scenes: Marion, making her fateful stop at the motel because of a merciless downpour; Marion, deciding to return the money she has stolen and taking a shower to cleanse her guilt away, only to lose her life; and Marion, in the trunk of her car which Norman Bates (Anthony Perkins) guides into a pond--slipping her into a watery grave.

Rain, therefore, typically plays a supporting role in film. Yet whether it moves characters to a critical path or intensifies their efforts to survive, this element wields greater power than appears evident at first glance. The natural grace of nature's moods proves deceptive in affecting human moods. Just ask Faber, a fully-functioning psychopath, who softens because, for him, he meets the right woman but at the wrong time and the wrong place...on Storm Island.

THE MOOD OF NOIR

Complementary to rain, mist, and shadows, we have the melancholy world of **film noir**. Jon Boorstin, who discusses lighting this dark world, argues for the pinpoint glare of "hard light" over the weak dispersion of "soft light." Hard light stems from a single source and gives a sharp edge to figures and background. Boorstin (1990, p. 24) contends that "...hard light has its own satisfactions. Used sparingly it can add a sense of drama, of eyeless sockets in cavernous faces, of men lurking beyond the glare of street lamps, of faces slashed by light knifing through the slats of a venetian blind. It is the light that put the 'noir' in 'film noir.'"

Thus, we enter a black world of jaded characters with nowhere to go, characters who realize that feeling alive means living life on the edge--even if the edge leads to murder. **Classic film noir** refers to "black film," specifically to black-and-white films of the 1940s, films like *High Sierra* (1941), *Double Indemnity* (1944), *The Postman Always Rings Twice* (1946), and *Out Of The Past* (1947).

Classic film noir represents an **abstraction**, a nightmare more surreal than real. The nightmare provokes viewers to imagine a dark landscape of seemingly endless tunnels and dead-end streets, populated by cynical personalities who spit on the 9-to-5 routine of making a weekly wage.

Men and women play each other as adversaries in the world of noir, duelists who find the adversity seductive and exciting. Their very union proves risky for them, and surely for those poor souls caught in the lovers' crossfire. Therefore, if a staid husband blocks the lovers' path to psychopathic happiness, he shall not last long in such company--as happens in *Double Indemnity* and *The Postman Always Rings Twice*.

But after murder, ...what? The culpable couple, unable to

experience the normal joys of life, finds a path strewn with thorns. The female often shows a stronger profile of psychopathy in classic film noir, using her feminine lures of secrecy and misdirection to full advantage. She is an **omega** woman, someone whose glacial temperament and mesmerizing beauty allow her to abdicate all responsibility for others (see Lesson 5 on "Character"). She desires wealth more than sex, since the sex is hers for the taking. Consequently, she will use a man she knows she **can** use, all the while professing her lusty affection for him.

Classic film noir designates an unforgiving era of Hollywood morality. No matter how clever and calloused the psychopath, she must fade out the loser. And, as in *Out Of The Past*, if she loses, the femme fatale will make damn sure that **he** loses, too. No one wins in a classic noir world. Whatever thrill she feels, she derives from deceit and from the superiority of knowing more than her victims.

The male psychopath, to survive, must not only remain somewhat immune to the perils of such femininity, but he must stay one step ahead of other characters who wish him harm. The task for Harry Lime (Orson Welles) in *The Third Man* (1949) proves a mite easier. The woman, Anna Schmidt (Alida Valli), is no omega personality. She loves Harry and is loyal to him, despite his cryptic dealings as a racketeer in war-torn Vienna.

Directed by Carol Reed and written by Graham Greene, the story begins when Holly Martins (Joseph Cotten), a writer of westerns down on his luck, comes to Vienna at Harry's urging. Holly, unfortunately, arrives just in time for his friend's funeral. Harry apparently meets with an accident: He is hit by a car, dies shortly thereafter, and three men transport his body away. Holly investigates and identifies two of the men, but the "third man" poses a mystery.

Holly's persistence in learning the truth leads him into an attraction for Anna, who discourages his attentions. But he also encounters danger as hoodlums chase him up a spiral staircase in one dazzling shot, and, by contrast, pursue him down to the post-war rubble of Vienna in a subsequent scene. Holly is at wits end, when, visiting Anna, he notices a cat nuzzling a man's feet in the shadow of a doorway. A cat, Anna informs him, that was fond of Harry.

Yelling for the man to come out, an apartment light goes on and bathed in the hard light is a man's face...Harry Lime's face. A classic film noir revelation: Harry with the mocking smile, Harry back from eternity. Harry, who promptly disappears, uses the labyrinth of Vienna's sewer system to vanish once again. Anna, however, offers the most sympathetic comment on Harry's resurrection: "Poor Harry. I wish he was dead. He would be safe from all of you, then."

Anna's assessment points to one of the psychopath's enduring strengths: a disreputable personality capable of performing foul deeds, yet a charming character who manages to retain the affection and loyalty of individuals for whom, frankly, he gives precious little in return. Orson Welles's Harry Lime possesses these useful qualities in abundance.

Indeed, he applies his natural gifts via a meeting with Holly aboard a huge Ferris wheel in the Prater, a deserted amusement park. But Holly has seen the ugly results of Harry's scheme, courtesy of Major Calloway (Trevor Howard): the illegal marketing of diluted penicillin that has caused too many sick children to perish. Harry, nonetheless, blithely waves away this ugliness, prompting Holly to challenge him: "You used to believe in God."

Harry replies smoothly, "Well, I still do believe in God, old man. I believe in God, and mercy, and all that, but the dead are happier dead. They don't miss much here, poor devils." What Holly hears in this rationale is the psychopath's convenient escape clause for irresponsible behavior: Don't fret for the victims, because the life they leave remains fraught with pain and suffering. Certainly this life appears sufficiently dreary in Harry's noir world.

The exchange of dialogue between Holly and Harry on the giant wheel brings their "friendship" of 20 years into sharper perspective. Harry fulfills the role of mentor, a teacher of cheap tricks and an instigator of trouble. The kind of trouble wherein, at least on one past occasion, he failed to give Holly a helping hand. We understand all too clearly that Harry treats Holly as he treats others under his influence: worse than they deserve, while using his considerable charms to keep them intrigued for morsels of his "wisdom."

Harry, however, has murdered. He even contemplates Holly's demise atop the Ferris wheel, until he learns that Major Calloway knows of his faked death. A police informant resides in Harry's coffin, his body previously carried from the scene of the "accident" by two of Harry's cronies, and by Harry as the third man.

Shifting gears with ease, as psychopaths do, Harry glosses over his threat and gives Holly a parting thought from Lime's Philosophy of Life 101: "In Italy for 30 years under the Borgias they had warfare, terror, murder, bloodshed. They produced Michelangelo, Leonardo da Vinci, and the Renaissance. In Switzerland they had brotherly love, 500 years of democracy and peace. And what did they produce? The cuckoo clock."

So, out of a volatile world of atrocities comes the creative juices to score magnificent works of art and commerce. Harry's sordid world, however, simply involves the murder of children using a compromised drug. Whatever magnificence awaits inspiration from these misbegotten deeds remains, as yet, undetected. Harry, naturally, worries not one whit over his lame analogy, but he overlooks his friend's reaction to the lost children. Holly now considers what he could not have imagined a few days ago: setting a trap for Harry.

The finale of *The Third Man* occurs in the appropriate noir world of Vienna's massive sewer system. Harry escapes into the labyrinth again, a sanctuary apropos of his endeavors, fleeing this time from Holly and squads of police. Escape routes to the streets above, always available to Harry before, now are blocked by officers. The elusive third man frantically evades his pursuers in the tunnels, splashing through the dregs of Vienna's sewerage, looking for the one sliver of luck that, heretofore, the fates have never denied him.

Wounded in an exchange of gunfire with a policeman, Harry scrambles up a ladder to find a hatch free of pursuers. From street level, we see his fingers curl through the grate, seeking to push his way to freedom at last...only the cover does not budge. The wheel of a car rests on the grate, keeping it and Harry firmly in place.

Nash and Ross (1987, p. 3376), in their review of the film, comment on Harry's "baleful expression" as he slips down the ladder and comes face to face with Holly. "Baleful" carries several shaded meanings, one of which is "menacing" and another is "miserable." Harry is unaccustomed to such terror, and even his powers of rationalization may not keep him from recognizing the end of a dark career.

The question of which mind-set Harry entertains--menacing or miserable--becomes academic because Holly fires the fatal shot. But the academic question is worth pondering: Does Harry still harbor a hope of escape, which means relying on his charm to take Holly off-guard and kill him? Or does Harry, believing he has played his last card, send Holly an unspoken invitation to shoot? The question has no ready answer, since both possibilities seem within Harry Lime's province of options.

Camera angles carry viewers into seemingly endless lengths of cavernous tunnels, illuminated sporadically by flashes of light that freeze figures in place. The gushing sewer water leaves an impression of pursuers and pursued grounded in inertia, slogging through timeless burrows that twist and turn--exemplifying the visual hell of a classic noir landscape.

Harry's psychopathic character does not falter as Faber did in *Eye Of The Needle*. Rather, Harry Lime's convoluted lifestyle creates too many enemies for him to avoid. He is wanted here, there, everywhere. Harry needs to leave Vienna, but his ego permits no such wisdom. The evil raconteur's faith in his subterranean landscape includes no recognition that such a haven can materialize into a tomb of ultimate judgment. Vienna's underground kingdom of refuse serves fittingly as Harry's final destination.

The film's postscript shows Anna walking (to where?) down a street. Holly, driving by with Major Calloway, gets out and waits for Anna to reach him. She reaches him, and she passes him without a word or a look. Anna views Holly as a traitor, someone who betrayed a friendship. Perhaps she had seen too much ugliness in her young life, so that Harry's unseemly ways did not dissuade her from loving him. Harry returned her affections with his own shallow feelings, but what little he offered Anna may have been more than she knew from other men in other places.

The quintessential noir ending reveals Holly staying put, smoking a cigarette, not bothering to glance after the departing Anna. Words will not heal their torn relationship. And this time, Harry can not resurrect himself to change the outcome. Holly is still down on his luck. Indeed, in killing Harry, he is worse for the experience of having known Harry at all. The mood of noir allows little tolerance for hope, and none at all for forgiveness.

MODERN FILM NOIR

The Third Man in color would not be *The Third Man*. The gloom and emptiness of Vienna's sewer maze could not retain its mystique in color. The deep shadows that Harry Lime used so seamlessly to mask his presence would surrender their intrigue if color became a requisite element in the noir world.

Does color violate the sanctity of film noir? **Purists** say yes. A classic noir world comes alive mostly at night, casting its lengthy shadows across figures and landscapes as if giving life itself the mark of Cain. Coloring this world, even with muted hues, introduces a measure of cinematic softness that purists find unacceptable.

Pragmatists, however, say baloney. The fundamentals of veering to risky relationships stay the same, whether in black-and-white or color (Palmer, 1994, pp. 27-28). Film noir appears to endure in different guises, although these bodies of work address the same basic yearnings and misdeeds as in the classic world--except now they exist in landscapes awash with color and a liberal moral set. Indeed, according to Robert Ray (1985, p. 159) in *A Certain Tendency Of The Hollywood Cinema, 1930-1980*, the "noir morality" extends to other genres, including certain screwball comedies, westerns, and even musicals.

Modern film noir, much to the purist's lament, embraces scenarios that carry "black film" beyond the confines of dark corridors and the hard light of grisly contempt. Admittedly, the downside of these modern changes dilutes the mystique and foreboding atmosphere of what purists mean by "noir." The upside, however, injects a constant in the noir world, whether black-and-white or color: A psychopath is a psychopath is a psychopath.

Judge for yourself as we provide a modern film-noir take on the mood and circumstance of three films--*Basic Instinct*, *Pulp Fiction*, and *Natural Born Killers*--that would not have seen the light of day in the censorship of the 1940s. And yet, through the psychopath's brand of dark humor, all three films capture the degradation of the classic film noir character.

PSYCHOPATHIC HUMOR

The psychopath who laughs with you denotes the psychopath who, secretly, laughs at you. An evildoer's **sense of humor** does not include sharing a laugh with friends, or becoming the butt of a joke. If the psychopath proclaims any capacity for self-mockery, watch out. The mood he invokes constitutes a ruse. A ruse that uses shared gaiety to prompt misdirection so as to mask the offender's true intent.

More likely, a psychopath's sense of humor concerns **playing games**, but only games that favor the advantage of winning.   Psychopaths truly dislike losing.   They dislike surprises, they dislike playing a supporting role, and they dislike a change in the rules...unless they do the changing. Mostly, psychopaths fear losing control, because losing control impairs their exalted sense of ego to maintain superiority. A theoretical case can be made that many criminals, and psychopaths in particular, operate from a perceived level of high self-esteem when dispatching violence (Baumeister, Smart, & Boden, 1996).

The psychopath's high self-esteem, imagined or real, constitutes his source of delight for duping those poor souls inferior to himself. This egotism lends itself to game playing, and to the harsh ridicule that relies on a form of merriment called **dispositional humor**.   Dolf Zillmann and Jennings

Bryant (1991, pp. 271-272) define dispositional humor as a dramatic exchange that allows the advantaged party to disparage and triumph over the disadvantaged party-- performed, of course, in a comedic spirit of winning and losing:

> ...Loveable and hateable characters must be developed, especially the latter kind. Pleasant, honest, and otherwise virtuous characters are mostly needed as targets for the abusive behavior of the "evil cast": those characters who display arrogance, snobbishness, vainglory, vanity, ignorance, bigotry, selfishness, egotism, contemptuousness, insensitivity, rudeness, brutality, or other utterly despicable traits.

Engineered by psychopaths, dispositional humor victimizes the target of humor well beyond "good-old-boy" hilarity. The psychopathic intent of this humor may serve as an end in itself: to cruelly ridicule the subject, say, by playing some demeaning practical joke. But psychopathic intent also reflects an instrumental use of dispositional humor, such as deliberately taunting a chosen victim to further the evil jester's nefarious scheme.

Basic Instinct (1992) produces a game-playing temptress, Catherine Tramell (Sharon Stone), who matches wits with an unstable detective, Nick Curran (Michael Douglas). Paul Verhoven's direction and Joe Eszterhas's screenplay bring out Catherine's wit and show that her arsenal of temptations is more than sufficient to send Nick reeling. The femme fatale relies variously on mockery, fast cars, lesbian foreplay, nudity, and even tears and the mystique of a shady life to cast a spell over Nick.

Most daunting to Nick, however, is Catherine's knowledge of confidential information about him--information that only Beth (Jeanne Tripplehorn), his therapist, should know. Nick, aware of the danger and excitement that Catherine represents, confides to his partner, "She's coming after me, Gus." What he does not realize is that, to Catherine, going after Nick entails a full-scale assault on the detective's senses. She seems vulnerable, she seems arrogant, she seems intimate, she seems distant, she seems gay, she seems mysterious, she seems murderous. She evokes moods that keep Nick off-balance and always a step behind in his pedestrian efforts to learn about the real Catherine Tramell.

Catherine tells Nick, "Pretty soon I'll know you better than you know yourself." Her professed intent concerns writing a novel about a detective who dies at the end. Catherine's books do not close with happy endings, a contemplation on the author's fatalistic view of life. She defends her morbidity by claiming, "Someone has to die." When Nick asks why, Catherine replies, "Someone always does."

Three (at least three) social institutions receive a humorous black eye in the melodrama of *Basic Instinct*. First, **an omega woman outwits the male establishment.** The interrogation scene places Catherine in the spotlight's glare as her inquisitors settle in the shadows to play their usual game of firing questions. But Catherine does not play conventionally. Instead, she sensually moves her legs to fleetingly reveal an absence of panties; she smokes in defiance of a no smoking ordinance; and she controls the conclave of uneasy males by doing what she does best: using her sexuality and her intelligence to disrupt the status quo.

Second, **Nick shows his disdain for therapy as a healing profession.** He is a mad dog when in close quarters with therapists, using blunt, blue, no-nonsense language to puncture the bland therapeutic line about childhood problems, the unconscious, and other psychoanalytic pablum. More provocatively, he previously engages in sexual relations with Beth, his police therapist. But, even though the affair appears dormant, Beth continues to see Nick as a client. Later, Nick, in a wild state over Catherine, promptly roughs Beth around, eventually propping her over a couch for an impromptu session, much against Beth's desire.

Finally, **a spoofing of carnal sex translates into the axiom that the only exciting sex is sex tied to a death wish.** Forget about the eroticism of sex in the sand, the elevator, or the guest room during a dull party. Nick and Catherine appear fated to meet, and destined to make their sexual relations compelling in basically one way: to transform sex into a flamboyant, memorable, and, most of all, dangerous experience.

This dangerous experience, of course, leads us to the ice pick. Given the age of ice cubes, the ice pick appears an artifact of bygone days. But the mood of *Basic Instinct* evokes those days in Catherine and Nick as two personalities who brush away modern formalities and probe for the kind of visceral emotions that seem timeless. Each party thrives on the dangerousness of the other, with Catherine, as always, holding the upper hand. After all, it is her forte, her game...and her ice pick.

Catherine's laughter may not coincide with our accustomed expectation of humor, but we must listen more carefully for laughter on the inside. She is the compleat psychopath who demonstrates a special flair for fostering puzzles. The puzzles, in turn, give Catherine a sly delight as she monitors her pawns and observes how they scurry about to find a solution.

With Nick, Catherine uses her secrecy and her misdirection to titillate him. Knowing he is the detective who will search tenaciously for answers, she teases him with her mystique and her masquerades. The games keep Catherine and Nick "alive," but are not designed for a long run. Each adversary proves too threatening to the other for mutual survival.

Catherine displays her vulnerability in two ways. She finds Nick attractive, but will give up too much control by embracing him: "I can't allow myself to care about you. I can't allow myself to care." Catherine guards herself against him, lest she endangers herself by sacrificing her dominance.

This dilemma leads Catherine to her most perilous enemy...herself. She refuses to take life conventionally, which means that only personal risk excites her. Catherine possesses the beauty and the money to live a comfortable existence, but she does not possess the complacency. She must take chances, and, as with other successful predators, she will ultimately take one chance too many.

Apart from the **game** motif, psychopathic humor also involves extremes of understated and overstated humor. **Understated humor** presents a safer artistic risk since actors underplay their roles, even as they engage in volatile acts, or find themselves in outlandish settings. The characters deliver their lines solemnly, oblivious to their personality quirks.

Does Quentin Tarantino's *Pulp Fiction* (1994), for instance, designate a new wave of modern film noir? Does this film satirize the mobster world by paying homage to those B movies that, in their day, took mobsters seriously? **Satire** refers to the dispositional use of irony, ridicule, and sarcasm directed at human folly and vice. But in psychopathic hands, the pattern of satire appears reversed. Those evildoers normally perceived as degenerates and fully deserving of ridicule, instead, deliver their own scorn upon others caught in disadvantageous positions. The ridiculed, in other words, become the ridiculers.

The screenplay by Tarantino and Roger Avary provides no progressive storyline in *Pulp Fiction* to deliver its characters from A to Z. Instead, we encounter vignettes that intertwine: A pair of low-grade opportunists, Pumpkin (Tim Roth) and Honey Bunny (Amanda Plummer), decide to blaze new trails and rob the diner they are in; a pair of hit men, Vincent (John Travolta) and Jules (Samuel L. Jackson), chit and chat over mundane issues involving foot massages and TV programs as they prepare to do a job for their boss, Marsellus Wallace (Ving Rhames); a fading boxer, Butch Coolidge (Bruce Willis), promises Marsellus he will throw his fight in the fifth round, but has no intention of doing so; Vincent squires Mia Wallace (Uma Thurman) at the bequest of her husband, Marsellus, to a night out that turns into a harrowing evening when Mia almost overdoses on Vincent's stash; Vincent accidentally blows off the head of a passenger in the back seat of a car, forcing Vincent and Jules to require the services of Wolf (Harvey Keitel), a cleanup man, to get them out of trouble; and, after Wolf's help, Vincent and Jules decide to eat at a certain diner...

Pulp Fiction offers us, not a linear storyline, but coincidental slices of low-brow Americana from all the B-movies you have ever thought of watching. The various plots occasionally crisscross past-and-present episodes, as we glimpse these characters over a weekend. Critic David Denby (1995, p. 228) refers to Tarantino's skewed use of past and present as "...*collateral* narration. What goes around comes around."

None of the vignettes find resolution by formula, and none of the characters declare the kind of brain power that might suggest a long lifeline. The film's mystic mood begins warped, and stays warped. Just as in *All About Eve* (1950), where we immersed ourselves in the theatre world, *Pulp Fiction* asks us to tag along in a mordant world of mobsters, enforcers, and betrayers. Everything is cheap, everything is lurid, everything is pulp.

Spotters of psychopaths will have a field day in this world. Marsellus, the glue to which all other characters adhere, possesses the greatest power and the most potential for dispensing evil. He does so brutally, although with one exception concerning Butch. Vincent, slouching and swaggering as a good enforcer would, appears destined to remain a hit man and unleash his malevolence by taking orders. Wolf, also at the beck and call of Marsellus, rises a cut above Vincent in the cleanup man's ability to control nasty situations. But Wolf, at heart, is a wolf who can make bad things happen with dispatch, and with nary a trace of his dirty work.

The odd man out in this cadre of ne'er-do-wells is Butch. He is a boxer who secretly goes against Marsellus and bets on himself to win. He does win and now must leave L.A. in haste to avoid Marsellus's minions. Butch, however, is no saint. When a cabbie informs him that the man he fought in the ring has died, and asks Butch how it feels to kill a man, the boxer replies: "I didn't feel the least little bit bad..." (Tarantino, 1994, p. 75).

An honest answer, but an answer tied to the boxer's beliefs that death, though remote, always looms as a possibility in the ring. (Quentin Tarantino shot a longer version of Butch's scene with the cab driver, one showing the boxer in a more sympathetic light. The edited scene that played in theatres gives Butch a more calloused demeanor.)

Butch's altruistic streak surfaces when, about to sneak away from two captors who are torturing Marsellus in the back room of a pawn shop, the boxer decides to return and save his boss. First, Butch selects a hammer as his weapon, then in an escalation of armament, he discovers a ball bat, a chainsaw, and, ultimately, a sword. The sword seems most appropriate for vengeance, and with it Butch saves Marsellus's unworthy hide. The boss agrees to forego his death contract on Butch if the boxer will leave L.A. pronto. This particular quid pro quo comes as close to honor among thieves as we will find in *Pulp Fiction*.

Jules, the other hit man, experiences what he calls "divine intervention." When he and Vincent eliminate some youths who have double-crossed Marsellus, a fourth man comes barging from the bathroom and fires point blank at the hit men--missing them altogether. Amazed at their stroke of fortune, Jules and Vincent blow away the fourth party.

Vincent discounts the incident as good luck, but Jules sees their escape as a sign. The sign, for Jules at least, indicates the need to embark on another career, more as a shepherd than as a hit man. He must walk the earth and find himself. This change of heart meets a stern test when Jules and Vincent are eating in the diner that Pumpkin and Honey Bunny decide to rob. Jules defuses the situation by getting the drop on Pumpkin (whom he calls Ringo), and dispenses a measure of Jules's new-found philosophy: "The truth is you're the weak. And I'm the tyranny of evil men. But I'm tryin'. I'm tryin' real hard to be a shepherd" (Tarantino, 1994, p. 158).

Translation: I'm THIS close to blowing your face away, Pumpkin, but I will not as long as you do what I say. And a subdued Pumpkin, not smart, but smart enough to know evil when he sees it, walks out with his arm around Honey Bunny, and the loot he has stolen from everyone in the diner. Jules even gives him the $1500 in his wallet, as if giving up his earthly possessions marks Jules's first real step from hit man to shepherd.

Logically, of course, psychopaths do not reverse their natures. Nor do we really expect Jules to do so in the sense of becoming someone 180 degrees altered from his former self. But Jules, if he can stay alive and free himself from the noir world of perverse loyalties and abbreviated life spans, may fare better than those denizens who find themselves too mired in this world to consider another life. Surviving appears to be as much a matter of luck as of style.

Where *Pulp Fiction* leisurely offers us an understated comedy on the banality of evil, Oliver Stone's *Natural Born Killers* (1995) swings in the opposite direction. David Veloz, Richard Rutowski, and Stone draw their screenplay from a story by Quentin Tarantino, investing the film with a potpourri of media antics: Keystone cops, the three stooges, Spike Jones--name the slapstick and you will find vestiges of the hooter, the tooter, and the old whoopee cushion in *Natural Born Killers*. **Overstatement**, indeed, accelerates to **over-the-top satire**.

For caricature (rather than character), we meet Mickey (Woody Harrelson) and Mallory (Juliette Lewis), two lovers, who, alone, would prove dangerous to anyone's health. Together, they embark on a 3-week rampage of 52 murders. Mickey even assumes the arrogance and authority to marry the two of them, while promising not to murder anyone on this special wedding day.

Supporting caricatures include (1) a hypersexual detective, Jack Scagnetti (Tom Sizemore), who eventually captures the lovers, and subsequently succumbs to the lethal lures of Mallory; (2) Warden McClusky (Tommy Lee Jones), a rabid publicity hound whose alienating presence helps to catalyze an uneasy prison atmosphere to a full-blown inmate riot; and (3) a frenetic tabloid journalist, Wayne Gale (Morton Downey, Jr.), who craves a sensational exposé so much that he becomes as bloodthirsty as his subjects.

Mickey and Mallory can imagine no philosophy deeper than pop culture, and no future grander than to live passionately for the present. As Mickey notes with a rare peep of insight, "We got the road to Hell in front of us." Translation: The two lovers can only be EVIL so long, before their capture becomes inevitable. But with capture comes adoration and mercenary devotion: adoration from fans taken by the lovers' derring-do of life and death, and mercenary devotion from the media vultures as they telescope Mickey and Mallory for a ratings bonanza.

After all, if a mad-dog killer's every word--spoken or written--draws media interest, and if groupies show themselves receptive to a notorious murderer's invitation of marriage, why not allow Mickey and Mallory to have their day? (Mickey and Mallory--even their names reek of commercial value.)   The carcasses of 52 victims, by comparison, receive hardly a back-page glance.

What thrashes about mostly in *Natural Born Killers* is a sometimes linear storyline chock full of chaotic intensity. The lovers' ludicrous odyssey comes apart at the seams with cinematic interruptions of black-and-white footage, grotesque animation, and unsettling flashbacks of young, innocent faces marred indelibly by adult brutality. For Mallory, sexual abuse from her degenerate father sets her heart on edge, made more macabre when she fantasizes life as a sitcom from hell. For Mickey, his frightening father makes an everlasting impression, whether the father merely has him witness untold violence, or whether Mickey receives the father's evil, up close and personal.

Notably, for a "natural born killer," Mickey's most discomforting moments surface when he confronts his scarred childhood. He prides himself on being that exceptional figure who kills well, kills often, and kills for the sheer joy of fulfilling his destiny. Mallory sings about being "born bad," subscribing to the same glorification of thriving as a natural predator of human souls. Mickey, especially, **must** believe in his predisposition to kill, because this one "gift" conveys his status to a feckless public, and to a news-hungry media. Hence, intrusions of childhood horror prove unwelcome and contradictory to his cultivated beliefs.

Whereas *Pulp Fiction* raises a corner of the rug to give us a deft look at the scum underneath, *Natural Born Killers* blows the muck in our face. The last laugh occurs when, after all the notables perish in a prison massacre, Mickey, Mallory, and Wayne Gale make their escape. Wayne, bloodied and bloody, finds himself suffused with the power of killing. He still carries his TV camera, and wants to get the ultimate interview with Mickey and Mallory.

But the duo have no plans to include Wayne. Thus, after frantically putting forth several pleas to avoid death, the journalist reminds his executioners of their trademark: They always leave one survivor to tell the story.   This time, however, Wayne's passion--the camera--proves his Waterloo. Mickey and Mallory inform the ego-stricken journalist that they do not need a survivor because the camera will tell their story. Indeed, the camera throughout *Natural Born Killers* has attempted indiscriminately to tell everyone's story.

So, goodbye, Wayne, and hello...Motherhood. Mallory hears the call of little feet. The closing passage projects a scene of love, serenity, and all the things that *Natural Born Killers* gave so little respect to during its murderous reign. Thus, we say farewell to Mickey and Mallory, now a family with two children (and one on the way), heading for the open road: bright, cheerful, content, and riding in a station wagon, no less.

MOOD INDIGO

A despairing version of *Natural Born Killers* occurs in *Henry: Portrait Of A Serial Killer* (1989). *Natural Born Killers* strikes a walloping mood of high-profile mayhem, whereas *Henry* drifts along at a meandering pace, quietly strewing its carnage to and fro. The difference amounts to a fanfare that transforms Mickey and Mallory into cultural icons, as opposed to gazing at characters, like Henry (Michael Rooker) and Otis (Tom Towles), who slowly dissolve into raw sewerage.

Henry, with no beginning or end, conjures up a series of short stories that chronicle the wandering evil of Henry, a drifter, and his dimwitted crony, Otis. Directed by John McNaughton from a screenplay by Richard Fire and McNaughton, the vignettes begin leisurely and end leisurely, fading slowly to black. Shorn of media histrionics and bereft of film noir's brooding signature, *Henry* supplies no purpose and, apparently, no public outcry to the murders that these disjointed stories tell.

We first see a woman's face, and, as the camera pulls slowly back, we note her unseeing eyes, her blood, her nudity, her loss of dignity, her death. The next scene shows a close-up of Henry's hand putting out a cigarette in the ash tray. The parallel suggests that Henry's act of discarding a cigarette differs little from his act of destroying a human life. Contrary to the malevolent exuberance displayed by Mickey and Mallory, Henry does not feel much.

What he does feel seems tied to memories of his whorish mother. Henry adds, "I don't fault her for that. It ain't what she done, it's how she done it." "How she done it" involves forcing little Henry to wear a dress and watch his mama have sexual relations with strangers. Henry claims to have killed his mother, but confuses the instrument of execution: Did it happen by bashing her, stabbing her, or shooting her? Did it happen at all? We do not know, but we do understand that Henry appears capable of about any atrocity (Carr, 1995, p. 341).

Murder, for Henry, becomes a matter of opportunity. Prospective victims are considered, and by some internal calculus, accepted or rejected. He sits in his car waiting for the "right woman" to come into view. The murderer follows one woman home, only to see her husband emerge from the house. Henry moves on. He is smart enough to realize that a surplus of victims await, and, eventually, he will find prey just as acceptable, and more accessible.

The chill of Henry's moribund attitude pertains to his **whimsical mood** in choosing, stalking, and murdering the characters in question. He encounters a lady walking her dog one evening. She is bitingly cordial to his questions about the dog, then tells him she must leave. Henry follows, pauses, then turns away. He decides that she is not worth his effort, but we do not know what dynamics feed into his decision. We just know that she escapes with her life because Henry makes a lazy judgment to pass.

His philosophy of life concerns never using the same gun twice, and always, always, to keep moving. Henry has no profound philosophy regarding his victims, other than to tell Otis, "It's either you or them. You know what I mean." Otis does not know, really, but killing intrigues him and he is willing to tag along. The uneasy relationship between the two murderers hits a fragile note, however, when Otis's sister, Becky (Tracy Arnold), comes into their lives.

Henry's bottleneck of emotions revolves about sex. He is

uncomfortable with the conventional signals, and finds his outlet through the stalking, murder, and grotesque positioning of bodies. Becky, a decent girl whose bad luck with men has made her wary, misreads Henry's polite behavior as someone worthy to pursue. She attempts to seduce him, but before any consequence results, Otis interrupts and Henry, relieved, goes out for cigarettes.

He returns to discover a drunken Otis raping Becky. A life-and-death struggle ends with Otis's bloody death, and his dismemberment in the bathtub. Dumping Otis in the river, Henry and Becky drive off, with Henry promising that he will take care of her. She looks at him and says, "I love you, Henry." After a pause, Henry responds, "I guess I love you, too." Underline "guess," because that word gives a true account of Henry's feelings: He has no clue as to what love is, and replies to Becky in the only way he can. After his perfunctory response to her, he asks if she wants to listen to the radio.

Henry knows the social buttons to push in misleading his victims, but he has no earthly idea how to relate romantically or sexually to Becky. He takes care of her as he takes care of his other targets, then leaves her in a garment bag by the highway. Henry drives away, adhering to his philosophy of moving along, prepared at a whim to select his next conquest somewhere down the road.

The harsh landscape, the rain, the shadows, the depraved humor--these mood pieces serve as buffers to soften the mundane realities of murder. Psychopaths in these pieces assume striking characterizations: an other-worldly alien in the Arctic; a replicant in future noir; a devious trickster in post-war Vienna; a seductive temptress who enjoys playing games; solemn hit men growling witticisms; and two murderers madly in love as they recklessly pursue their notoriety. These players make themselves known in unusual and unnerving fashion.

But Henry? We find no buffer with Henry. Instead, we encounter a tragically warped personality calmly taking lives in a landscape too normal for cinematic comfort. No wintry blasts, no desolate environment, no games, no cushion to feather reality's sickening blows. *Henry*, allegedly based on the murderer Henry Lee Lucas, patterns the man's character more than his actual deeds. And his character offers none of the mystique that we expect to discover when filmmakers offer us murder as entertainment. Henry is just a hollow man who trudges by, killing as apathetically as he lives: a psychopath without the customary adornments of cinematic grace.

Aside from the desire to murder, the one link between *Henry* and *Natural Born Killers* concerns the television camera. The camera sails along with Mickey and Mallory, documenting their riotous trail of devastation. In Henry's hands, however, the camera shakily records a morbid scene of Otis murdering a woman. A gutter action that reflects a gutter mentality, with none of the grandeur and hype of Mickey and Mallory's world. Indeed, we see in Henry no media phenomenon, no personable individual worthy of media attention, except for his dedication to murder.

Stripped of the usual cinematic appeals, the man reveals no looming monster or exceptional deviousness or spry wit in his nature. Most unsettling, he's just...Henry.

Lesson 8

Materialism: The Power Of Plenty

Cinematic psychopaths murder for external power, status, and money--a common denominator of outward reasons more or less material in nature. But psychopaths also murder for revenge, sex, and just for the hell of it--denoting a cluster of inward reasons shrouded in subjectivity.

Material psychopaths assume themselves quite the entrepreneur by substantively bettering their power base. But they do not always succeed, frequently because the aspirations expressed exceed the capabilities endowed to them. Psychopaths often desire more rewards from life than they merit. Hence, there is nothing so inviting as a tangible goal just beyond the materialist's grasp, and no one so obsessing as the psychopath who will cheerfully lie, cheat, and steal to acquire that goal.

Likewise, **spiritual psychopaths** toe the line as restless wolverines eager to commit mayhem for the sake of mayhem. Forget material needs and concentrate on individuals who create morbid fantasies of vengeance, lust, and the joy of killing. They become warped souls, acting out inner demons that speak of nameless, torturous desires, too deeply ingrained in the mind's cavities to ever see the light of day.

Evil's materialism and evil's spirituality keep the psychopath a busy ne'er-do-well. The evildoer, moreover, does not always maintain a slate of outer and inner transgressions that prove conveniently neat and tidy. Reasons to kill can be complementary so that, as in *A Shock To The System* (1990), a murderer like Michael Caine's Graham Marshall terminates adversaries for external power **and** the thrill of escaping unencumbered.

Tangible and intangible motives mingle, although the cinematic psychopath gives priority to one or the other as a guiding light. A **motive** prompts the question, **Why?** What primary reason does the malevolent personality entertain to explain his or her evil actions? If external power represents the goal, then any feelings of exuberance in this quest serve as a means to an end. The intangible motives of lust or revenge prove subservient to the main material concern of attaining superiority. Intangible motives in this scheme prove pleasurable, though still instrumental to the offender's chief aim of exercising manifest power.

Thus, **secondary motives** are **instrumental** in support of primary motives, and **primary motives** are **expressive** of the psychopath's fundamental desires. Sometimes the primary motive expresses outer needs like overt power, status, and money; and sometimes the primary motive expresses an inner orientation hellbent on lust, revenge, or the thrill of dusting a victim off. Although evildoers may indulge in both kinds of motives, ultimately they find one orientation--favoring outward accomplishments or fulfilling inner fantasies--more pertinent to satisfying their most urgent desires.

The difference in primary and secondary motives becomes a matter of emphasis. The compleat psychopath's habitual commitment to a goal reflects his overriding concern, whether the goal consists of ruthlessly pursuing a financial empire or engaging in a string of sexual assaults.

THE MOST PROLIFIC MOTIVE

Given these instances of tangible and intangible motives, an interesting twist in films concerns the consequence of one particular rationale. This rationale persists as, arguably, the most prolific motive for cinematic murder, and can encompass either a material or a spiritual act of violence.

The motive in question concerns a **fear of exposure**. The fear proves instrumental in nature, since the psychopath's actions involve a defense of maintaining the status quo. Malignant personalities, in other words, must remain unfettered to pursue their material or spiritual desires. The motive to stay free is secondary, although this incentive, if unfulfilled, can prove lethal to the psychopath.

The psychopath's first order of business is to stay in business. It does not require a film buff to recall any number of movies in which the villain attempts to sanction one or more victims to preserve the evildoer's nefarious plan. Espionage agents, for example, spend most of Alfred Hitchcock's *The Thirty-Nine Steps* (1935) searching for the hero, Richard Hannay (Robert Donat), because he can expose their political agenda.

A later Hitchcock thriller, *I Confess* (1953), makes fear of exposure its central premise: A killer confesses his crime to a priest, Father Logan (Montgomery Clift), knowing that the confidentiality of his confession is inviolate. True to his calling, Father Logan refuses to breach this vow, even when the police come to suspect **him**. The matter resolves itself when the killer finds himself exposed by other means, but the idea remains potent: Fear of exposure will drive criminals to extreme measures.

The number of innocent victims can mount precipitously to guard against disclosure, as evidenced from Lesson 2 when we tracked George Brougham (Kirk Douglas) in *The List Of Adrian Messenger* (1963). Tallying up a bombed aircraft and other craftily-arranged accidents, George killed 107 people to prevent the exposure of his grand scheme for inheriting the wealth and grounds of Gleneyre estate.

Fear of exposure, furthermore, can apply to a range of circumstances, beginning with a select intimacy and spiraling to situations of tragic scope and breadth. The preservation of intimacy, family, and reputation rules the thoughts of Judah Rosenthal (Martin Landau), a recognized ophthalmologist in Woody Allen's *Crimes And Misdemeanors* (1989). Judah's sterling status as a beloved father and humanitarian suffers from a two-fold blemish: (1) He has earlier engaged in some questionable financial practices; and (2) he has a mistress, Dolores Paley (Anjelica Huston), who finds herself increasingly agitated when Judah refuses to leave his wife.

Judah's rationale to resolve his problem with Dolores progresses from repulsion to acceptance. One solution, says Jack (Jerry Orbach), Judah's brother, is to eliminate Dolores, permanently. Judah shakes his head, "I can't do it. I can't think that way." Ah, but he can. Later, when Judah finds it impossible to sleep on a stormy night, he turns from the staircase on the first floor, just as a prodigious flash backlights his figure. This transfixed moment ushers Judah into an imaginary conversation with Ben (Sam Waterson), a Rabbi and friend to whom Judah shares his dilemma. Ben advises Judah, as expected, that he should trust in God and tell his wife of the affair.

Judah, however, believes his wife will be hurt too deeply. He responds that "God is a luxury I can't afford." Instead, Judah turns once more to Jack, who has Mafia connections. Jack consoles him with the thought that, for the right money, Dolores will no longer pose a threat. Judah comes to see the act as simplicity itself: "I push one button and I can sleep again nights." So easy, so clean, so quick, but, unfortunately for Judah, so short-lived.

He quickly succumbs to a stricken conscience of anguish and self-loathing. Judah even jeopardizes his safety by visiting Dolores's apartment just after the murder. He gazes down at his late mistress, her eyes open. She lies in quiet repose, a benign, tranquil look on her face, as if she had slipped effortlessly from life to death.

Judah, however, does not readily put her convenient murder behind him. He agonizes, he rhapsodizes, he eulogizes to his brother: "It's pure evil, Jack. A man kills for money. He doesn't even know his victims...There was nothing behind her eyes if you looked into them. All you saw was a...black void."

"Eyes" play a continuing refrain during Judah's trail of tears: The refrain begins with Judah's earlier, rather smug acknowledgement that (a) "The eyes of God are on us always," to (b) his profession as an ophthalmologist, to (c) the deteriorating vision of his patient and friend, Ben, the Rabbi. Ben, a man of virtue, goes blind. Judah, a man who professes virtue, arranges a murder and sees all too painfully the lesser man within him.

Fear of exposure proves horrendous for Judah, given his years of investment in family and reputation. Exposure means **everything** comes tumbling down: his loss of freedom, loss of family, loss of respect, loss of friends, loss of all that Judah has learned to value--and taken for granted. The only telling question now concerns Judah's moral skirmish. Can he live with himself and continue the good life, knowing that he is responsible for Dolores's death? Can he finally learn to abdicate responsibility?

Judah, in another fantasy, visits his house of birth and imagines himself gazing upon his family at mealtime, years ago. The members respond to Judah's predicament by detailing his options: He should take the moral high ground and confess his complicity; or he should take the amoral path and not weaken himself with assumptions of God's scrutiny. The thought of one member, however, stays with him: "And I say if he can do it and get away with it, and he chooses not to be bothered by the ethics, then he's home free."

This last option would not be the Rabbi's choice, but it is an escape that Judah slowly begins to assimilate as a psychopathic defense. He occasionally experiences a "bad moment" thinking of Dolores and of what he did, yet the moment passes, as, no doubt, will subsequent moments: "I mean this is reality. In reality we rationalize, we deny, or we couldn't go on living." Hooray for Judah, he is comfortable again. Too bad for Dolores, who emerges only as a fleeting "bad moment."

Thus, we can envision the psychopathic cushion that softens a killer's fear of exposure. Wealth and connections help Judah Rosenthal to wheel away former intimacies and transform them into distant shadows. What happens, however, when fear of exposure encompasses a far-reaching operation? What consequences arise when we change our mind-set from an intimate matter to a sweeping cause, knowing that the fear of exposure can exert considerable urgency upon the characters at either extreme?

The political thriller *Black Sunday* (1977), directed by John Frankenheimer and written by Ernest Lehman, Ivan Moffat, and Kenneth Ross, acquaints us with devotees of a Palestinian terrorist group, the Black September Movement. Stated simply, these terrorists want to share their suffering with others, especially Americans. Their wildly improbable plan involves commandeering the Goodyear blimp on Super Bowl Sunday, and unleashing an explosion of lethal darts onto the stadium crowd--a crowd that includes the President of the United States.

An Israeli agent, Major Kabakov (Robert Shaw), seeking to counter the Palestinian scheme, lies wounded on a hospital bed long enough to wonder about his years of killing: "You know for 30 years I have been killing and murdering. What have I achieved? Same world, same wars, same enemies, same friends, and same victims." Kabakov, perhaps experiencing a midlife killing crisis, begins to doubt his penchant for assassination.

The Major has already committed one grievous mistake: An Israeli raid gave him the opportunity to kill a highly resourceful Black September agent trapped and helpless in a shower; but, with the creeping doubt that another death would accomplish little, Kabakov spares her life. The agent, Dahlia (Marthe Keller), now finds it necessary to assassinate Kabakov, since he can expose her presence and scuttle the "Black Sunday" plan.

Kabakov, moreover, must shoulder the responsibility for other lives lost--lives taken by Palestinian agents fearing exposure of their plan. These deaths include Kabakov's closest friend, murdered at an opportune and vulnerable juncture by Dahlia. Therefore, lives sacrificed to preserve a hair-raising scheme of Super Bowl massacre trace back to Kabakov's humane gesture of allowing Dahlia to live. The point is pounded home to the Israeli agent by a Russian official: "Here's her face, look at it. After all, in a way, she's your creation, Major Kabakov."

The irony of this tragedy surfaces at the story's end when

Kabakov, in a helicopter, and Dahlia, in the Goodyear Blimp, face each other with their automatic weapons. Dahlia freezes for one tense moment as she recognizes the man who granted her life. Kabakov, not about to make the same mistake twice, fires first and kills an assassin who has caused him and others untold harm.

Had Dahlia died in that shower, would the resulting deaths still have occurred? This question of "What if?" proves difficult to analyze, except to say that a less resourceful terrorist than the seductive Dahlia may have made fear of exposure more likely and the Super Bowl plan too risky for consideration.

Thus, fear of exposure denotes the psychopath's dedication to maintain a coveted lifestyle. Thinking of our Cognitive/Emotional Model of Evil, the better the appearance of propriety and misdirection, the more accomplished will be a psychopath who functions to distance himself or herself as a suspect. Clearly, after a faltering start, Judah Rosenthal manages this feat with greater aplomb than does the assassin, Dahlia, saddled as she is with her rabid terrorist mind.

THE MATERIAL PSYCHOPATH

Fear of exposure assumes different complexities, depending on the psychopath's platform of power. The **power of plenty** refers to acquiring more and more material resources, thereby freeing the psychopath to cast aside certain constraints. Assuming a measure of protection against exposure, he can, for example, deliver his scintillating brand of evil with greater boldness.

A dictator, like Saddam Hussein, orders atrocities--even against family members--without effective reprisal, although political considerations prevent him from running amok. Too, the **megalomanic** in a James Bond or Indiana Jones film behaves as a supreme creature, worrying little about fear of exposure due to the technological fortress that surrounds his godliness. Indeed, the megalomanic may flaunt his magnificence, daring the forces of justice to a duel of good versus evil.

Material dominance, in other words, lessens the dangers associated with fear of exposure. Because **materialism** refers to the tangible comforts of life, we can envision how power, status, and wealth relate to such outward desires as control, superiority, and greed. These desires propel material psychopaths to external goals that prove primary and expressive of their true calling. Therefore, when we speak of a material psychopath, we do not think in terms of impassioned pursuits like sexual lust. The material personality may engage in sexual lust, but does so incidentally to the primary practice of satisfying his or her material demands.

Cinematic events can occur, however, so that power, status, and financial wealth appear indistinguishable. Indeed, attaining power (control) suggests that status (superiority) and wealth (greed) naturally tag along as tight partners. Exceptions arise, of course. The individual may receive an honorary title and thereby gain status, although he or she fails to realize any increase in power or wealth. Or a person may enjoy considerable power and status, yet function as a philanthropist to defy Scrooge and disdain the greed of hoarding excessive wealth.

But compleat material psychopaths recognize external power as a fundamental goal. Acquiring power means that status and wealth also likely emerge as manifestations of this greater influence. And yet the three branches of materialism do not prove interchangeable, since, if they were, we would have no need to discuss power, status, and wealth separately. Just collapse the three into one, say, power, and talk about this element.

The need for all three branches derives from what psychopaths deem important to their ego. The simplest scenario indicates that they use the **power of plenty** to concentrate on a prestigious position or to accumulate a surplus of material goods. Because material psychopaths vary in their signature of outward desires, however, these villainous entrepreneurs will express differences in how they seek and utilize the materialism of utmost concern. But whatever their power priorities, they always want more.

PSYCHOPATHIC POWER

Because power may be real or imagined, the psychopath proves just as dangerous relying on imagined power. If an evildoer pumps himself sufficiently to believe that he can accomplish his goals, even without the material means to do so, havoc and tragedy will ensue. Thus, rather than assume a close-knit similarity between power as control, status as superiority, and wealth as greed, reality dictates that the three material desires are not only distinguishable but complex. And the cinema, on select occasions, hints at this complexity.

The compleat evil of Hannibal Lecter (Anthony Hopkins) in *The Silence Of The Lambs* (1991) allows him to feel suffused with power from within: his overwhelming intelligence; his considerable charms at misdirection; and his ability to dupe and distance others from the truth. But Lecter has no tangible means for gaining the kind of freedom and autonomy that he desires. Hannibal as a captive offers no restrictions on inner power, although, until he escapes, his material comforts prove quite limited.

Contrary to Hannibal Lecter's unique presence, movies seek to infer inner power by visualizing the more easily portrayed trappings of outer power. The cinema has invested power in the military code of conduct (*A Few Good Men*, 1992); in political bureaucracy and covert operations (*No Way Out*, 1987); in recreating Adolph Hitler's master race (*The Boys From Brazil*, 1978); and, literally, in commanding the Ark of the Covenant (*Raiders Of The Lost Ark*, 1981). Each film reflects a thirst, not for power in the abstract, but a power expressive of materialism.

Cinematically, power favors a materialistic goal. The "show-and-tell" approach prevails whereby filmmakers find it preferable to present viewers with power as a tangible expression. Material psychopaths become especially suited for this quest since, whether true or imagined, they believe that tangible power rightfully belongs to them. And if these evil souls happen to score high on physical attractiveness, intelligence, and, of course, callousness, they can realize a shot at real domination.

Meredith Johnson (Demi Moore) is beautiful, bright, and seduces her victims with a practiced ease in *Disclosure* (1994). What she lacks, for evil's sake, is a course under the tutelage of Ms. Manners. Meredith, frankly, does little justice to the psychopath's potential for secrecy and misdirection. Her arrogance and hard looks transmit a sharp image of someone ruthless and formidable. Otherwise, she possesses all the requisite cognitive and emotional skills to shatter the glass ceiling, and succeed in the wild and wooly world of high-tech electronics.

Based on Michael Crichton's novel and directed by Barry Levinson from a screenplay by Paul Attanasio, *Disclosure* encompasses a Monday-to-Friday period in the turbulent life of a Seattle cyberspace company. The firm's president, Bob Garvin (Donald Sutherland), desperately seeks to bolster his company by merging with a more conservative corporation. This transaction can strengthen the high-tech firm financially, and, more importantly, plant $100 million in Garvin's pocket.

Several prospective themes hover about the dynamics of completing this merger: (1) The nagging threat of job insecurity, so feared in the workplace today, and what this threat does to the workers and their families; (2) the helplessness of subordinates who find themselves reduced to guessing about far-reaching decisions made by an elite few; and, oh yes, (3) a case of sexual harassment in which the male learns how much he stands to lose when a powerful female victimizes **him**.

Meredith performs a power seduction of Tom Sanders (Michael Douglas), a former lover who finds himself competing and losing a cherished executive position to Meredith. During the course of her sexual groping, Meredith gasps "...Now you've got all the power...Got something I want..." Namely, she wants Tom's penis in her mouth, and he is sorely tempted to accommodate her. But Tom's happily married with two children, and incurs Meredith's wrath when he draws away from her to a family that Meredith has no capacity to understand or value.

The materialistic pursuits of power occupy all concerned. Meredith and Tom's failed sexual encounter merely constitutes a passion that ultimately falls under the jurisdiction of a higher materialistic priority. Even Tom's lawyer, Catherine Alvarez (Roma Maffia), puts the matter to him bluntly: "Sexual harassment is not about sex. It is about power. She has it, you don't." What Tom does have is a load of trouble. Bob Garvin and Meredith want to oust him as a threat to the merger, and they strive to do so without any digressions of conscience. Both white-collar manipulators translate the cognitive trait of abdicating responsibility and the emotional attribute of lacking remorse into a very practical, business strategy.

Bob Garvin and Meredith Johnson represent two of three psychopaths who rise from the workplace to deliver Tom through five days of living hell. Meredith, surprisingly, offers the least interesting characterization. She wears her evil too openly and fails covertly to deflect Tom's interference. Meredith comes firing out of the chute, strident and brash, behaving as if she has no need to bother with secrecy or misdirection. Consequently, her bullish approach to make Tom appear incompetent boomerangs, and leads to a lesson about psychopathic success: If you are a compleat evildoer, you learn the value of discreet manipulation so that your victim gains no advantage to use what you know against you. Meredith has no problems with callousness or zealousness, but she is an unmitigated disaster in other respects.

Bob Garvin, understanding this lesson, divulges his callousness only to those players close to him in power. He behaves as "positive power plus" when addressing the company's rank and file, masterfully transforming his personality to that of an inspirational trend-setter. The team leader speaks enthusiastically of his products and his employees in the jargon of one who knows how to sound good while saying very little.

But Garvin pushes another button and behaves as "negative power plus" when in a huddle with his confidants. He snarls and snorts and admonishes them to work harder to subvert Tom's sexual harassment suit. Garvin, the "team leader," wails, "This is America, goddammit. The legal system is supposed to protect people like me."

Finally, it is Meredith who gives Garvin a weapon he can use against Tom, when she says, "He hasn't told his wife yet." This revelation prompts an evil grin from Garvin, because, now, Wham!--he has an opening to exploit. And, better still, his power permits him the luxury of appearing to remain aloof even as he personally instigates the next round of dirty tricks.

Philip Blackburn (Dylan Baker), the third and most intriguing psychopath, functions as Garvin's emissary of bad tidings and misinformation. Anyone who has tried to wrestle a secret from another knows about the disparity of power that attends such a lopsided relationship. Blackburn possesses only that power ascribed to him by Garvin, but this messenger uses his special status to tantalize the troops with rumors and innuendoes.

Philip enjoys knowing that others know he is privy to a fount of desired information. The internal market for company gossip accords him status as a feared yet indispensable personality. Blackburn seldom answers questions directly, shading what he "hears" in slippery prose to keep his inquirers twisting in the wind. Aware, for example, that Meredith has the position sought by Tom, Blackburn nonetheless couches the bad news to Tom as tentative: "The rumor is you're getting passed over." Tom then asks Blackburn directly, "Phil, am I out of a job?" Blackburn, knowing that Garvin wants to give Tom a "lateral transfer" from Seattle to Austin, instead dodges the question and says, "You gonna be okay? You want a Prozac?"

Philip Blackburn, nonetheless, harbors a disdain for all parties concerned. He savors the cruelty in toying with those pathetic peasants who long to be his confidants, but he finds himself weary of being the "leg man" who must carry out management's amoral activities. Blackburn has no fondness for either camp, although, as a survivor, he knows well the source of his power and where his allegiance must lie.

Interestingly, his sense of functioning as an "outsider" plays on Blackburn's need for acceptance. He possesses no real power as an executive, and he enjoys only a guarded status with the workers. He is neither fish nor fowl, but a chameleon who changes colors, yet remains a worm at heart.

Consequently, Philip's trickiest bit of magic involves maintaining his self-esteem, even as he executes Garvin's skullduggery.

Late in the game, Blackburn slyly leads Tom to believe that the company wishes to make amends, and that Meredith will be transferred elsewhere. The company, however, plans to dupe Tom and expose him as "incompetent" to run his division. Blackburn, therefore, congratulates Tom on winning, but does so with the intent of lulling Tom into a trap. Then, after setting up the ambush, Philip pauses and smiles. "Hey, friends?" Tom, taken aback, says, "What?" Blackburn responds, "I hope you still think of me as a friend." Tom clearly does not. But Blackburn points a finger at him as a "friendly" parting gesture to suggest, lamely, that Blackburn, the two-faced go-between, harbors little conception of the deep enmity Tom and others feel toward him.

An incriminating answering machine tape and other contrivances prevent Tom from succumbing to the company's ruse. The real corporate world would have shown Tom as no match for the likes of Bob Garvin and Philip Blackburn. Cinematic reality, by contrast, sees Meredith on her way out--although she vows to return one day in a stronger leadership position and unleash more chaos. Meredith also denies that Tom outwitted her in the scheming. Her parting condemnation underscores the ruling difference between male and female power in the corporate hierarchy, and Meredith faults that power for abandoning her: "I'm only playing the game the way you guys set it up, and I'm being punished for it."

Bob Garvin and Philip Blackburn, playing the game of executive survival, exhibit greater agility than Meredith to accommodate power's fickle tune and remain in place. The fact that the two powermongers do not inspire trust becomes neutralized by the equally important fact that the company pays the bills--and Garvin and Blackburn represent the company.

Thus, power in its many guises governs the passions of mere mortals in *Disclosure*. External power becomes the primary motive and sexual lust the secondary motive in this tactical game of move and countermove. A more discreet and patient Meredith, for instance, may have successfully seduced Tom **and** retained her position of authority. Regardless, the cinematic theme suggests how the rules of sexual conduct can change precariously when such passion occurs under the auspices of a materialism that takes no prisoners.

PSYCHOPATHIC STATUS

Status registers as one of the perks of materialism, because status and power normally realize a natural partnership. Certainly, if psychopaths elevate themselves via the thrust of new-found material power, their status also realizes ascendance. The power may prove circumscribed at times, say, when functioning as a gang leader in *Boyz N The Hood* (1991), or when aspiring to a modest management position as does George Eastman (Montgomery Clift) in *A Place In The Sun* (1951). But whatever the power gained, status customarily goes up rather than down.

Sometimes, though, rank per se becomes the apple of a psychopath's eye. Recognition as a celebrity can inspire the psychopath, aside from the power that lends itself to such visibility. Thus, the real treat may involve the prestige or notoriety that surrounds status, whether it occurs as an actor, a corporate headhunter, a daredevil, a bank robber, a politician, or...a television journalist.

Suzanne Stone (Nicole Kidman) of Little Hope, New Hampshire views status with a devotion to pop culture that trails back to childhood. She shares her philosophy with us in *To Die For* (1995), using the ubiquitous television camera as her benefactor: "...there are some people who never know who they are or who they want to be until it's too late. And that's a real tragedy in my book. Because I always knew who I was. And who I wanted to be. Always" (Henry, 1996, p. 111).

Granted, Suzanne exhibits the superficial credentials to be a television journalist. Her husband, Larry Maretto (Matt Dillon), extols Suzanne's apparent virtues: "She's so pure, delicate, and innocent. You just have to look at her, and you want to take care of her for the rest of your life."

Larry's life, as it turns out, will not be long at all. Suzanne's milky-cream image shields a vacuous mind, a dark heart, and a soul dedicated to climbing that ladder of ambition. Larry, who foolishly wants children, eventually does not compute for Suzanne's one-track brain. Once she decides that he must go, he goes, Poof!

Suzanne ingratiates herself with two teenagers, Jimmy (Joaquin Phoenix) and Lydia (Alison Folland), to develop a scheme in which they will help remove Larry from her path. She exerts considerable sex appeal on the dense Jimmy, forever trapping him with her fleshly charms; and she promises the slow-thinking Lydia that the two of them will advance together, professionally.

To Die For rests loosely on a true murder case in which a New Hampshire schoolteacher, Pamela Smart, convinced her 16-year-old lover to kill Pamela's husband. The film, however, draws primarily on Joyce Maynard's fictionalized account of that murder (Lippy, 1996, p. 150). The screenplay by Buck Henry (1996, p. 109) intersperses Suzanne's brief TV career and her precipitous decline with disjointed scenes and monologues. Speaking to the camera, friends and victims discuss Suzanne's character and ambition in what amounts to, really, a rather simple tale of status.

The bottom line of Suzanne's wilful persuasion is that Jimmy and a companion in the crime, Russell (Casey Affleck), ambush a surprised Larry at his home. Jimmy's hand trembles as he clutches the pistol and aims at Larry, because he also sees Suzanne doing her weather report on the local TV station. But Jimmy is too taken by Suzanne to do anything except pull the trigger. Goodbye, Larry; and, soon, goodbye, Jimmy.

Suzanne's character countenances no middle ground, only peaks and valleys. She is bright as in upbeat, and always, always professional in her "documentaries" for the station. She represents, in short, a truly frightening creation in her unrelenting pursuit of professional status. Suzanne's crafted image depicts the banal tone of television reporting, whereas her shadowy self uses those people she momentarily needs, then casts them aside.

Suzanne's potential for secrecy and misdirection never reaches full stride, because she does not possess the *savoir-faire* to protect her "clean image" from her malevolent self. She portrays the beautiful psychopath who expects others to accept her desires to better herself. But Suzanne entertains these desires by running hot or cold, depending on what her career demands. She bungles the virtues of secrecy and misdirection, naively alternating the cosmetic Suzanne and the dark Suzanne once too often.

Larry's death and the suspicions that encompass Suzanne as the mastermind behind the act do not faze her. Indeed, she finds herself drawn like a magnet to the tabloids and the TV cameras. Suzanne weaves a fantasy about Larry as a cocaine addict, with Jimmy and Russell as his suppliers. Even when the police wire Lydia to trap Suzanne into a confession, Suzanne insists that she is clear of this horrid tragedy: "I'm a professional person for Christ's sake. I come from a good home. Who do you think a jury would believe?" As she utters these last words to Lydia, Suzanne seamlessly makes her "exit" on the "up" escalator, giving Lydia a smile and a calculated little wave of her hand. Adios, you poor fool.

Suzanne manages to compartmentalize her complicity in Larry's murder, although she knows in her own way of knowing that the rules of a conventional life are not for her. But, now, notorious, and loving the publicity and the offers of a Hollywood story, Suzanne also ranks as an amateur in the murder department. She makes enemies of Larry's parents with her fabrication of Larry's "cocaine problem," and she has never convinced Larry's sister, Janice (Illeana Douglas), that she, Suzanne, was anything other than a status-climber.

Legally, Suzanne appears beyond punishment. But the Maretto's connections to the Mob offer another solution. A hit man dutifully materializes, persuades Suzanne of his Hollywood interest in her, and cons her into an abandoned wooden structure next to an ice pond. When we last see Suzanne Stone (her professional name), she is **in** the ice pond: A dignified repose, translucent just beneath the ice. A pose, perhaps, that Suzanne might have approved as an image suitable for TV viewing.

Status proves more complex in the adolescent fantasies of *Heavenly Creatures* (1994). Pauline Parker (Melanie Lynskey) and Juliet Hulme (Kate Winslet) depict real characters who plan and perform a murder in 1954 at Victoria Park, located in Christchurch, New Zealand. A two-year friendship, bolstered by imaginative visits to the "Fourth World," leads to the calculated murder of Pauline's mother, Honora Parker (Sarah Peirse).

These facts hardly do justice to the dynamics that bring the girls together, or to the mystic alliance they create when embarking on breathless sojourns with their fantasy figures. Juliet, vibrant and outgoing, sparks their Odysseys into a Fourth World of light and dark forces. But Juliet also experiences severe mood swings that prompt her to gush with optimism one moment and plummet into despair the next. Pauline, although witty and imaginative, contrasts Juliet's demeanor by projecting a more inward, forbidding countenance. The girls' strengths and weaknesses complement each other, permitting reckless experiences of pleasure and pain that neither girl could have experienced alone.

The two fall in quickly at the girls' high school in Christchurch. Juliet admires Pauline's earlier bout with bone disease, and Pauline commiserates with Juliet's ongoing susceptibility to tuberculosis. It is Juliet's attitude, however, that foretells the tone of their mutual admiration when she says, "Cheer up! All the best people have bad chests and bone diseases! It's all frightfully romantic!" (Walsh & Jackson, 1995, p. 186).

"Frightfully romantic," frightfully so. Pop-culture celebrities of the day, Mario Lanza and James Mason, assume saintly status with the girls, although Juliet rejects Orson Welles as "The most hideous man alive!" because of his villainous role in *The Third Man* (see Lesson 7). During their excursions into the Fourth World, Welles returns to haunt both girls as a Plasticine figure of evil and cunning.

Inevitably, reality and fantasy mix, mingle, and fuse. Pauline and Juliet accord themselves status as superior beings who change names to suit their fancy, who irreverently belittle royalty and the reigning heroes of the 1950s, and who believe

themselves misunderstood by everyone. Pauline, in particular,
ultimately views her mother as an outsider and, worse, as an
obstacle to the girls' togetherness.

The families, still, are slow to realize the growing intensity
of this "togetherness."   Nor do family members readily
comprehend the spellbinding sexual attraction that Juliet and
Pauline share.   Honora does observe the girls' playful
intimacies with early concern, but she says nothing and has
little inkling of the enthrallment that Juliet and Pauline imbue
to their daydreams.

Pauline nurtures a developing, irrational hatred of her
mother, a hard-working woman who reminds the young
teenager too much of the blue-collar world of her existence.
Juliet, in turn, adores her parents but plunges into melancholy
over their casual yet distant affection for her. They leave
Juliet for extended periods of time, doing so in one instance
when she suffers another round of tuberculosis and must be
confined to a hospital. As her father tells her, "Cheer up, old
thing...four months will fly by in no time."

Discovering little common ground with the families, Juliet
and Pauline immerse themselves in each other...and the Fourth
World. This enclosed universe gives rise to an exclusivity that
places the girls, in their eyes, beyond all others. Even the
girls' schoolmates, who may best relate to Juliet and Pauline's
parental alienation, fail to meet the intellectual and
imaginative standards that the two romantics establish for their
fictional kingdom. Pauline's poem emphasizes this unique
attainment (Walsh & Jackson, 1995, p. 200):

> 'Tis indeed a miracle, one must feel, That two such heavenly creatures
> are real,...Hatred burning bright in the brown eyes with enemies for
> fuel,...Icy scorn glitters in the gray eyes, contemptuous and cruel, Why
> are men such fools they will not realise,...The wisdom that is hidden
> behind those strange eyes...And these wonderful people are you and I.

The question of psychopathy is complicated by the girls'
presumed expressions of madness. Are they mad? Pauline
believes so when she proclaims that she and Juliet are "stark
raving MAD!" But Pauline also shows calculation when she
informs Juliet, "I know what to do about mother...We don't

want to go to too much trouble...some sort of accident...People die every day." And later, Pauline admits in her narrative that she has no qualms of conscience: "So the next time I write in this diary Mother will be dead. How odd--yet how pleasing."

And how sad. The brutal bashing of Honora by Pauline and Juliet leaves lifeless a mother who displayed her affection for Pauline more openly and genuinely than did Juliet's mother for Juliet. How sad, too, that a mother gives life to a daughter who, with utter wickedness and immaturity, desecrates that miracle by taking the mother's life.

Tod Lippy (1995b, p. 217), in his interview with screenwriters Frances Walsh and Peter Jackson, reveals the truth behind *Heavenly Creatures* as well as the reluctance of many people to relive the 1954 murder of Honora Parker. Pauline's diary entries became the main source of information and inspiration for understanding the girls, and for creating their haunting dreams of a netherworld. A fantasy world that ultimately intruded on the reality they swore to disdain.

Mad? No, not according to a jury, who found Pauline and Juliet guilty of murder in August, 1954. Both girls were released in 1959, and lost themselves to anonymity thereafter (Juliet later became a writer of mystery novels). The court, however, made one stipulation very clear: "It was a condition of their release that they never meet again" (Walsh & Jackson, 1995, p. 216).

To Die For and *Heavenly Creatures* build to murder with a style and verve that suggest an inevitability of doom for the victims, Larry Maretto and Honora Parker. The lurking intelligence in both films depends less on linear storytelling and the act of killing, and more on how the killers managed the digressive process of getting from A to Z. Note that in the beginning neither Suzanne Stone nor Juliet Hulme and Pauline Parker appear to display the evil wherewithal to premeditate murder. But by story's end, the three characters transpose their vibrant images of womanhood to a malignant corruption of psychopathic femininity.

Suzanne clearly lacks the gift of imagination that Juliet and Pauline project with such relish, yet all three characters sully themselves in their amateurish attempts at murder. A harsh boundary divides reality from fantasy, and these young women simply fail to appreciate the difference. For Suzanne, the difference lies in the fact that she does not possess the intellect to think ahead or to waver from her self-appointed path to fame. For Juliet and Pauline, their restless intelligence charms them into believing that a superiority in traversing the Fourth World also extends to the real world--to Pauline's mother, and to murder.

Thematic suggestions for either film, therefore, must consider the ugly revelation of how distant fantasy and reality can become. The revelation, admittedly rather brief for Suzanne, shows the perils of an **assumed status**. People like Bob Garvin in *Disclosure* possess real power and real status to execute an evil directive, and possibly to do so with impunity. But individuals lacking real power, such as Suzanne, Juliet, and Pauline, find that an evil directive based on assumed status offers no net to cushion the Great Fall. The fantasy of assumed power and assume status prompts a superiority that vanishes once the dictates of reality take effect.

PSYCHOPATHIC GREED

Notice that "Psychopathic Power" and "Psychopathic Status" denote titles of the previous segments. It becomes essential to identify calloused expressions of power and status as psychopathic, since other modifiers of power and status contain the flexibility to assume healthy interpretations. Responsible individuals can use power wisely and beneficially; these same individuals also can claim a deserved status for their good works.

"Greed" does not enjoy this possibility of benevolence. **Greed** indicates an inherent disposition to selfishness and possessiveness, two traits that psychopaths easily embrace. A greedy opportunist, therefore, can become irrational about money. Treasure hunters may even become paranoid, which occurs in such different vehicles as *The Treasure Of The Sierra Madre* (1948) and *It's A Mad Mad Mad Mad World* (1963). But mental disturbance does not prove interchangeable with psychopathy (see Lesson 4), since **psychopathic greed** designates a particular form of selfishness and possessiveness that remains quite sane and calculated. The psychopath, even so, will take extreme measures to capture the treasure in question.

Satire has taken its measure of buffoons in power, pompous fools occupying high rank, and driven souls who view the world in dollar signs. Greed, in particular, brandishes a form of tunnel vision that lends its foolish characters and their capers to sundry kinds of disparaging humor. Some psychopaths, for instance, enjoy the power that money can supply, but also care about money...as money.

Imagine, then, the elegant practice of murdering select victims according to a sliding scale of payment: The more difficult and important the target, the higher the price a client must pay for a job well done. *The Assassination Bureau* (1969) springs from a Jack London and Robert Fish story that details such a practice in pre-World War I Europe. Directed by Basil Dearden from the screenplay by Michael Relph, this macabre premise translates cinematically into a frothy, playful tale of showing how the wealthy's appetite for more wealth can lead to chaos.

Sonya Winter (Diana Rigg), a budding feminist of journalistic ambitions, detects a pattern of assassinations that resemble "Murder as a fine art." She takes her suspicions to a newspaper entrepreneur, Lord Bostwick (Terry Savalas), and asks for financial backing to probe the organization of killers. He says okay, and off she goes.

Sonya meets the Bureau's head, Ivan Dragomiloff (Oliver Reed), who quickly stuns her with his philosophy about killing: "Money is life...The lack of it has killed more people one way or another than a 100 assassination bureaus. In my case, human life is possibly the most expendable commodity we possess. It's so easily replaced..."

The idea, Dragomiloff says, is for the Bureau to accept commissions only on those individuals who need killing. Whereupon Sonya replies that she knows a person who bears the sins of pride, avarice, and murder. She commissions the Bureau to murder...Ivan Dragomiloff. Sonya then dumps

20,000 pounds on his desk as the fee.

Ever the gentleman, Dragomiloff finds her boldness and the commission a sterling challenge. He will match himself against the skilled assassins of his own organization. When the members gather in a Knights of the Round Table setting, he informs them of his plan: "It means, my friends, that you must kill me--or I will kill you."

Unknown to Sonya, Lord Bostwick holds a seat on the Bureau; and, unknown to Ivan, Bostwick spins a devious plan to ensure that Dragomiloff shall fail. Ivan's death will permit Bostwick to indulge in an appetite more important to him than money--namely, as a megalomaniac, the power to rule Europe. He even adds an additional 10,000 pounds to the fee as an incentive to get the assassination performed quickly.

Greed no doubt helps to accumulate the wealth that the Bureau members enjoy, and greed becomes paramount in bringing the members down, one by one. Explosions and narrow escapes follow, overlaid by the tumultuous signs of an eroding peace among European countries. To Ivan, the impending war poses a grave concern from the standpoint of sound finance: "It's purely a matter of business. How can we charge our sort of prices with everybody happily killing each other for a shilling a day?"

The Bureau's philosophy regarding who deserves to die does not pass scrutiny, but the psychopathic mood needed to accomplish the "commissions" flourishes nonetheless. The Bureau's jargon, moreover, aids in cushioning the veiled fact that its members constitute killers for hire. "Killers for hire," of course, does not compute in their vocabulary. Instead, the members' designate themselves as assassins, not killers.

Ultimately, even the straitlaced Miss Winter begins to appreciate the practicality of such a scheme. And when Ivan saves the day, the King of England is there to knight his gallant champion, **Sir** Ivan Dragomiloff. "Virtue has been rewarded," Ivan tells Sonya. Indeed, Ivan's virtue suggests one of those rare occasions whereby psychopathy seems to have assumed a robe of financial respectability, however shallow its rationale in justifying murder as a financial enterprise.

A darker satire lurks in *The Last Seduction* (1994), directed by John Dahl and written by Steve Barancik. Recall from Lesson 5 that females who play **omega roles** are shockingly beautiful women, possessed of an icy disposition (Wilson, 1994, p. 150). Visualize Bridget Gregory (Linda Fiorentino) as the quintessential omega seductress, a feline creature who uses animal eroticism as currency to snare unsuspecting (and even suspecting) victims to do her bidding.

The point of calling *The Last Seduction* a satire rides on Fiorentino's portrayal of Bridget as a sultry lass who runs hot and cold, but never lukewarm. She is bigger than life, she is in your face, and she wants what she wants--pronto! Do not mess with Bridget because Bridget will always be a step up and a day ahead, ready to have a good laugh at your expense.

Bridget's husband, Clay Gregory (Bill Pullman), rivals her in amorality and in street smarts, but he proves less cunning regarding Bridget's future plans. Clay makes his big mistake after selling a stash of "pharmaceutical cocaine" for $700,000. The mistake? When Bridget calls him an idiot, he backhands her to the face. What Clay learns rather quickly is that you never, ever, turn against an omega. Never. Ever.

Bridget, we suspect, has designs for the $700,000 anyway, but the slap serves as a catalyst to hasten her departure. And depart she does, leaving Clay in the shower, thinking that he will have no trouble paying his debt of $100,000 to a loan shark. Unfortunately for Clay, $100,000 of nothing is not merely nothing. It means that someone will execute a thumb job on him as the loan shark's sweet reminder of how quickly interest on $100,000 can escalate.

Temporarily in hiding from an anguished Clay, Bridget finds herself in Beston, New York...Smalltown, USA. Walking downtown, she encounters townspeople who greet her as they pass, a friendliness so alien to Bridget that she quickly climbs in her car for relief. The people of Beston, naturally, have no inkling of the force within their midst.

One individual in particular, Mike Swale (Peter Berg), falls under her spell. Mike has suffered a bad marital experience in Buffalo, and he returns to Beston unsure of his future. After meeting Bridget in a bar, he still remains unsure of his future and completely baffled by her unpredictability. She swallows him sexually, lies to manipulate him, and utters words he longs to hear so she can keep the relationship alive.

But Bridget performs these maneuvers in a no-nonsense fashion, so that Mike knows the sex is perfunctory and the lies are lies, yet he can not stay away. One scene in a bar drives home the opportunism that can light up the inscrutable eyes of an omega. Bridget and Mike work at the same insurance firm in Beston, and Mike, at a pool table, begins talking about his job. Bridget could care less, except that Mike makes reference to the credit records of cheating husbands.

The camera at a low angle begins to move closer to Bridget, seated at the bar. As the camera pulls in, she begins to ask questions about the scheme, creating a visual tension for viewers who, now, know her well. Omegas do not ask idle questions. The questions have a purpose, but Mike does not immediately recognize Bridget's inquiries. When the youth finally comprehends her brainstorm, he desires no part of it.

Bridget, who excels at improvising, wants to sell murder as a service to wives whose husbands are having affairs and using credit cards that the wives can not touch. Accessing this information through insurance files, Bridget engages in a trial run to show that, once a beleaguered wife discovers the husband's sexual and monetary transgressions, she may contemplate a murder for hire. If not, Bridget, who remains anonymous, can always claim to be kidding.

Bridget works the credit game as a ruse, however, to seduce Mike into helping her murder Clay. Bridget manages this feat in two ways that would make any psychopath proud. First, she becomes available to him sexually, but only when he acquiesces to her desires. Psychologists refer to such rewarded acts as behavior modification, although they would hardly appreciate Bridget's venomous intent.

Second, Bridget uses personal information against Mike that he, trustingly and shamefully, shares with her. Mike married a woman he thought was a woman in Buffalo, but, lo and behold, his bride was a man. Little does Mike realize that he would have a better chance at happiness with his male bride than with Bridget. She (1) parlays Mike's shame by deviously frightening him to go to New York with her; and (2) she subsequently uses the secret to anger him, causing Mike to incriminate himself in the murder of Bridget's husband, Clay.

Mike believes initially that he is killing a man called Cahill, a name that Bridget previously places on the mailbox in the apartment building. Mike being Mike, he finds himself unable to murder "Cahill." Then, during his bout with morality, Mike learns the truth from Clay, who has deduced Bridget's dastardly plan: Clay tells Mike that if he carries out her scheme, he, Mike, will go down for the job.

Enter Bridget. She calmly takes charge, and, before Mike's horrified gaze, the omega female forces mace down Clay's mouth, sending him to a toxic death. Bridget then infuriates Mike about his secret in Buffalo, and, as Mike assaults her, she opens a 911 line for the operator to hear. Clay is dead, Mike is snookered, and Bridget is free--game, set, and match.

Behind bars, Mike implores his lawyer that "There might be one thing" to use against Bridget to show her complicity in Clay's murder. The Cahill label on the mailbox would substantiate Mike's version of the events. Hmmm. Do you believe that Bridget finally succumbs to a careless bit of forgetting?

Think again. We last see Bridget climbing into a limousine, comfortably embracing the lifestyle of someone richer by $700,000. We also see her finger a label, and set fire to the label. Sadly, for Mike, no more Cahill, ergo no more Mike. He plays his one trump card, but loses to a superior adversary. And Bridget? Well, Bridget rides off into the sunset, free and clear, and dangerous as ever.

The Assassination Bureau and *The Last Seduction* capture greed by imposing a sly viewpoint. Characters in *The Assassination Bureau* deliver a mischievous twist to murder, taking advantage of those twits whose love of money carries them to oblivion. Even Ivan, who manages a better perspective on greed than his competitors, views money as a standard for negotiating anything--including a sliding scale for murder. *The Last Seduction*, by comparison, gives us Bridget as an omega woman who laughingly seduces her male victims with panache. She knows she is evil, and she glories in her natural gifts: A temptress who makes it clear that you play with her at your peril.

Both films offer their themes in a reckless spirit of larceny, themes that emphasize the ludicrousness of what some people will do to fatten their pockets. The movies have in common a peculiar **grin of wickedness**: Each film attests to the love of money as evil, but it is the smile that makes all the difference. The cinematic smile counts because it compromises goodness and charms us into thinking of greed as a sporting amusement. Or, as Gordon Gekko proclaims in *Wall Street* (1987), "Greed is good."

When the smile lacks cinematic charm, however, greed becomes a loathsome and heavy burden to bear for the sake of entertainment. *Shallow Grave* (1995) gives us three shallow people in a prickly triad of contrarious personalities. Juliet (Kerry Fox), a doctor, David (Christopher Eccleston), a lawyer, and Alex (Ewan MacGregor), a reporter, enjoy promising professional careers. But as roommates searching for a fourth tenant, the three cruelly put down prospects. They garner harsh laughter at each prospect's expense, suggesting that their strange camaraderie, in tandem, orchestrates a collective psychopathic character.

Directed by Danny Boyle and written by John Hodge, the story begins when the three castigators meet Hugo (Keith Allen), an enigmatic figure who charms them sufficiently to become the fourth roomie. When Hugo hands over a wad of cash as an advance payment, David, the most unrestrained personality, leans down and rubs his nose across the money: "Well, it certainly smells like the real thing."

David's adolescent gesture foretells of portentous events. First, Hugo does not last long. The roommates quickly find him lying nude and very dead on his bed. How Hugo dies proves less interesting than what he leaves behind, namely, a suitcase full of loot. The money keeps Hugo on the bed for a period of time, so that Alex and Juliet can talk David out of calling the police.

David, the most conservative of the group, reluctantly succumbs to their urgings. They must separate the teeth, hands, and feet from the rest of Hugo to make identification difficult, and they must transport their fourth roommate to the country and into a grave just deep enough to hide him. David, who appears least prepared to dismember Hugo, performs the grisly task because he draws the short straw. This apparently chance occurrence proves devastating for all concerned by story's end.

Juliet and Alex impulsively spend a portion of their windfall on a videocamera. When David discovers the camera, he becomes enraged: "You paid 500 pounds for this?" Juliet, smiling, replies, "That's what it cost, David." But David, more perceptive, says, "No, no. That's what you paid for it. Five hundred pounds is what **you** paid for it. We don't know how much its cost us yet..."

The cost, as it happens, proves enormous. David moves himself and Hugo's suitcase to the loft, forging the first wedge in the trio's relationship. The episodes that follow represent a series of improbable incidents. First, David kills two thugs in the loft as they search for Hugo's stolen money, and, second, David drills a number of peepholes through the ceiling so that he can keep an eye on...his two "friends."

Juliet, sensing who has the controlling hand, shifts her allegiance from Alex to David, so that Alex becomes the odd roomie out. But David has his own agenda. He finally brings the suitcase down, preparing to leave. Juliet says, "David, you forgot to wake me," whereupon she blocks the front door. Alex exhorts Juliet to let David leave, and, when she refuses, David slugs her on the chin.

The tragedy that ensues deteriorates into a death struggle. David, who discovers his shadowy self when he dismembers Hugo earlier, and when he kills the two thugs, decisively plunges a knife into Alex's shoulder. David pauses, gathering himself for the *coup de grâce*, when, from behind, Juliet stabs him in the throat.

Juliet's face, projecting an unfolding expression of cold calculation, leans over Alex and says, "You did the right thing, but I can't take you with me." Then, instead of removing the knife and ministering to Alex's wounds as a doctor would, Juliet drives the knife farther and pins Alex to the floor. Leaving Alex effectively immobilized, she grabs the demon suitcase and heads for the airport.

The game, however, is still afoot. The police find Alex, conveniently pinned to the floor. But now Alex is grinning, as a musical chorus sings in the background "It's my happy heart you hear," and, true enough, the chorus sings of Alex. Because beneath the floor lies the money. Juliet, the winner of Hugo's suitcase, finds it full of paper.

The ridicule that Juliet, David, and Alex unleash so joyfully against others ultimately manifests itself into a greed that overwhelms their fragile alliance. David, though now a corpse, still narrates for us at the movie's end: "Oh, yes, I believe in friends. I believe we need them. But if, one day, you find that you just can't trust them anymore, well, what then? What then?"

What then? Then, you have nothing. Even Alex, the most impulsive and least likely character to gain the money, does not exhibit the patience necessary to preserve secrecy and enjoy his wealth. Instead, we see three flawed personalities, who, together, project a callousness and deviousness that leave no room for trust or compassion. Despite their duress, had any two of the three bonded as trusting partners the outcome could have realized a happier ending.

Shallow Grave, unlike *The Assassination Bureau* and *The Last Seduction*, provides no sense of crocodile merriment to bolster its tale of greed. Juliet, David, and Alex simply shed their civility and slip into psychopathic portrayals to show, at best, evil's mediocrity. Evil, to be adored, demands a masterly finesse. The material target of this finesse - - power, status, or an insatiable love of money - - calls for something more than a series of evil actions by the numbers.

Greed as a theme carries no nobility of its own, and therefore requires a helping hand to forge a worthwhile message. Whether we consider the lighthearted humor of *The Assassination Bureau* or the sardonic trysts in *The Last Seduction*, these films at least embellish greed with a wink as well as a shiver. The humor of *Shallow Grave*, however, remains conspicuously absent. Ultimately, we find the selfishness and acquisitiveness of Juliet, Alex, and David too anxious and uninspiring to make us delight in their characterizations as evildoers.

THE SAD TIGER

What happens, finally, if an evildoer desires money but enjoys **no** material power, **no** status of merit, and **no** wealth? Secrecy and misdirection assume a heightened importance under these miserable conditions. The psychopath must take risks of personal safety that an insulated manipulator like Bob Garvin, the executive in *Disclosure*, need not take; and the psychopath must possess powers of persuasion for cajoling or threatening the victim to his way of thinking. The lone psychopath's power, here, depends on his intellectual strategy to pull himself up via a bootstrap operation.

Red Lynch (Ross Martin) in *Experiment In Terror* (1962) fits this profile as he targets a bank teller, Kelly Sherwood (Lee Remick), to "withdraw" $20,000, a modest yet manageable theft. Directed by Blake Edwards from the screenplay and novel by Gordon and Mildred Gordon, the film shows how a lack of material resources forces the villain into close contact with his victim.

Lynch must use his **powers of persuasion** to enlist Kelly as a reluctant ally. These powers include (1) threatening to kill Kelly and her younger sister, Toby (Stefanie Powers); (2) informing Kelly that he has killed twice before; (3) warning her that others are watching, and that he can gain access to her and to Toby at any time; (4) bluffing at random times that Kelly has violated their secrecy...to see if she has done so; (5) and offering to cut her in for 20 percent of the loot--a gesture he seems unlikely to honor.

Lynch must engage in these intimate, psychological tactics to ensure that Kelly preserves the secrecy critical for the plan's success. The line of confidentiality becomes a tightrope for each personality: Lynch's only chance for the $20,000 hinges on Kelly's complicity, and Kelly realizes that her best chance to survive depends on Red Lynch not knowing that she has disclosed the scheme to John Ripley (Glenn Ford), an FBI agent.

Thus, the cunning yet endangered psychopath, unaware of Kelly's disclosure, keeps his game alive through misdirection--relying on the powers of persuasion mentioned earlier and assuming various disguises. He dresses, during one scene, as a dowdy woman to rendezvous with Kelly in a ladies' restroom. Lynch clearly thrives on the risk and excitement of such meetings, his exuberance made more frightening by an asthmatic voice that wheezes forth a labored, no-nonsense evil.

But Red Lynch allows another chink in his psychopathic armor to hasten the evildoer's complete exposure. He fails to abdicate all responsibility and remorse when the FBI learns that he is paying the expensive hospital bills for an oriental boy who needs a hip operation. Perhaps the asthmatic Lynch shares a moment of compassion with another outsider, disabled so young. Whatever the rapport, Lynch ultimately becomes more prey than predator.

The outcome of his incongruous charity resolves into the furry form of a sad-faced tiger, bought for the boy by Lynch. A chain of cause-and-effect events traces the tiger to a toy shop; and from this shop to a heretofore unknown address given by Lynch; and at this address, FBI agents find Toby, Kelly's younger sister taken hostage as Lynch's trump card.

Kelly agrees to meet Lynch at Candlestick Park during a Giants' baseball game to pay him the money. Now, however, John Ripley and his colleagues no longer need play passive for fear of Toby's fate. The agents can act more aggressively, and do, ultimately corralling Red Lynch at the pitchers mound, where the outwitted and outmanned psychopath dies in grand style, wheezing his last pathetic wheeze. Thus, the man's demise, aside from Kelly's breach of secrecy as an informant, can be attributed in no small measure...to a sad-faced tiger.

The power of plenty sports a rule of thumb: Possessing manifest power makes more power easier to obtain, along with status and wealth. And make no mistake, the material psychopath will reach for more of the same. Such power can lessen the ruthless personality's susceptibility to the Great Fall--if the personality's ego remains in check--as illustrated by Bob Gavin's slippery ethics in *Disclosure*, and Bridget's use of money and her omega ways to entrap her lover and kill her husband in *The Last Seduction*. The more external power white-collar psychopaths realize, the more insulated they become from the repercussions of their ruthless conduct.

But for solitary figures of little material consequence, like Red Lynch, bluffs and threats at the street level of personal safety endanger the psychopath's precarious livelihood. Prognosis for the Red Lynchs of the world appears bleak and predestined to failure: The psychopath of proletarian means encounters too few resources and too much goodness to expect a long life.

Lesson 9

Spiritualism: The Power Within

Cal Hockley of *Titanic* (1997) and Bob Ewell of *To Kill A Mockingbird* (1961)--what can these distant personalities possibly share in common? Hockley (Billy Zane) characterizes a haughty, Edwardian upper-class aristocrat and Ewell (Collin Wilcox) a sneering, prejudiced dirt farmer. What dynamics bring these disparate characters to the same, unbecoming conduct of attempted murder? Answer: revenge...and social class.

Hockley desires to kill a commoner, Jack Dawson (Leonardo DiCaprio), for stealing Rose (Kate Winslet), Hockley's "exclusive property." One sad note amid the tragic tales associated with the Titanic is that Cal Hockley confuses love and possession. He finally divines between these experiences, but does so too late to reclaim Rose (Parisi, 1998, p. 161).

Atticus Finch (Gregory Peck) defends a black man wrongfully accused of raping a white woman in a small southern community of the 1930s. When Atticus questions Bob Ewell, the woman's father, about the accusation in court, Ewell views the cross-examination as an insult to his social class. The malcontent seeks revenge by attempting to murder Atticus's children, Jem and Scout (Phillip Alford and Mary Badham). He fails when the children's protector, Boo Radley (Robert Duvall), intervenes and stabs him to death.

Social history proves a mitigating factor in the orientation of Cal Hockley and Bob Ewell to the people "beneath them." Specifically, social history in the context of social class sets the tone for fostering revenge. The chasm of social class between Cal and Jack prohibits Cal from "dirtying" himself with someone like Jack--except that Rose changes the rules. And Bob Ewell, having grown up with the vested belief that whites are superior to blacks, can not abide Atticus's challenge to the contrary.

Social history, then, adds to the motivational complexity of revenge as an apparently straightforward act of retaliation. The act appears comprehensible in one sense--getting even-- but the reasons for getting even often claim a torturous past. Whether aboard the Titanic or couched in the Great Depression, revenge assumes the tenor of the prevailing *Zeitgeist*, the spirit of the times.

THE SPIRITUAL PSYCHOPATH

We manage a better understanding of individuals who identify themselves through their material desires. Even if these materialists represent nothing better than psychopathic lowlifes, the fact that they seek external power, visible status, and obscene wealth strikes a note of understanding. Most of us do not behave as compleat psychopaths, but we remember moments when more power, greater status, and certainly a pot full of money would have been highly appreciated.

Spiritual psychopaths, by contrast, denote alien creatures. The power that interests them is the **power within**, regardless of society's prepossession to recognize manifest authority. No one really wishes to fall under the charms of a psychopath, outward or inward. But if we faced the hellish selection of one or the other, which beast should we choose? Do material and spiritual psychopaths play the same grim game so interchangeably that our "choice" becomes the tiger...or the tiger? Or do we find sufficient contrasts in material and spiritual desires that the outcome actually makes a difference for the victims?

Both types of psychopaths tread common ground via our model of evil: Cognitively, they engage in calculating secrecy, cultivate misdirection, and abdicate responsibility. Emotionally, material and spiritual psychopaths evidence a lack of remorse, and thrive on their exaltation of superiority. Glancing at the basics of what it takes to become a compleat psychopath, the model in its elementary form applies to both material and spiritual psychopaths. The two evil types also share a **fear of exposure**, detailed in Lesson 8, although the psychopath who claims few financial resources proves more vulnerable to discovery.

Because we can not assume a convenient world of 100 percent independence when classifying characters, spiritual and material psychopaths must acknowledge the cognitive and emotional essentials of survival. They honor these essentials so as to negotiate and sustain their evil presence. But the two characterizations differ when one personality chooses to emphasize spiritual interests, and the other personality focuses on material matters. A defining separation of spiritual and material psychopaths, therefore, concerns their **preferred orientation**.

Material and spiritual evildoers differ (1) in the clarity of motives that obsess them; (2) in the predominance of fantasy that governs their behavior; and (3) in the nature of victimizations that result from their evil designs. Had Cal Hockley been content to let the authorities deal with Jack Dawson for "stealing" the necklace given to Rose, a material understanding would have surfaced. But for Cal to personally fire a pistol at Jack poses a breach of decorum--Titanic or no Titanic. His considerable standing and influence make the mismatch with Jack appear as a dastardly act and a loss of gentlemanly control. Even upon losing Rose, Cal's elite status in society will allow him to find a sterling replacement for her. The problem, of course, is that Cal Hockley wants "his" Rose.

Revenge consists of righting a real or imagined wrong in a vindictive spirit of punishment. The inherent nature of taking revenge indicates a desire to experience the power within and make the victim suffer. Thus, wealthy Cal Hockley, despite his social status, exercises the same gut-level mentality as the impoverished Bob Ewell: Evildoers gratify themselves by causing the victim, or someone symbolic of the victim, pain.

Spiritual forces, unlike material motives, permit less tolerance for targets captured in the spiritual psychopath's maelstrom of desires, be it revenge, lust, or the joy of killing. The material con artist views the victim as secondary to the ultimate goal--more money. But the spiritual predator sees his prey as primary, a fixation from which the victims may not survive.

Spiritual psychopaths eventually come forth as monsters whose feelings have gone berserk, and yet these manipulators fail to show the expected emotional symptoms: They do not surrender themselves to expressions of schizophrenia, paranoia, or depression. Instead, any delusions that place spiritual psychopaths at a disadvantage are soon altered to better fit the conquest at hand. Their turmoil within--be it lust, revenge, or a craving to kill--lurks behind a creative facade of benign behavior. The predators' strange predilections allow them to find excitement through their victims--and the victims must be "just so" in appearance and demeanor. "Just so" to indulge the savage beast.

THE SERIAL MURDERER

One popular cinematic profile associated with spiritual psychopaths concerns that of the **serial murderer:** someone who selects victims according to morbid fantasies or through a fear of exposure, and who has killed an assumed three or more victims over an extended time period. Movies have exploited the mental dungeons of serial killers since silent films, commercializing these creatures into a franchise. Consider this sampling of cinematic serialists since 1919:

The Cabinet Of Dr. Caligari, 1919; *The Lodger*, 1926; *M*, 1931; *Night Must Fall*, 1937; *Shadow Of A Doubt*, 1943; *Arsenic And Old Lace*, 1944; *And Then There Were None*, 1945; *Monsieur Verdoux*, 1947; *The Bad Seed*, 1956; *Peeping Tom*, 1960; *Psycho*, 1961; *The Manchurian Candidate*, 1962; *The List Of Adrian Messenger*, 1963; *The Boston Strangler*, 1968; *No Way To Treat A Lady*, 1968; *Ten Rillington Place*,

1971; *Pretty Maids All In A Row*, 1971; *Frenzy*, 1972; *The Day Of The Jackal*, 1973; *The Texas Chainsaw Massacre*, 1975; *Halloween*, 1978; *Murder By Decree*, 1979; *Time After Time*, 1979; *Eye Of The Needle*, 1981; *Nightmare On Elm Street*, 1984; *Tightrope*, 1984; *The Deliberate Stranger*, 1986; *Manhunter*, 1986; *Black Widow*, 1986; *A Shock To The System*, 1990; *Henry: Portrait Of A Serial Killer*, 1990; *The Silence Of The Lambs*, 1991; *Man Bites Dog*, 1992; *Raising Cain*, 1992; *In The Line Of Fire*, 1993; *Kalifornia*, 1993; *Romeo Is Bleeding*, 1993; *Serial Mom*, 1994; *Copycat*, 1995; *Just Cause*, 1995; *Seven*, 1995; *The Usual Suspects*, 1995; *Scream*, 1997; and *Kiss The Girls*, 1997.

Many titles exist aside from these 44 entries, but the chronology of films listed represent the more notable efforts regarding originality and/or production values. Certain entries relate to real cases, such as *The Boston Strangler*, *Ten Rillington Place*, *The Deliberate Stranger*, and *Henry: Portrait Of A Serial Killer*. These cases focus on sex as a motive, but not the kind of sex that we might joyfully pursue in the comfort of our boudoir.

Actually, sex does not reveal itself in any simple fashion throughout the list. Thirteen films become embroiled in money and politics as reasons for the serial killings, whereas the remaining titles give us murderers who slaughter for revenge, fear of exposure, the joy of killing, or for reasons too obscure to unravel. Sex no doubt resides somewhere in this web of dark intentions, although the relatively forthright act of, say, rape for the sake of rape does not appear prevalent in the films sampled.

Five of the 44 films portray females as serial killers, ranging from lighthearted figures (*Arsenic And Old Lace*, *Serial Mom*) to more somber characterizations (*The Bad Seed*, *Black Widow*, *Romeo Is Bleeding*). Gender differences in the movies and in reality show that the females' *modus operandi* favor a material over a sexual motive for serial murder, and that females engage in luring rather than stalking tactics to claim their victims (Wilson & Hilton, 1998; Pearson, 1997, p. 170). The victims, unfortunately, find themselves just as dead either way.

Serial killers are predominantly male, however, and their orientation to spiritual rather than material conquests leaves us with a disturbing question: Exactly what do serial killers gain when they satisfy the lust to murder? Consider Hannibal Lecter as one who attains the profession of a psychiatrist, and, with his intellect, clearly appears capable of living a materially comfortable life. Lecter, however, gives precedence to his inner life, a cavern of dreadful cravings that only he seems to phantom.

This harrowing void of untold savage pleasures becomes the **Mystery that frightens us all**. From an external perspective, the climb for material goals gains legitimacy because society endorses this aspiration. Power, status, and wealth: We see, we hear, we touch, we smell, we taste--the senses leave no doubt that we are in the presence of a known reality.

The Mystery, however, of traveling to an inner sanctum dictates a different universe. We go now where the senses can not easily guide, a journey into the unknown. Add to this secrecy our feelings of unease, feelings that relate to temptations of the flesh and other desires, and the Mystery assumes bolder proportions. Our conscience tell us that we shall never succumb to lust in the way that a Hannibal Lecter lusts. And yet, a thirst for the flesh, or for the sheer exuberance of killing does not seem beyond our perverse dreams. We mollify ourselves that any hint of these urgings shall surface as no more than harmless echoes of the real thing. And yet, and yet...

THREE MURKY MOTIVES

One distinguishing feature between outward and inward psychopaths concerns **clarity of motive**. A motive asks the question, Why? What reason does a murderer entertain to murder? Material reasons involving dollars and cents, owning more real estate, acceptance into a prestigious membership, claiming the big office on the top floor--these tangible gains speak for themselves, although, of course, none justifies murder.

But the motives of a spiritual psychopath fail the clarity

test. Revenge, as we observed, only appears simplistic. A closer examination reveals that "getting even" fails to rival the obviousness of the materialist's gain. A loss of behavioral control seems more in order, not to mention the dangers of exposure that these inner motives bring on the perpetrator.

Frankly, the spiritual psychopath emerges as a loser. The repetition of murdering out of hatred, carnal desires, or the thrill of inflicting pain does not suggest an upward path. Instead, these apparently senseless motives indicate a downward slide, a deterioration of the psyche. The inner-directed creature, imprisoned by his fantasies, proves quite frightening. We can imagine him as more likely to self-destruct than the outward psychopath, even though he may assume powers of superiority and godliness.

M offers moviegoers the first sound film to explore the cravings of a child killer, and to present these cravings as uncontrollable impulses (Lang, 1997, p. 228; Thomson, 1977, p. 172). Interestingly, this 1931 film also represents an early cinematic foray into forensics, noting that the killer's taunting message to the press appeared to have been written on a rough table; that the remains of a particular brand of cigarettes, called Aristons, had been found at the crime scenes; and that whistling was heard in the vicinity of the crimes (the killer, when in predatory pursuit, enjoys whistling bars to "Hall of the Mountain King" from Grieg's *Peer Gynt*).

The fictional case in *M* draws upon the true exploits of Jack the Ripper, who wrote letters to London newspapers during his killing spree in 1888, and on the career of Peter Kürten, who murdered numerous women and children in Dusseldorf, Germany from 1919 to 1930. One bit of satire that the director, Fritz Lang, brings to the film concerns the parallel practices exhibited by law enforcement and the underworld in Berlin. The police find themselves having to calm fears and quell riots, whereas underworld figures realize that "This beast has no right to exist." What also bothers the gang members, naturally, is that they can not concentrate on their business of thievery until the killer is captured, or, better still, terminated.

Peter Lorre as the child killer Franz Becker shows us a

pathetic man who takes enormous risks in choosing children as victims; children whose deaths will leave him little recourse of escape once Judgment Day arrives. Graham Greene (1995, p. 403) praises the terrifying vividness of Lorre's performance: "I still remember the expression of despairing tenderness he turned on his small victim, the hapless struggle in his face against a habit he could not break."

Considering the delicacy of dramatizing such a struggle, no one expected in 1931 to see a child being murdered. Indeed, a filmmaker must always show care in harming a child, not to mention circumventing the taboo of depicting a sexual assault against a child on screen. Fritz Lang used a wiser approach, still effective today, of asking the audience to imagine the horror (Lang, 1997, p. 218):

> *Everybody* in the audience--even the one who doesn't *dare* allow himself to understand what really happened to that poor child--has a horrible feeling that runs cold over his back. But everybody has a *different* feeling, because everybody *imagines* the most horrible thing that could happen to her. And this something I could not have achieved by showing only one possibility--say, that he tears open the child, cuts her open. Now, in this way, I force the audience to become a collaborator of mine--by *suggesting* something I achieve a greater impression, a greater involvement than by showing it. To go down to a simple thing: a half-dressed girl is much more sexy than a nude one.

And, inevitably, Judgment Day arrives. A blind beggar selling balloons hears the familiar tune being whistled as the killer courts yet another child with gifts and charm. The beggar alerts an ally who spots their target. The ally chalks his hand with the letter "M" and rushes up to Becker, slapping his hand on Becker's back: M, the sign of Cain, the scarlet letter of death, and, for Franz Becker, the mark of a child molester and killer. The little girl unwittingly attempts to brush off the M but does not succeed. Becker, detecting the tell-tale letter through a reflection in the store window, goes wild-eyed with fear. He is branded, and the chase commences.

The police find Becker's room with its rough table and Ariston cigarettes, but the thieves go one up on law enforcement: They locate Franz Becker and submit him to an underworld tribunal, arranged to eradicate this monster from their midst. The gangsters give lip service to a "defense attorney" for Becker, an attorney who can say little more than that the killer belongs in a mental institution.

But it is Lorre as Becker who bursts forth with an anguished, riveting plea for survival: "You are all criminals because you want to be. But me--I can't help myself...I don't want to kill, I must." The tribunal's judgment reduces Becker's fate to an either/or proposition. Either Becker pleads for his life in the only way possible, lying to his peers so as to buy what sympathy he can. Or, he truly has no clue regarding his compulsion to kill children, only that he is at the mercy of this dreaded repetition.

The gangsters know what proposition must occur, but before they can pass judgment the police arrive to pluck Becker from one court and plop him in front of another tribunal. Becker now faces real judges in all their autocratic splendor, a body appearing pompous and staid in juxtaposition to the freewheeling emotions of the underworld court. Nonetheless, the legitimate tribunal proclaims Becker's destiny by stating "In the name of the people"...and that's all we hear. The camera then cuts to a mother who says "--and if they take his life? Will that bring our babies back to us?"

The movie ends without proscribing Becker's fate. True, his death would provide closure of a sort for the grieving mothers. But from another vantage point, his survival might speak to a more progressive, understanding nature of mental disease. The problem for us, however, does not concern this dichotomy. Our problem resides with Becker's motive--**what was it**? If we consider Franz Becker a spiritual psychopath, we must recognize that whatever symptoms he evidenced as an allegedly disturbed personality, he cloaked those symptoms through deception, stealth, and cunning.

Franz Becker exhibits a **character disorder**, the kind of disorder that will make him accountable for his misdeeds. He knows right from wrong, and he harnesses his emotional misgivings so that feelings of remorse shall not incapacitate him. What we have left to argue concerns his compulsion to molest and murder children. A compulsion to kill is not an explanatory motive. This state of mind indicates intent, but fails to explain how and why Franz Becker acquires his destructive habit. The story never details the killer's past, so we must rely on our imagination to produce the reasons for Becker's psychopathy.

Speculating about inner motives for criminals like Franz Becker can lead to elaborate scenarios. Spiritual psychopaths entangle themselves in convoluted beliefs, a potpourri of fears and hatreds that frequently stems from a tortuous childhood. Mark Lewis (Karl Boehm) constitutes such an example, portraying outwardly the handsome blond chap with a quiet disposition and an obsessive affinity for the camera's eye. *Peeping Tom* (1960), directed by Michael Powell and written by Leo Marks, chronicles Mark's voyeurism to peep at his voluptuous female subjects using the legitimacy of a camera.

Movies, when they choose to present a motive for the villain's destructiveness, usually propose a stark, simple-minded explanation to justify the evildoer's dark obsessions and compulsions. Mark, however, does not present himself in the coarse fashion of a leering psychopath. Instead, his ambition concerns an elusive quest to film genuine **fear**--the kind of fear expressed just before a victim realizes that she will die.

Mark, moreover, occupies the dual position of both predator and prey: He suffered as the unwilling subject of his father's sadistic leanings to "create situations for provoking fear." The father's scientific purpose involved filming his son's fear reactions throughout the boy's childhood. Thus, one scene shows Mark awakened by the glare of a light so that his father can record the kid's reaction to a surprise visitor--a lizard placed next to him in bed. (The director Michael Powell portrays the father, and his son plays Mark as a boy.)

Given a dispassionate father who viewed his son as a scientific case study, what can we expect? What we find, ultimately, is a Mark who appears shy and withdrawing on the outside, while masking a tumultuous inner existence that drives him to murder. Mark can not leave fear alone, and, just as his father filmed the son's responses of fright, so Mark pursues the same goal by using women as prey. The difference between father and son becomes magnified, however, when Mark bypasses lizards and the like to register the female's fear--just before he spears her with one leg of his tripod. Specifically, he attaches a mirror to the camera so that his victim can see her own grotesque reaction before dying.

Another difference between father and son pertains to Mark's insignificant stature relative to the father's accolades as a respected biologist. Mark works at a film studio, but as a "focus puller" who lines up shots for a scene. He aspires to become a director and has a "director's chair" in his dark room, although we know that his ambition will never reach fulfillment.

To earn extra money, he uses his camera to film girls in pornographic poses on the second floor above a magazine store. The owner, who runs this operation, prompts Mark to recite the one creed that always sells magazines: "Those with girls on the front covers, and no front covers on the girls." A case in point unfolds when one customer enters and requests two newspapers. The customer then hesitantly asks about special magazines, the kind that, well, you know, are under the counter. Obtaining his special magazines the man prepares to leave, only to be reminded by the store owner that he has forgotten his two newspapers.

Still, where is the "sex" for Mark? Carol Clover (1992, p. 174) underscores Mark's dual role as a doer (cinematically assaulting his victim via the camera) and as a spectator (reliving the scene as a viewer). The problem, however, concerns understanding the arousal that Mark really experiences when gazing at the screen. He may find erotic pleasure in controlling his victim's final moments; he may perversely indulge in masochistic delight at seeing someone suffer as he suffered from his father's machinations; but he also may feel only disillusionment at failing, again, to capture the ultimate fantasy of how fear should appear on film. These options (and others) show the difficulties of assessing the undercurrents of a psychopath turned inward.

Mark offers no sexual overtures to the one woman, Helen Stevens (Anna Massey), who edges into his life, attracted to the man and his nefarious ways. Mark's passion seems

centered on his precious camera, rather than channeled into
the possibility of a normal relationship with Helen. Indeed, as
James Twitchell (1985, p. 293) speculates, "...it becomes clear
as we see Mark fondling the camera in his lap: the instrument
is sexual." A detective in one scene asks to see the camera out
of curiosity, prompting Mark to display nervousness and a
tentative reaching out until he has the camera back "safely" in
his hands.

Realizing the point is arguable, let us make the assumption
that Mark's passion remains his search for the quintessential
moment of fear. Whatever libidinous fallout occurs from this
passion must relinquish center stage to the face of fear, the
one defining expression that a face delivers to the camera's eye
before annihilation: the moment that Mark seeks as
perfection, the moment that becomes his hallmark experience
with the gods. Nothing can rival such lusty attainment for
him, certainly not sex as a mere carnal attraction.

Given this assumption of perfection, the stage is set for
Mark to realize his ultimate experience in only one way. Can
you guess the face of fear that the camera's eye will finally
capture?   Mark's date with destiny is hastened by his
encounter with a nemesis: Helen's mother (Maxine Audley).
Ms. Stephens can not see, a condition so alien to Mark that he
becomes unnerved when introduced to her, a blind woman
who constitutes the antithesis of all Mark understands and
cherishes. What irony. Actually, what an adversary, because
Helen's mother "sees" Mark far more perceptively than do
others, including her daughter.

Earlier, the mother tells Helen, "I don't trust a man who
walks quietly." Helen replies, "But he's shy." Whereupon the
mother says, "His footsteps aren't. They're stealthy." Later,
confronting Mark in his upstairs darkroom--where she feels
quite at home--the mother challenges him with a telling
observation: "The blind always live in the rooms they live
under."

Mark acknowledges the mother as a dangerous threat to his
plan, and he almost makes her his next victim.   But the
turmoil to kill again runs its course, and he resigns himself to
the one fate--his fate--that has proven an unconscious staple

of his plan from the beginning. Mark even allows the mother to caress his face, as he comments wryly, "Taking my picture?" Yes, she is. And, yes, she knows he is a very disturbed soul.

The disturbed soul, as we have declared before, does not represent a fully functioning, compleat psychopath. Mark engages in psychopathic practices, murdering his victims by calculation and deception, and, in one instance, referring to his next victim as another "opportunity." But he exercises poor behavioral control, so that whether we speak of secrecy, misdirection, or the abdication of responsibility, Mark does not acquit himself well on these cognitive practices.

Nor does Mark attain the exuberance desired in his quest for the supreme, cinematic reaction to fear. His only psychopathic strengths appear fixed in an abdication of responsibility and a lack of remorse for the women murdered. Mark displaces any assumption of blame or feelings of remorse through his frustration that each murder falls short of artistic perfection on film. He cares more about finding the pluperfect face of fear, than in facing the realism that he has taken three lives.

The final life taken, therefore, must be his life. Helen's protests and the police siren's wail shall not deter him. Mark positions the sharp leg of the tripod next to his beloved camera, and prepares to move toward the apex of his existence: "When they felt this spike touching their throats, and knew I was going to kill them, I made them watch their own deaths. I made them see their own terror as the spike went in. And if death has a face, they saw that, too" (Clover, 1992, p. 170).

Does Mark see what he desired to see, his face alive with the fear of all fears? We do not know. Whatever face the camera's eye recorded, it also detailed the needless sacrifice of four lives, inspired by the absurdity of a spiritual motive for the kind of perfection that comes with death.

Reality and fantasy vary in obvious ways, such as determining which of the two domains will likely prevail. First impression suggests that reality holds the upper hand and more capably intrudes on daydreams comprised of imaginary schemes. Mark's disregard of reality and the inevitable exposure awaiting him ended his fanciful career; he realized that his imminent discovery permitted only one more opportunity: to use himself as the sacrificial lamb.

What happens, however, if a clever murderer can manipulate reality so as to fulfill his personal odyssey? What happens if the spiritual psychopath's fantasy is simply beyond anyone's comprehension, save the killer's? Reality then becomes a universe to curry in the psychopath's favor. A serial killer can use the depressing reality of a city's sprawling decadence to mask his true motive, to thwart police who know the city's gloom all too well, and to make death a personal horror by realizing which buttons to press.

We first meet William Somerset (Morgan Freeman) in his nondescript apartment. We notice a chess set on the kitchen table. We see Somerset fastidiously knotting his tie. And, in what passes as a well-worn ritual, we observe that he selects meticulously from his bureau the tools of his trade, which include a badge and a switchblade. William Somerset is a detective, seven days from retirement, seven days more in the hellhole of a dark, grimy, damp city that will remind viewers of *Blade Runner* revisited.

Seven (1995) tells the story of Somerset, of David Sims (Brad Pitt), a new partner just beginning his career, and of a diabolical murderer. The serial murderer uses those seven days to unleash a searing experience of dread and fascination that neither Somerset, with his years of wisdom, nor Sims, in his restless dedication, fully understands...until the murderer wins. Sims, flashing those youthful credentials of eagerness and impulsiveness, wants to barge ahead and run the beast down. Somerset, introspective and more observant, desires to understand the murderer's grand scheme of invoking the seven deadly sins. Both detectives realize that the sins comprise sermons, yet they fail to anticipate the enormity of their adversary's planned devastation.

Directed by David Fincher from a screenplay by Andrew Walker, the film details how the seven deadly sins--Gluttony, Greed, Sloth, Lust, Pride, Envy, and Wrath--become the ominous handiwork for a killer's hidden quest. The early deaths, illustrating Gluttony, Greed, and Sloth, display gruesome arrangements that seem to mesh with the city's decay. Gluttony, for instance, pictures a hugely overweight man sitting at a table, tied securely, and forced to eat himself into oblivion. The police find him, expired, face down in a swamp of spaghetti.

The true despair, however, is the city. The monstrous deaths agitate police, yet create nary a ripple among the city's denizens. They have inured themselves to the sleaze they call home, to the cavalier commerce of sex and drugs, to the degradation of everyday existence, to the incessant sirens that reverberate day and night. Man's inhumanity to man does not become monstrous enough to distract the streetwalkers' attention for long. Somerset has endured this apathy for years. When David's wife, Tracy (Gwyneth Paltrow), asks him how long he has lived here, he answers, "Too long." Later, she tells him of her feelings, summarized by the admission, "I hate this city."

Tracy is there because David is, and David is in Dante's inferno because he hopes (plans) to make a difference. Somerset knows better, although the two detectives simply find themselves unprepared for the evil that awaits. Somerset retains his pessimism, adding prophetically, "You know this isn't going to have a happy ending..." He is right, more right than he will care to be again.

Somerset's pessimism concerns, first, the philosophy of the job. The job involves solving murders, which means finding clues that lead, more often than not, to other clues rather than to final solutions. And, second, his cynicism centers on the serial killer in question: "This guy's methodical, exacting, and worst of all, patient." These truisms mean little to Sims, who favors actions over lectures. Sims is convinced that the beast will be caught, and...he is, but not in the manner that either detective can imagine. Fantasy, in this scenario, rules reality with an evil hand.

On Sunday, the seventh day, the beast enters the precinct station. Heretofore, he has materialized more as a dark apparition, a gothic figure who killed five people (adding Lust and Pride to his agenda), left clever clues, and led police on a dreary chase through hell. But now, the beast surrenders himself. "John Doe" (Kevin Spacey) has no past, and no identity (he sliced off the tips of his fingers to thwart efforts at fingerprinting). Although sporting the contradiction of a bland demeanor even as he is covered in blood, John insists on harboring a secret about two more bodies--or so he says.

John Doe will pinpoint the final two victims and confess, but only if Somerset and Sims drive him to his chosen destination. They agree, and as the two detectives are preparing themselves with a wire for communication, Sims appears to assume a stricken look, and says, "You know..." Somerset gazes at him and replies, "Yeah. What?"

But David never answers. This puzzling moment poses the possibility that Sims, however briefly, may have glimpsed the darkness of a soul like John Doe. The sight, however, proves fleeting and fails to warn him of the exactitude of the beast's treacherous ways. Once the detectives agree to John Doe's conditions, they are at the mercy of their captive.

During the drive, with the detectives in front and the beast in back, Sims drones on about how insignificant the killer will become in two months. Somerset, meanwhile, seeks to draw the murderer out, knowing that something is terribly wrong. And John Doe tells them of his intentions, but does so cryptically, using his own esoteric language and logic. He turns to Sims and reminds him that, in an earlier incident, he could have killed him: "I spared you. Remember that, detective, every time you look in the mirror at that face of yours for the rest of your life--or should I say for the rest of what life I've allowed you to have."

They arrive at a desolate locale, flanked by high tension wires. David moves John Doe some distance from the car, as Somerset goes to a van that he spots moving toward them. The driver has a box for Sims, a box that he places on the ground. Somerset looks at the box, thinking bomb, although this potentiality does not seem fitting for the devilish mind he is striving to understand. Using his switchblade he slowly opens the beast's present, and finds...Tracy's head.

Two deadly sins remain, Envy and Wrath. Somerset haltingly relates the horror to Sims, and Sims begins his struggle between sworn duty and punishment. The beast gazes benignly at David and says, unnecessarily, "It seems that Envy is my sin." That leaves Wrath, sending David into a maelstrom of agony as the life worth living has been ripped from him.

John Doe provokes, desiring death as the capstone of his masterly plan. David convulses, slipping wildly from torturous grief to sheer hatred. And Somerset pleads, asking for a sliver of reason from a partner gone ballistic: "David, if you kill him, he will win."

The beast wins. Just before John Doe's blessed departure, he closes his eyes, the picture of serenity awaiting salvation. David, conjuring up an image of his loving Tracy, crosses the line and explodes in rage against the evil that has claimed his humanity.

Somerset, watching as a police car carries David away, now finds a reason to stay around in Dante's city. The retiring detective had used a metronome when he slept, as if to mark time until the next despairing day. Why submit oneself to such a relentless existence? But now he faces a challenge worthy of staying, worthy of making him **want** to stay. If anyone can bring David back to the living, Somerset can. As the scene fades, we hear the wise detective's resolution: "Ernest Hemingway once wrote, 'The world is a fine place, and worth fighting for.' I agree with the second part."

FANTASY'S INSIDIOUS TRIUMPH

Clarity of motive becomes an elusive task. Even the spiritual psychopath's professed reason of why he kills need not depict the truth of his evil desires. Indeed, he may hardly know the truth himself. Material psychopaths, although not always transparent, offer the more tangible proposition of focusing on money, and on the power that money can buy.

The spiritual psychopath, however, fails to encourage such closure. Exactly what prompted Franz Becker, or Mark Lewis, or John Doe to kill? Settling on elementary notions of lust or hatred or the thrill of murdering does not really explain their abnormal actions. Whatever these killers gained psychologically from their destructiveness, they indicated less concern over material benefits, except as a means to pursue morbid fantasies.

When the film's storyline addresses motive for a spiritual psychopath, the motive too often indicates a vague and bizarre tale--such as John Doe's quasi-religious mission in *Seven*. (How did John's thinking become so devout, and so deviant? What were the origins that led him to choose the seven deadly sins for furthering his obscure cause?)

Or, the cinematic motive arises from a horrible experience in childhood, but an experience too singular to reasonably drive an entire life. In *Halloween* (1978) a six-year-old boy, wearing a mask on trick-or-treat night, stabs his sister to death after she has made love with her boyfriend. We assume that the child, already deranged, simply plays the games that Halloween suggests to him (Crane, 1994, p. 15; Telotte, 1987, p. 116). But, cinematically, we never learn about the etiology of the boy's mental disturbance. What **was** his problem?

Filmmakers, of course, concern themselves less with explanations, and more with art and commerce. They desire a film that audiences will pay at the box office to enjoy. Discussing the vagaries of growing up in a dysfunctional family does not provide an entertaining prospect. Why worry about how John Doe of *Seven* or Michael Myers of *Halloween* began their early years? The reasons why prove more fascinating if viewers are teased with a mysterious past (John Doe) or a silent childhood crystallized through one catastrophic incident (Michael Myers).

The spiritual psychopath's motive for killing, therefore, represents a **cinematic contrivance**: Realistically, it is too equivocal, too simple, or too unimportant to be taken seriously. Dramatically, however, the mysterious or horrendous motive serves to conjure up a malevolent personality of frightening proportions. If we have no clear idea of why a serial killer murders, we must assume that something dark and demented is happening "inside."

Hence, whereas the material psychopath enhances his security by acquiring greater external power, the spiritual psychopath tortures and murders to revitalize his inner existence. But how to examine this creature? He kills and kills, and we do not really know why. Does a back door exist that permits us to probe the serial killer's psyche? Perhaps an alternative view that affords us another perspective on an introspective killer?

One stratagem for finding this perspective involves the tandem of fantasy and reality. **Fantasy's world** speaks to the subjective, the intangible, the privacy of an inner dominion. Fantasy knows no social constraints save for the limits of the fantasizer's imagination. Good and evil, sense and nonsense-- the style and content of this netherworld become the "secret with a grin." We control pertinent information, and we do so smugly. Conventionally, anyone suspicious of what we harbor in our mental paradise must await our willingness to disclose the desired details. We know what others must discover.

Fantasy runs into trouble, however, when the fantasizer decides to transpose his hidden desires to **reality's world**. Dreamers can, of course, make reality work for them when they address their fantasies creatively; thoughts that find illumination through an invention, a song, or an architectural edifice. These fantasizers reflect a perceptiveness by delivering impressive, substantive transitions from thought to action, a feat much easier to accomplish in movies than in real life.

But evil fantasies traverse the bridge too, fostering a marriage that entangles morbid fancy with harsh reality: an unwholesome union engineered to provoke intense cruelty. Under these circumstances crossing over to reality pitches the fantasizer into a roar of startling developments, none or few of which the killer anticipates during his dream scenarios.

John Hinckley Jr., prepping himself to assassinate President Ronald Reagan, found in the movie *Taxi Driver* (1976) an apparent inspiration for changing his image. James Clarke (1990, p. 52) argues that John Hinckley never attempted to immerse himself in the character of Travis Bickle, the assassin played by Robert De Niro. Instead, Hinckley knew and despaired of his own aimless existence, and wished to alter that existence by making himself known to society, and especially to actress Jodie Foster, with whom he had an infatuation.

Hinckley may have attributed a hero status to Travis Bickle, and then parlayed that status to himself by attempting to assassinate the most powerful individual in the free world. Whatever he imagined, it seems unlikely he had a sufficient sense of reality to fantasize that his "heroism" would place him in the mental institution of St. Elizabeth's Hospital in Washington, D. C. What John Hinckley Jr. accomplishes for us, however, is the recognition that fantasizers need not disappear into their daydreams. Rather, dreamers like Hinckley retain a personal identity, while using fantasy to bolster the belief that, indeed, they **can** deal with reality. The relationship of fantasy to reality, therefore, designates more than a static difference between two worlds. Sadly, these two domains form a contrarious alliance that carries the dynamic intensity to afflict all participants: the dangerous, the cynical, the obedient, and the innocent.

Note, for example, a progression in relating fantasy to reality across our three films: *M*, *Peeping Tom*, and *Seven*. First, we know that Franz Becker molests and kills children, yet we have no conception of his fantasies. We believe that the fantasies help to fuel his compulsive behavior, but these mental aberrations remain unknown to us. Furthermore, once detected, the child killer finds himself at reality's mercy, completely dependent on society's laws to decide his fate. Franz Becker illustrates the dangers of living out sexual fantasies amid the soldiers of society. Soldiers, who show a feverish dedication to take him out of circulation.

Second, compared to Franz Becker, we **do** learn more about Mark Lewis and his imaginative strivings to capture the quintessential fear reaction--that special fear expressed on the threshold of death. But we also observe Mark's tenuous hold on reality, and on how his fantasy world proves no match for the harsh dictates of punishment when reality smothers fantasy. Once the police close in, Mark must end his "experimenting" and use himself as the final subject. He fails to ponder the ways and means of maintaining misdirection, of finessing reality to evade the police so that he may continue his quest. Thus, considering Franz and Mark and their vulnerability to society's demands, we can score Reality 2,

Fantasy 0.

Finally, we meet John Doe and his crusade to mock the seven deadly sins. Granted, *Seven* introduces us to a more despairing reality than in the previous two examples, although law enforcement does manage to maintain a nebulous sense of order. And, because John appears no more suited to live according to the law's dictates than did Franz Becker or Mark Lewis, the easy answer suggests that John Doe also loses to the overwhelming foe that reality poses. After all, David Sims emptied his gun into the beast at movie's end, did he not?

The problem with *Seven*, however, concerns the manner in which John Doe appraises the law and utilizes its imperfections for his own aggrandizement. John knows about police mentality, and he uses this knowledge to help fantasy gain ascendance. Yes, the beast dies, but he dies expectantly, the penultimate gesture of a spiritual psychopath who taunts and tantalizes the guardians of justice.

John understands the detectives' intense curiosity about his motivation to kill, and he teases this curiosity to complete his spiritual fulfillment. The beast, promising a full confession, maneuvers the detectives to a desolate field where he springs his surprise. Somerset and Sims have no conception of this surprise, despite their training and experience. John Doe, moreover, realizes well before either detective that he is not the final victim. He knows that sin (Wrath) belongs to young Sims. A tragedy ensues as fantasy, and, in a hellish cost to all concerned, defeats reality.

Seven outperforms *M* and *Peeping Tom* in providing a more enigmatic portrait of the serial killer turned inward. But *Seven* also propounds a timeworn lesson for the psychopath, namely, that fantasy's insidious triumph plays no favorites. Experiencing renewed "inner power" by killing again and again does not protect the spiritual psychopath from society's punishment. The serial murderer, like John Doe, must contemplate reality as an existence to bastardize in his favor. To ignore the advantages that reality offers as a resource becomes tantamount to the spiritual psychopath shooting himself in the back. John Doe compromised reality's lawfulness, whereas Franz Becker and Mark Lewis did not.

THE FINE ART OF VICTIMIZATION

The spiritual psychopath may well baffle law enforcement as to when and where the next execution will occur, but his inner life also calls for escalating episodes of omnipotence to demonstrate the beast's godlike superiority. Serial murderers do not always content themselves with the kind of sameness that borders on a perverse inertia. The killings can become more frequent, more gruesome, and increasingly risky to the predator.

Indeed, the serial killer's worst enemy, apart from himself, is his victim. To think of a serial killer alone is to think in a vacuum. The murdered victim gives him a history, a presence, the semblance of a characterization. Using the victim as a channel of information does not guarantee capture, but the attraction of predator to prey provides forensics experts with opportunities for detection that work against the killer.

A **victim**, consequently, represents someone who dies, but does not wish to die; or someone who survives, managing by skill or luck to escape the killer's lethal clutches. Compiling an overall list, the "someone" can be anyone: members of an ethnic group, the homeless, prostitutes, authority figures, preschoolers, gays, students, hitchhikers, wayward teens, or, for that matter, wayward adults.

More important for our purposes, the victim becomes someone special to the killer. Because money seems less a priority for the spiritual psychopath, a question arises regarding the criteria that guide such a predator to his prey. The spiritual psychopath chooses his victim according to...what? Hair style? Age? Overall appearance? Vulnerability? Stridency? Celebrity? That certain smile? The single trait or combination of traits that beguiles the serial killer also offers him a concrete vision of his morbid fantasies. The victim "fits," and that is bad news for the victim.

Jack the Ripper, the serial killer par excellence, registers a faint profile in the autumn of 1888 when he intensifies his butchering, respectively, among five prostitutes: Polly Nichols, Annie Chapman, Catherine Eddowes, Elizabeth Stride, and Mary Kelly. To wit: The profile derives from speculations on Jack's motivation for seeking prostitutes; from evidence of a letter written by him; and from a canvassing of potential suspects based on the five crime scenes. The absence of useful eyewitnesses, however, leaves only the five victims to tell Jack's woeful tale.

Commercially, the Ripper constitutes a godsend. His assumed stealth, his imagined identities, his apparent sexual lust or hatred in choosing streetwalkers--these characteristics paint a ghostly figure of evil. An evil perfect for diverse interpretations through books of fiction and nonfiction, magazines, comic strips, stage plays, even a musical (Rumbelow, 1988, Chapter 8). Jack has portrayed royalty and working class, has been revealed as Sherlock Holmes and as a mad brigadier general (Jack D. Ripper), has stalked his victims disguised as a woman, and...has **been** a woman.

Cinematically, Jack runs the gamut from exploitation films on carnage (*The Ripper*, 1985), to science fiction comments about violence (*Time After Time*, 1979), to sociological statements disparaging the English class system (*Murder By Decree*, 1979). Jack's murders in and of themselves are insufficient to captivate audiences. Another dimension becomes necessary to show that Jack's slaughterhouse offers more than the standard fare of gore and guts. An **ulterior motive** lurks, hidden by the blood.

The ulterior motive in *Time After Time* (1979) aspires to a noble enquiry, namely, how our proneness to violence carries all too nimbly over time and space. Written and directed by Nicholas Meyer from a story by Karl Alexander and Steve Hayes, the story begins when Jack (David Warner) steals H. G. Wells's time machine and spirits himself beyond a precarious existence in Victorian London to a more anonymous presence in modern-day San Francisco. Sad to say, Jack feels quite at home in 'Frisco, exclaiming that "The world has caught up with me, and surpassed me. Ninety years ago I was a freak. Today, I'm an amateur." As proof, ladies of the evening begin to bite the dust with less outcry and less concern than in Jack's former Victorian haunts.

Enter H. G. Wells (Malcolm McDowell), who labors not only to accommodate his staid London upbringing to a cavalier

San Francisco, he must (1) cope with the amorous entreaties of feminist Amy Robbins (Mary Steenburgen); (2) attempt to alter future tragedies by slipping back in time; and (3) fend off a revitalized Jack. Wells, of course, manages this tall order, eventually consigning Jack to a hellish infinity via the time machine.

The inventor earnestly proclaims, "The first man to raise a fist is the man who's run out of ideas." But Wells, even with his foreknowledge of who will die, fails to prevent these murders. His success in banishing Jack the Ripper pales under the realization that any hope of eliminating future violence lays dashed to despair. Evil carries an enduring passport to chaos, whatever its time and destination.

Murder By Decree (1979) presents Jack the Ripper as myth, conjured up by a secret order of Freemasons. The story, originally written by Bob Clark using Sir Arthur Conan Doyle's famous characters, was directed by Clark from a screenplay by John Hopkins. The Freemasons espouse brotherly love as their mission, although sisterly love becomes another matter. The ulterior motive they must protect involves one of their own, Prince Albert (Eddy), who has bed and wed a commoner, Anne Crook, procreating a baby from their "marriage." The marriage may be a sham, but the baby is not. When Eddy tires of the arrangement, Anne finds herself remanded to an asylum. Note that the primary motive for the Freemasons involves fear of exposure (see Lesson 8). Now, one problem remains: Where is the baby?

Sherlock Holmes (Christopher Plummer) and Dr. Watson (James Mason) do not piece together this story until the deaths of Polly Nichols, Annie Chapman, Catherine Eddowes, and Elizabeth Stride lead the sleuths to Anne Crook (Genevieve Bujold) and the pitiful residue of her life. She is mad, although through her madness Holmes finally comprehends the murders. The four prostitutes, and, ultimately, Mary Kelly, die yet again. This time, however, they perish for political reasons, and not from a Ripper hellbent on lust alone.

These torn and tattered ladies learn of Anne Crook's relationship with Prince Albert, and one, Mary Kelly, knows of the baby's whereabouts. Mary is the last to die, tortured by the Ripper creation who searches for the infant. Discovered too late by Holmes and Watson to save her life, Holmes chases "Jack" to the docks for a final confrontation. After an eerie struggle, the Ripper dies by strangling in a fisherman's net.

So much for Jack, but what about that baby? Holmes, in a searing indictment against the prime minister and other noblemen, trashes the Freemasons' motivation that they found it imperative to protect the royal status quo by murdering five women (actually six women, as Holmes learns to his grief that Anne Crook has taken her life in the asylum).

The famous detective strikes a bargain with the secret order: He will say nothing of their dastardly scheme in creating a fiendish sex killer to cover Eddy's errant ways, if - - if - - the baby stays unharmed. The Freemasons agree, although Holmes leaves them with a parting thought: "I will always have the death of Mary Kelly on my conscience. And you, prime minister, will have the deaths of Anne and all those tragic women and their agony on yours."

What we learn, however, concerns the hunt for an allegedly spiritual psychopath - -Jack the Ripper - -as misdirection to mask the true motive, fear of exposure regarding a royal figure. The material and the spiritual can blend in chaotic fashion, so we must rely on following the film's lurking intelligence to finally unravel the puzzle.

RETRIBUTION

Do we see a pattern here? Realistically, victims of serial killers appear democratic with respect to age, appearance, and even gender. But cinematically, the favored victim remains female: Sometimes she is a temptress, sometimes a loser, possibly an innocent. Regardless, she will likely possess a beauty and charisma that only the movies can provide.

Given the idea of **genderisms** - -of overplaying differences between the sexes - -the prototypical female victim in film behaves foolishly, placing herself at grave risk: She screams and panics, making the killer's task more convenient; and her demise serves, not to mourn the victim's fate, but as a warning for other carefree females to proceed with caution (which, of course, they seldom do).

Hardly a glowing profile of the stressed female, although no one said that film had to play fair with the fine art of victimization. Women in distress from a serial murderer prove more believable and entertaining than men facing the same horror. Hence, females in jeopardy become saddled with acting imprudently, and thereby pay dearly for their sexual allure (*Psycho*, 1960; *Dressed To Kill*, 1980; *Kiss The Girls*, 1997), and their ignorance (*Pretty Maids All In A Row*, 1971; *Halloween*, 1978; *Scream*, 1997). They pay through an off-putting moment of lethal judgment, usually carried out by the grip of strong hands or the swish of a sharp blade.

Occasionally--only occasionally--will a film redeem the beleaguered female and accord her the primary responsibility to launch a counterattack. The formula for such **female retribution** includes the female earning her redemption: First, she must suffer the slings and arrows of considerable misfortune; and, second, she must work like a pack mule to achieve vindication by outwitting the male psychopath via the slimmest of margins.

The odds of success in besting a clever psychopath, especially for a woman, are overwhelming. After going through hell and high water just to persevere, the female must harbor the savvy to play a psychopath's game in a psychopath's way. She becomes a little psychopathic herself to overcome evil's propensity of ravaging her as victim. Namely, she thinks like her adversary by being secretive, using misdirection, and abdicating responsibility for her actions. It also helps if she not only does not care how he suffers, but feels a surge of joy over kicking the bastard into eternity.

Our cinematic 3/2 formula, therefore, may elevate the retaliating female a mere notch above the enemy that she seeks to dispatch. But unless the female victim can rely on a stalwart hero to avenge her, she must shift mental gears and fend for herself. Thus, she stops thinking like a victim, and begins thinking like an aggressor. A transformation occurs from the polite, sheltered woman to a woman rife with resolve and vindictiveness. She becomes a reckoning force, someone voracious, someone like psychiatrist Margaret Ford in David Mamet's *House Of Games* (1987), drawn from a story by Mamet and Jonathan Katz.

Patient #1 asks psychiatrist Ford (Lindsay Crouse), "Do you think you're exempt from experience?" Ford replies with a perfunctory "No," although we suspect she does not truly appreciate the question's pertinence for her. One session later Patient #2 tells Ford, "Man, you're living in the dream--your questions--cause this is a real world."

Margaret's questions relate to the psychobabble of therapy, and apparently underscore the sum total of her life. The psychiatrist's life and her best-selling book, *Driven*, derive from the same fabric. Like her patients, Margaret Ford drives herself compulsively, to the point that she permits little time for simple pleasures, such as having lunch with a friend.

But Patient #2, a compulsive gambler, changes this routine when he talks Margaret into helping him--**really** helping him--beat his addiction. The commitment sends Ford to a dingy recreation parlor, the House of Games, where she meets Mike (Joe Mantegna), a con man whose world of trickery and deception intrigues the good doctor.

Mike makes Margaret a proposition: If she will help him win his money back from a hard-nosed poker player, he will cancel the debt owed him by Margaret's gambler patient. She agrees, her job being to detect a "tell," a telling mistake made by the hard-nosed opponent of playing with his ring when he is bluffing a hand. The player guards himself against this cue when Mike's present, but, by leaving the table momentarily, Mike believes the player will relax and indulge in the "tell" for Margaret to spot.

True to form, the player fingers his ring, Margaret spots, and Mike returns to bet a wad of money--only to lose when the player lays down a club flush. What has gone wrong? Mike appears baffled at why the "tell" failed to work. Regardless, the opponent wants his money NOW, and brandishes an automatic to enforce his demand. Mike does not have the $6000 needed to pay off, so Margaret, enthralled and feeling responsible though she did nothing wrong, writes a check to cover his losses. But then she decides not to pay. She reaches that decision because the player's gun shows a dribble of water, which no self-respecting gun should ever show.

The gun is a water pistol, the game a scam, and Mike absolves himself by revealing to Margaret how his world operates. She almost loses $6000, but, taken with the excitement of his world compared to the compulsive regimen of her patient-to-patient therapy, Margaret plays down a crucial fact: Mike would have happily pocketed her money, had she not been so observant.

The material psychopath and the con artist boast a seamless history. Taking advantage of people through charm and finesse denotes the psychopath's creed: a perfect mix for duping the greedy individual (the mark) who desires an easy score. Mike offers the disarming admission that he is a con man, and, yes, he does terrible things to people by fleecing them, but that is what he does for a living. Mike even uses his candor to set Margaret at ease, allowing her to believe that if he tells her he cons people, he will not con her. She is wrong.

Mike "frankly" tells her, "It's called a confidence game. Why? Because you give me your confidence? No. Because I give you mine." Mike sets Margaret up for a fall, even as he explains to her how the game works. The assertive psychiatrist concentrates so intently on researching this diverting turn of human nature that she has no conception of becoming a mark herself. But a mark she is, figuring in an elaborate scheme that, among other acts of duplicity, involves Mike's pretending to use someone else's hotel room so he can make love to her. Unknown to Margaret, all events that appear spontaneous, are not.

The scheme culminates when Margaret insists on helping with another game, "the briefcase left behind"--an attache case that presumably contains $80,000 and is "forgotten" by a man leaving in a taxi. Mike, his partner, Joey (Mike Nussbaum), Margaret, and a convention delegate (the unidentified mark), stare at the money. Next, the four are in a hotel room, arguing about how to handle cash that appears likely to be illicit gains, probably from drugs.

The game goes horribly wrong when Margaret discovers that the "mark" is an undercover police officer. The possibility of seeing her professional reputation in tatters causes Margaret to lose control, and she declares, "I can't be here." A confrontation ensues and Margaret shoots and kills the officer in a struggle, whereupon Joey laments, "She's killed this man. The bitch has killed us dead."

Mike, Joey, and Margaret make their escape when she steals a red convertible at their urging, only to find that Joey has forgotten the money. Margaret offers to replace the cash, which is on loan from the mob, to prevent Mike and Joey from becoming an endangered species. Mike then spells out the scenario: He must leave town, and she must return to her professional life. Mike likes to preface his rationalizations with the expression, "Listen to me." "Listen to me" denotes a "tell," a signal that Margaret might have used to wonder about her $80,000. Instead, shaken by the killing, she follows Mike's orders...until a misstep blows the scheme open.

Margaret's gambler patient, who began the scam by enticing her to the House of Games, drops in to secretly gloat and say goodbye. But, inadvertently, Margaret observes him leave in the convertible that she "stole." A discreet trip to the House of Games allows her to eavesdrop on Mike, along with the "slain officer" and others as they re-create the con. This revelation devastates the psychiatrist, who always prided herself on maintaining an upper hand over patients and the crises that life brings.

Margaret confronts Mike in the back room of an airport terminal--the man who raped her (under false pretenses), who took $80,000 of her money, and who humiliated her by violating her trust and professional status. The loss of money comprises a material insult, but Margaret can always write another book to cover any financial pinch. No, Margaret's primary need involves revenge: Spiritually, she needs to reestablish her professional sense of superiority. Publicly, Margaret still retains her external, professional status, since no one knows of her participation. But inwardly, she feels betrayed and belittled. The only way to accomplish salvation is for Mike to admit defeat. He must beg her forgiveness so that she can walk away, her self-esteem intact.

A compleat psychopath facing a coldly distraught woman

with a gun would have postured appropriately and expressed the words necessary to survive. But Mike commands too much pride as a craftsman of cons to play the self-serving whiner. He refuses to beg, refuses to give Margaret the satisfaction she craves, and prepares to leave. "If you walk out that door, I'm going to kill you," she says. Betting his life on a possible bluff, Mike replies, "I don't believe you." Margaret says, "What is life without adventure." Mike turns toward the door and Margaret shoots him full of holes. To the con man's credit, he maintains his arrogance even as the breath of life slowly leaves him.

We next encounter Margaret in a plush restaurant having lunch with a colleague. Margaret reminds her friend of something the friend once impressed upon her: "And you said when you've done something unforgivable you must forgive yourself. And that's what I've done, and it's done." The colleague, not realizing that the "something unforgivable" is murder, finds pleasure that Margaret has listened to her.

The friend leaves to take a phone call, and Margaret, noticing that a woman at an adjacent table has just used an attractive lighter and replaced it in a handbag, leans toward the woman and asks her to identify a salad at the salad bar. As the woman examines the bar, Margaret deftly steals the lighter, lights a cigarette, and rewards her newly developing inner self with a slight, playful smile of triumph.

We leave Margaret Ford at an arc of fulfillment in her private and professional existence. She uses a colleague's psychological advice as pabulum to justify her murder of Mike, a grave offense for which the idea of "forgiving herself" seems all too fortuitous. But Margaret believes in such lingo, just as she believes that murdering her nemesis--even though he did not submit to her--proves her mastery over him and his crew, not to mention the police. No one suspects, at least no one who can touch her. Now she realizes a new enjoyment from life, a dark exuberance that we have previously recognized as the psychopath suffused with narcissistic adoration. Margaret Ford finds herself enamored of her own marvelous abilities: a new calling, a fresh agenda...a psychopath's awakening.

Retribution also provokes a camaraderie of "us" against "them." We sense in *House Of Games* that Mike perceives Margaret as a ready mark because of her professional snobbery, her curiosity about his world of cons, but, too, because of her gender. Females attempting to match males in a man's universe of deception and strategy usually find themselves disadvantaged, as did Margaret, despite her skills.

For Margaret, retribution involves reasserting her superiority over players like Mike who had worked to bring her down. But what happens if the stakes of retribution soar to affect one's very survival? What happens if a woman must again thread her way through a masculine world, whereby she seeks to scam a family of street-wise males? Males, incidentally, who hog the spotlight, and who expect women to hover effeminately in the background, until called upon.

Bound (1996) gives us a woman, Violet (Jennifer Tilly), who wants out of this hobbling existence. But she needs a female partner to help her with the daunting task of outplaying the guys at their own game. The partner, Corky (Gina Gershon), has just completed a 5-year stretch in prison for "redistributing the wealth." The landlord puts her to work in a Chicago complex refinishing an apartment, located conveniently next door to Violet and her mob-connected boyfriend, Caesar (Joe Pantoliano).

Caesar struts forth like a bantam rooster, feisty and oblivious to certain warning signals, although, as the women learn, this cocky guy proves smarter than he appears. Caesar has grown up with the mob mentality that women symbolize "them," attractive broads who enjoy the good life in return for staying at the mob's beck and call. Caesar thinks that he understands women, that he understands Violet, that he knows what makes her tick.

What Caesar does not know is that Violet finds herself sexually attracted to Corky, and Corky, slow to trust anyone, begins to reciprocate. Corky, tattooed and tomboyish, appears a rough-and-ready personality compared to the restrained Violet with her little-girl voice. But looks are deceiving, and the two lesbians count on this deception to extract two million dollars from the mob. Violet proposes the scheme to Corky, who replies: "You have no idea what you're asking. How much trust it takes two people to do something like this."

Indeed, trust becomes an elusive realization, especially for two women who have yet to appreciate such a golden relationship. Corky went to prison because a woman she trusted betrayed her. And Violet knows that Caesar's feelings for her run like skim milk. Neither female can afford a mistake. Unlike Margaret Ford, whose concerns centered on her self-esteem and not her life, Corky and Violet will pay dearly if discovered.

The plan proves fiendishly simple and refreshingly feminist. Caesar receives two million dollars in bloody money--literally bloody money--which he must wash and dry and present to members of the Marzzone mob family. Violet creates a diversion, allowing Corky to steal the cash, leaving the suitcase filled with paper. The key to the plan's success, however, hinges on a macho rivalry between Caesar and the family's psycho son, Johnnie (Christopher Meloni). The two males hate each other, and Violet uses this hatred to convince Caesar that Johnnie has stolen the money to make Caesar look bad. Johnnie's purpose, of course, is to have the family eliminate Caesar.

The film, written and directed by Larry and Andy Wachowski, shows how masculine arrogance can lead to an array of stupid acts. One such act is that Caesar thinks so little of Violet's brainpower he never considers the possibility of a scam. But instead of fleeing, as Violet expects, Caesar decides to stay and expose Johnnie as the thief. This plan goes awry, and, when the smoke clears, three mob members are dead, including Johnnie. The defining moment occurs when a mob chieftain tries to talk Caesar into handing the gun over, and Caesar slowly closes his eyes, knowing that he has reached a point of no return when he fires.

The cocky mobster, though shaken by his own actions, is a psychopath at heart. He has not survived the precarious protocol of mob membership all these years by going into denial. Caesar phones an enforcer, Mickey (John Ryan), to buy time. When Mickey asks if he has the money, Caesar replies smoothly, "Oh, yeah, Mick, I still got the money.

Staring right at it." A perfect psychopathic answer by someone who has no idea where Johnnie supposedly hid the cash.

The loot, actually, resides in a bag inside a pail of white paint, next door to Caesar's apartment. Caesar, preparing to run, learns of Violet's treachery when he catches her making a phone call to Corky in the adjacent apartment. The call, while risky and foolish, reflects Violet's need to know that she can still trust Corky. The outcome, unfortunately, reveals Caesar's true malevolence. He ties up both women, then gazes at Violet: "What did she do to you?" Violent answers, "Everything you couldn't."

It is the worst possible answer for a man who finds himself unable to understand the lesbian attraction ("Everybody knows your kind can't be trusted"), and who is in no mood to care. Caesar wants his money, and prepares to cut off Corky's fingers, one by one, until somebody talks. A timely interruption by Mickey diverts Caesar from his purpose, and forces him to free Violet and enlist her help to keep Mickey from discovering the murders. Violet escapes, as does Corky, leading to the climatic scene between Caesar and Violet in Corky's apartment.

He finds the money as the overturned pail of white paint spreads around him like a spotlight at center stage. Caesar has the money, but Violet has the gun. The hoodlum goes into his shallow, macho philosophy of how well he knows her, yet how little she knows him. He closes his lesson with a confident challenge: "You don't want to shoot me, Vi. Do you. Do you? I know you don't." Violet gazes at him for a moment, then the years of adversity and subordination rush out in a lethal burst of hatred: "Caesar, you don't know shit," whereupon Violet, like Margaret Ford, blasts her nemesis into oblivion.

Caesar collapses, spread-eagled in red and white, a man whose psychopathic shortcomings cause him to underestimate Violet as a thinking, feeling female. He never quite believes that Violet cares more for another woman--a woman!--than she cares for him. Nor does he fully comprehend that his five years with Violet can possibly leave him so ignorant of her potential for retribution.

We next see Corky and Violet with a new truck, a new life, and two million dollars. Corky slyly glances at Violet and asks, "Know what the difference is between you and me, Violet?" Violet answers, "No." Corky replies, "Me neither." The two ladies have lived shady lives, relative to the pure in heart. But they experience a depth of feeling for each other that represents still another sensitivity lost to the bubble-gum machinations of a drone like Caesar, now deceased.

The burning question still demands an answer: How goes the spiritual psychopath? Because the beast looks inward, he offers us no ready frame of reference for comprehension. The Mystery of his ways and means fascinate, as long as the human puzzle stays intact. But if the Mystery retreats and Evil's true face takes form, an ugliness perseveres.

So, what can we say? We do know that he baffles us regarding the lack of a clear motive, as portrayed through the creature's enigmatic relationship with his victims. We also know that the fine art of victimization, whether it revolves coarsely around hatred, lust, or excitement, makes him vulnerable. Thus, the potential for retribution, however expressed, can undermine the spiritual psychopath's very existence.

Perhaps the parting thought should come from a last look at Caesar. His desire for the two million dollars labels him a material psychopath, and makes his motive understandable. But another dimension intrudes concerning the mobster's ongoing relationship with Violet. We can shudder at her fate, had he triumphed. Whatever his mob-mentality thinking, this Caesar would have functioned as a roaring, spiritual psychopath. The money in hand, his priorities changed, he would prepare to brutalize Violet for reasons that go beyond her attempting to steal his money. "Us" and "them" assume a vindictiveness in the war of males versus females. The spiritual psychopath engages in this war with relish--and, for Caesar, he would have done so for reasons that have nothing to do with material wealth.

Or at least that is the direction Caesar might have taken, had he lived. Which, of course, he did not.

Lesson 10

Justice And Keyser Söze

So, who is Keyser Söze? Captain Renault, when he flippantly gave the order to "Round up the usual suspects" in the 1942 classic *Casablanca*, likely would have distanced himself from the motley crew who appear for a lineup in the 1995 film noir *The Usual Suspects*, directed by Bryan Singer.

The apparent key to deciphering the five suspects' true intent rests with Dean Keaton (Gabriel Byrne), a fallen cop trying to go straight. The five suspects know but do not trust one another, yet the remaining four realize that they need Keaton and his smarts to pull off a job. Keaton's reluctance to participate does not last long and the game is afoot.

The suspects, unwittingly, have previously fouled the plans of an enigmatic mastermind, Keyser Söze. This shadowy figure may or may not exist, but screenwriter Christopher McQuarrie (1995, pp. 7-49) conjures up an ephemeral, villainous presence who rates marquee space alongside Hannibal Lecter. Söze, or whomever, informs the suspects through his lawyer, Kobayashi (Pete Postlehwaite), that they owe him, and that the debt involves taking down a Hungarian mob in a supposed drug transaction. The suspects can keep the money themselves...if they survive.

A freighter, anchored in San Pedro, California, becomes the nebulous arena where the suspects and the mob collide. Their confrontation leads to bullets flying, bodies scorched, and the unnerving discovery of...no drugs. Indeed, apart from the 27 bodies located by the police, only a lone member of the five suspects emerges alive: one Verbal Klint (Kevin Spacey), also known as the Gimp and the Pretzel Man because of a disabled left hand and a maimed left foot turned inward.

Interrogated in a police sergeant's office, Verbal blandly begins to ramble about being in a barbershop quartet in Skokie, Illinois, and picking beans in Guatemala. But a U. S. Customs agent, Daniel Kujan (Chazz Palminteri) cuts to the chase, convinced that Verbal knows Keaton did not die in the fiery holocaust at the pier. Kujan, moreover, believes the slippery Keaton is Keyser Söze, a name that visibly upsets Verbal.

One other survivor, the freighter captain, lies in a burn ward. He has met Keyser Söze, but the police must wait until the captain can give the sketch artist a description. Meanwhile, Verbal Klint's narrative provides the **only** comprehensive details of who and what led to the massacre.

One puzzling development to Sergeant Rabin (Dan Hedaya) concerns the powers on high who give Verbal full immunity from prosecution. Or, as Rabin puts it, "I'm telling you that this guy is protected from up on high by the Prince of Darkness." Given this ominous sign, Verbal recites a horrifying tale wherein a younger Söze encounters Hungarian thugs who have raped his wife and threatened to kill his family. Before the hoodlums can act, Söze shoots and kills his family and the thugs, leaving one terrified soul alive to send word to the organization: "They realized that to be in power you didn't need guns or money or even numbers, you just needed the will to do what the other guy wouldn't." Keyser Söze had gone farther in stating his will than would most gangsters, however degenerate.

A Satanic undercurrent pervades Verbal's story, fueling the mystery of Keyser Söze and his trail of evil. One suspect, Hockney (Kevin Pollak), stands by a truck during the confrontation, greedily counting his blessings at finding the presumed drug money. Abruptly, he is shot from behind. A closeup of Hockney's features shows him turning slowly to the camera, in order to view the suspect that he never dreamt could rise forth as his master. When Hockney turns, the light on his face intensifies to a blinding glare...as if he now gazes upon Lucifer in the flesh, before dying.

Verbal professes his fear of Söze: "How do you shoot the devil in the back? What if you miss?" Kujan, however, believes that Keaton arranged the raid, and not for drugs but as a setup to kill a witness under the mob's protection, a man who had seen Keyser Söze (i.e., Keaton). Verbal disagrees, vowing to think of Keaton as his friend, and, embittered, departs to collect his belongings from the property officer.

Kujan, convinced that he squeezed what he wanted from Verbal, sits in the sergeant's office and lazily scans a crowded bulletin board. Then, an evil echo sparks his comprehension, replete in its revelation to show the bulletin board as an instrument of sardonic trickery: Kujan notices a poster citing a barbershop quartet in Skokie, Illinois; and a flyer listing Guatemala as a vacation paradise; and, after dropping his coffee mug in disbelief, the agent observes that the mug is made of...Kobayashi Porcelain. Verbal has nimbly adapted innocuous background items to embellish his narrative. The slow-as-molasses Pretzel Man is Keyser Söze, the honeydewed narrator--once here, now gone--leaving the arrogant Kujan roasting slowly on a spit.

We observe Verbal, gathering his property and limping down the street, at first haltingly, then more confidently as the left foot magically corrects to give Keyser Söze a full stride. He leaves just before Kujan's rush to the street, and just ahead of a fax sent from the hospital, showing Verbal as Söze. The conundrum, however, is this: Keyser Söze could have escaped at the pier, yet he allowed customs agents to capture him? Why?

One devilish answer pertains to his exuberance at manipulating others and playing the game. Keyser Söze, as Verbal, can revel upon hearing how Kujan has learned to "spot murderers," and how Kujan sees himself as so much smarter than the slow-thinking Gimp. Söze weaves his version--the only complete version we witness--of what happens before and after the slayings. Then, executing the equivalent of a graceful bow, he exits moments prior to having his identity exposed--the *coup de maître*.

We retain no firm idea of the true storyline, other than what Verbal Klint tells us. Nicholas Christopher (1997, pp. 260-261), in his analysis of *The Usual Suspects*, notes a cacophony of language references throughout the film, for example, using "Verbal" as a name, and selecting the Hungarian language and its obscure origins, for which a customs agent must find an interpreter. Too, snippets of narrative and dialogue surround Verbal's departure and offer retrospective hints to his identity:

> ...A babble, at first, which then comes stunningly clear as crucial bits of dialogue and voice-over from the film flow past us, assembled so as to demonstrate that all along, buried in the lines we heard throughout the story, was an inexorable line leading to the fact that Verbal was Keyser Söze. Poised at the center of his web. A film about storytelling on its deepest level after all had to be a film about language in the end. About Babel. Which of course is the Hebrew for Babylon, the city where in Genesis the Lord did "confound the language of all the earth" so that the people "may not understand one another's speech."

Keyser Söze's maze of babble and deception fosters an elaborate scenario of secrecy, misdirection, and a false profession of friendship (Verbal for Keaton). But most notably, Keyser Söze presents himself as the enfeebled Verbal, the masochistic role of a personality subject to contempt and derision for his disabilities and his timid ways.

If we accept Keyser Söze as the Devil, what the **devil** is the Devil thinking? Step back from the trees and examine Söze's overriding purpose: He wishes to kill a witness, held by the Hungarians, who can identify him. The film's usual suspects, who unknowingly cause him a minor setback with a truck hijacking, also face termination as they storm the freighter to do his bidding. Söze succeeds in killing the witness and the suspects, but his Satanic overview presumably fails to account for the ship's captain surviving. Now, after the cumbersome plan plays out, and lives are lost, Keyser Söze has been identified, regardless.

Did he have prophetic control over all that transpired, and

just wished to create a bit of mischief? That is, did Söze allow the Hungarian captain to live so as to fine-tune the mischief and escape by a few breathtaking seconds? If not for Satanic joy, then what? The entire operation becomes null and void in any realistic sense. Keyser Söze wishes to eliminate a prospective witness, but is fingered, nonetheless.

Perhaps Söze's closing line best captures the moral of his well-laid scheme (a sentiment also encountered in Lesson 3): "Greatest trick the devil ever pulled was convincing the world he didn't exist...And like that (poof!), he's gone." Be he the devil or an ardent disciple, Keyser Söze appears untouchable. Evil wins in grand fashion, and the only justice meted out becomes Keyser Söze's justice: an improbably contrived revenge that ultimately tallies forth as an indulgence in Satanic tomfoolery.

JUSTICE

The Usual Suspects constitutes a film oddity in that (1) no sterling hero emerges who allows us to place our eggs cozily in one basket; (2) the one soul we **most** sympathize with is Verbal Klint, a master of misdirection; and (3) some part of our shadow self roots for Keyser Söze's contempt of authority and for his vanishing act.

Justice, in other words, gets roughed up. Keyser Söze murders the innocent and not-so-innocent with seeming impunity. He is not a nice man, especially if his pedigree turns out to be more than mortal. But in seeking cinematic closure, viewers either must accept the story's sense of deranged justice--Keyser's Söze's justice--or leave in the unsettled state of witnessing justice mocked.

Because evil can give justice a bad name, it helps to understand how this code of conduct fares in reality, and in the artful expanse of the cinema. Justice in the abstract makes for interesting discourses on points of morality and retribution.   One camp, for example, desires equitable punishment for murderers and musters principled support for life imprisonment without parole, whereas an opposing camp favors the kind of retribution that stems from capital punishment.

Justice applied, however, denotes a different universe of rules and consequences. Philosophical discussions aside, the practice of justice bears on the mechanics of determining and dispensing punishment. Criminal offenders either face death, incarceration, freedom with contingencies, or freedom unfettered. Whether these outcomes seem right or wrong in the abstract, in practice the judicial system assumes responsibility for dictating real verdicts in real time.

Real justice dispatches its share of controversial verdicts, as in the O. J. Simpson case. Simpson's release provoked ideological forays concerning the integrity of American justice and its haphazard application through our judicial system. But if the Simpson trial suffered from a lack of focus, the lumbering pace of due process did highlight the adversarial advantages and disadvantages attending each side. And, regardless of issues pertaining to justice in the abstract, O. J. Simpson left a free man, at least from further criminal prosecution of the two murders charged against him.

Real justice, at times painfully slow and digressive, still commands a resolution. The jurors' decision in the Simpson case may not indicate vindication to many observers, but the jurors' unanimous verdict constitutes an act of real justice. The power behind that verdict set O. J. Simpson free. Therefore, the checks and balances of due process, however well or poorly executed, comprise the heart of our judicial system. The system customarily reflects advocates who sort through evidence and pick their way to a conclusion. By contrast, the system typically does not give sway to surprising revelations that miraculously convict or clear the accused.

Cinematic justice, however, dotes on the implausible, the improbable, the last-minute windfall that accords underdogs a victory from the villain's omnipotent control. Frankly, the scant hope of convicting a murderer means high drama for filmmakers. High drama portrays the hero as disadvantaged, down on one knee and gasping for breath. Our hero (the protagonist) must now confront a villain (the antagonist) of immense skill and perspicacity. More often than not, make that **much** more often than not, the hero somehow prevails. The murderer's domination collapses through a vortex of unexpected, and, at times, bizarre developments.

True, in films revolving about matters of legal justice, viewers can observe the fundamentals of due process: They probably know the *Miranda* warning by heart, and they likely appreciate the highlights of trial procedure, the judge's absolute presence, the legal skirmishes between opposing counsel, and the mystique of jurors as they harbor their unknown quantity. But when viewing films centered on legal justice as entertainment, moviegoers receive less exposure to the finer points of law, and to the tedium that due process can impose in expounding these finer points.

What viewers **do** see most frequently involves final judgments that rely on startling advancements, sometimes legal, sometimes illegal, sometimes outrageous and hugely fortuitous, but advancements almost always designed to prompt a melodramatic resolution. And, most frequently, films will stretch logic razor thin to accommodate this brand of justice, even if the accommodation involves a last-minute epiphany. Keyser Söze, in other words, personifies that rare stroke of evil who the cinema lords allow to go poof! with the wind.

THE AMBUSH GAMBIT

Cinematic justice can not afford undue realism, since legal tedium and the finer points of law do not facilitate popular entertainment. Entertainment requires that cinematic justice indulge viewers by avoiding tortoises and embracing hares; by compromising complexity in the service of simple clarity; and by cutting to the chase.

Thus, George Brougham (Kirk Douglas), our resident psychopath in *The List Of Adrian Messenger* (1963), seeks to arrange a lad's death. Unknown to George, his adversaries use the murderer's very preparations to arrange **his** murder. George, underestimating the opposition, succumbs to a surprise maneuver that proves lethal (see Lesson 2).

Ripley (Sigourney Weaver) of *Alien* (1979) finds herself trapped in a small space capsule with the alien who has decimated her crew. What to do? The drooling creature savors its prey, watching Ripley strip to her undies and climb into a space suit. The slow-thinking invader does not grasp Ripley's trickery until it is too late: She depressurizes the cabin and blows the predator into space, an unexpected move that solves her problem nicely.

Even Mother Nature can pull a fast one. Remember Rhoda (Patty McCormack) of *The Bad Seed* (1956)? We learn in Lesson 2 how her girlish charms effectively mask the child's psychopathic orientation. Rhoda's selfish immaturity, therefore, gives her no reason to worry about a lightning storm as she troops through the rain to retrieve a trinket at the dock. Zap! A lightning strike ensures that Rhoda no longer poses a threat to anyone. Although sudden and highly improbable, this climatic action reduces the little psychopath to a charred heap, bringing her dangerous potential to an abrupt end.

These three films rely on concealment and surprise, using the **ambush gambit** to dispatch a formidable villain. Indeed, the malignant personality may well persevere if not for a startling turn of events that transform almost certain victory into devastating defeat. A film's "ambush logic" can seem a bit lame on occasion, as in Rhoda's case of sheer bad luck. But, lame or not, the ambush motif functions to free the hero from an apparently hopeless situation, send the scheming villain into a tailspin, and supply an entertaining finale for movie viewers.

The ambush gambit offers a dramatic tactic for undermining the psychopath's masterful performance. Imagine, then, how this tactic finds expression when the psychopath brushes against the kind of cinematic justice that the judicial system executes. Agatha Christie's *Witness For The Prosecution* (1957), directed by Billy Wilder from a screenplay by Wilder, Harry Kurnitz, and Larry Marcus, dramatizes just this sort of legal entanglement. Leonard Vole (Tyrone Power), a drifter and itinerant inventor, desires the help of a barrister, Sir Wilfred Robarts (Charles Laughton), to defend him against a murder charge. The prosecution accuses Vole of murdering an older woman, arguing that he falsely befriended her to inherit an 80,000-pound estate. Vole says he is innocent, and relies on the testimony of his wife, Christine (Marlene Dietrich), to give him an alibi.

But Christine, as a witness for the prosecution, refuses to support Leonard's story. Instead, she claims a previous marriage, declaring that Leonard is not her legal husband. (Vole could have claimed status as a "putative spouse," meaning he **thought** he was married, and might have kept Christine from testifying against him; however, had he done so, the putative spouse ruling would have scuttled the storyline in *Witness For The Prosecution*. See Bergman & Asimow, 1996, p. 186.)

Christine's damaging testimony almost sinks Sir Wilfred's case, until he receives an apparently serendipitous phone call from an unknown source. Before this source--a Cockney woman--mysteriously disappears, she shows Robarts a packet of letters written by Christine to a lover. The letters indicate that Christine perjured her testimony in an attempt to frame Leonard for murder so that she might leave him.

Sir Wilfred recalls Christine to the stand and confronts her with the letters. Distraught and disheveled, she screams "Liar!" at him as Sir Wilfred makes his case and the jury finds Leonard Vole not guilty. Everyone for the defense appears jubilant...except Sir Wilfred. He suspects that the letters represent a good fortune too convenient for curmudgeons like himself: "It's a little too neat, too tidy, and altogether too symmetrical, that's what's wrong with it."

What's wrong with it, as he soon learns, is that the witness for the prosecution has outwitted him. Christine and the Cockney woman are one, a ruse that enables Christine to incriminate herself as a lying witness. She commits perjury by giving "false" testimony against Leonard, thereby producing the desired outcome of setting him free. And Leonard needs his freedom, since, alas, he **did** murder the old lady. Christine's original testimony was not really false: She told the truth about Leonard's movements, but later misled Sir Wilfred and the court into thinking that she had lied.

Thus, we encounter Ambush #1: A psychopath commits a murder, and relies on a loving yet duplicitous wife to rescue him dramatically from almost certain doom. Ambush #2 arrives when Christine realizes that Leonard's endearing charms belong to another sweetie. Leonard "gallantly" offers to finance Christine's forthcoming legal burden, but he leaves no doubt that their relationship is history and that a new, younger damsel has replaced her.

Sadly misjudging Christine and her rage at his disloyalty, Leonard finds himself unsuspecting when she grasps a letter opener and plunges said letter opener into his heart. He collapses to the floor, dead. Leonard, on the threshold of victory, becomes yet another psychopath too egocentric to worry about the danger of recklessly discarding a woman who passionately loves him.

Thanks to the ambush gambit, cinematic justice triumphs. If the triumph does not happen according to the letter of the law, at least retribution prevails. And Sir Wilfred, who witnesses Leonard's "execution," now finds himself with a new client.

Real justice, nonetheless, seldom relies on such contrivances outside the legal arena to solve a murder case. What the judge allows as evidence, what counsel can unearth for and against the defendant, what the court permits the jury to hear and see--these dynamics constitute the usual raw material from which a verdict derives.

Cinematic justice and real justice manage a closer alliance when the ambush gambit occurs naturally, as from the legal jousting of attorneys via examination and cross-examination. *Anatomy Of A Murder* (1959), directed by Otto Preminger and written by Wendell Mayes, dramatizes the murder case of one Lt. Frederick Manion (Ben Gazarra). Manion walks into the Thunder Bay Inn and fires several shots at the proprietor, Barney Quill.

Mr. Quill's demise means that Manion needs a lawyer, and that lawyer becomes Paul Biegler (James Stewart). Biegler spends more time fishing the back lakes of Northern Michigan than he does nurturing his law practice. The lawyer, however, must contend with Maida (Eve Arden), his secretary, who prods him to take on work so she can get a new typewriter. Biegler's other helpmate, Parnell McCarthy (Arthur

O'Connell), shuffles forth as a retired attorney given to booze and to arguing fine points of law from the "old brown books."

Manion's public elimination of Quill prompts Biegler to meet with the accused at the insistence of Manion's wife, Laura (Lee Remick). She claims to have been raped by Barney Quill, hence Frederick Manion's apparent motivation for plugging Quill into eternity. Still, the director, Otto Preminger, poses a recurring question concerning Laura Manion's credibility: Did a rape really occur? Witnesses attest to Frederick Manion killing Barney Quill, no problem there. But no one observes the alleged rape between Barney Quill and Laura Manion.

Biegler's initial meetings with Manion are not encouraging. He finds the lieutenant surly, reticent, and a mile or two shy of boyish charm. Manion subscribes to the "unwritten law," the ancient belief that a husband can freely defend his honor when another man sexually compromises the husband's property. Frederick Manion argues that he had a time-honored "right" to go after Barney Quill (Bergman & Asimow, 1996, p. 236; Harris, 1987, p. 80).

Biegler quickly dismisses that primitive notion as having no legal standing. He also excludes other possibilities such as killing Barney Quill by accident or out of anger. The murder was surely no accident, and Manion waited an hour before confronting Quill, a delay suggesting premeditation rather than the lesser charge of manslaughter. So, what defense **can** Frederick Manion claim?

Paul Biegler surreptitiously guides the lieutenant to the one workable defense that may allow him a chance for freedom. The lawyer begins by saying, "You're very bright, Lieutenant. Now let's see how really bright you can be." He waits as Manion gropes for the best defense, a defense the lieutenant finally stumbles upon with the realization, "I must have been crazy."

Cinematically, convincing Manion to embrace an insanity defense appears acceptable. Realistically, however, Paul Bergman and Michael Asimow (1996, p. 236), in their book *Reel Justice*, question Biegler's ethical conduct when he coaches Manion to an insanity plea:

For all his country-lawyer innocence, Biegler's lecture probably violates
the attorneys' code of ethics. A lawyer can help a client tell a story in
a credible way, but cannot create the story the client tells. But
Biegler's lecture guides Manion towards the one story that might
produce a not-guilty verdict. Of course, violations such as Biegler's
rarely come to light. They take place behind closed doors, and are
protected by attorney-client confidentiality. Ironically, for all the rules
that regulate how evidence comes out publicly in court, stories typically
take shape in lawyers' offices, out of the reach of those rules.

Ethical or not, Manion has his defense but no money to pay
Biegler. Paul decides to take the case and collect his fee later,
knowing that the enlightened lieutenant will now use the
insanity defense, regardless of who becomes his lawyer. This
seemingly small shift in negotiations, won by Manion,
illustrates the psychopath's opportunism. Manion, still
unconvinced as to the gravity of his situation, gains
satisfaction at wresting back a modicum of control. He has a
lawyer who must now depend on him for payment in due
course. "Due course" to a psychopath means "in the distant
future," a time reference too indeterminate to cause him any
loss of sleep.

Manion's defense pertains to **irresistible impulse**, a state of
mind by which he felt compelled to kill Barney Quill
(Bergman & Asimow, 1996, p. 234). If the lieutenant believes
that Quill raped his wife - - whether the rape really occurred or
not - - the lieutenant can claim he could not stop himself.
Under the rules of irresistible impulse, right or wrong does not
matter. Manion may realize his actions are wrong, but he will
be helpless to change the outcome. What Lieutenant Manion
really thinks, of course, we never learn.

Interestingly, when psychiatrists for the defense and
prosecution declare their views on irresistible impulse, the
prosecution's psychiatrist offers a stronger position. Because
Manion did not display prior neurotic reactions, even in
combat, the prosecution's psychiatrist suggests that no
emotional foundation exists for developing the kind of dazed
behavior claimed by Manion in killing Barney Quill. The
psychiatrist's damaging testimony makes Manion's use of
irresistible impulse seem a very convenient legal excuse for

murdering the tavern owner.

Given the precarious defense of irresistible impulse, and given prosecuting attorney Dancer's (George C. Scott) inference of Laura Manion's promiscuity, Paul Biegler and associates find themselves in trouble. Promiscuity and rape do not blend seamlessly in jurors' minds. Laura's alleged promiscuity suggests that a rape did not happen. If the jury believes that Frederick Manion recognizes this possibility, then his defense of irresistible impulse proves more difficult to accept. The lieutenant's delay of one hour before killing Barney Quill becomes a critical time period. Manion may have spent that hour planning Quill's death, a premeditation that speaks of first-degree murder.

Time for an ambush, and the bait for this ambush turns out to be...a pair of women's panties. Laura Manion's panties, in fact; panties that she clearly identifies and claims Barney Quill ripped from her during the rape. The lingerie in question remains missing until Mary Pilant (Kathryn Grant), who also runs Thunder Bay Inn, locates the item in the hotel laundry.

Dancer zeroes in on Mary Pilant, eager to discount the ripped panties and the article's evidence of a possible rape. Almost nose to nose with the witness, he makes his critical prosecutorial mistake when he chooses to attack Mary's character (after all, it worked with Laura Manion, so why not Mary Pilant?).

Customarily, a careful lawyer asks those questions for which he already knows the likely answers. Hence, counsel merely waits for the witness to confirm his suspicions. But Dancer savors the thought of clinching his case in dramatic fashion, so he dispenses with caution. The prosecutor heatedly challenges Mary Pilant's relationship with Barney Quill, accusing her of being his mistress. Mary replies emotionally that she was not Quill's mistress, that Barney Quill was... Dancer moves in: "Was *what*, Miss Pilant? Barney Quill was *what*, Miss Pilant?", whereupon Mary blurts out the incisive answer: "Barney Quill was my father."

Ahhh. Ambush successful. Dancer fades away, and cinematically, so does the prosecution's case. Biegler, of course, knew of Mary Pilant's status, but felt no compunction to share this information with the prosecution. Mary's tentative admission that her father may have raped Laura Manion, and the presence of the ripped panties, serve to give Frederick Manion his verdict of "not guilty by reason of insanity."

Real justice would not have showcased such a thorough reversal of fortune. The ripped panties, despite their dramatic introduction, do not offer sufficient proof that Barney Quill raped Laura Manion. He could, for example, have ripped and kept the panties in a moment of mutual passion with Laura. Cinematic justice, however, dictates otherwise.

And, technically, considering the verdict of "not guilty by reason of insanity," Lieutenant Manion should have been remanded to a mental institution for therapy until he could no longer pose a danger to himself or to others (Bergman & Asimow, 1996, p. 238). This outcome does not occur in the film. Instead, as Biegler and McCarthy pull up at the trailer camp to collect their heartily earned fee, Frederick and Laura Manion have vacated the premises: no lieutenant and, alas, no fee.

Manion's farewell note underscores the lieutenant's triumphant departure: "...so sorry but I had to leave suddenly. I was seized by an irresistible impulse..." What better way for a psychopath to celebrate his freedom than by tweaking the defense team with the very idea that set him free. A defense team, we should add, who worked so tirelessly on his behalf.

Comparing Frederick Manion to our model of evil, we find the lieutenant a strong candidate for secrecy (we suspect deception, but we **still** do not know the truth); for abdication of responsibility (he killed in combat, and he has no problem in deciding to kill Barney Quill); for no remorse concerning his actions (he claims a lack of memory, but more likely he simply does not care that Quill is gone); and for exuberance (Manion's eyes glisten with attentiveness as the attorneys recount the actual killing).

Manion's one deficiency pertains to his use of misdirection, or better put, the lack of it. He presents himself as a man of animal prowess, a physical man, cunning and perhaps lucky enough to find his way out of bad situations. But he is never a man of charm or geniality. Rather, with one exception, Manion maintains an aloofness from everyone, including Laura: To illustrate, she offers to light his cigarette in one scene, yet he ignores her and lights it himself.

The one exception occurs when he opens his arms to embrace Laura after Dancer emotionally tears her apart on the stand. Aside from this brief moment of comfort, Manion expresses little regard for anyone, save himself. The lieutenant maintains an enigmatic presence and reveals only a shadow of what counsel--defense and prosecution--believe that he knows. His selfish and uncommunicative nature keeps defense and prosecution from comprehending the whole truth. A whole truth, the skeptics will charge, that permitted a psychopath to beat the system.

THE PSYCHOPATH'S PLAYGROUND

Imagine the material psychopath who seeks a long-term goal, and who must covertly arrange a series of maneuvers to keep himself in line for the final payoff. Imagine, too, a psychopath who plays this game in an arena that encourages secrecy, misdirection, and a fluid allegiance to the individual in power. Imagine, in other words, what it takes to survive a long and "honorable" career in English politics. Masterpiece Theatre dramatizes this survival in a 3-part series based on the novel by Michael Dobbs and adapted for television by Andrew Davies, with Parts 1 and 2 directed by Paul Seed, and Part 3 by Mike Vardy.

Francis Urquhart (Ian Richardson as F.U.) begins *House Of Cards* (1990) by placing a picture of Prime Minister Margaret Thatcher face down. He then slyly confides to the camera, "Even the longest, the most glittering reign must come to an end someday." Francis desires the title himself, but, as his party's chief whip, he knows that timing is everything.

Smiling modestly, he denies his ambition by deprecating himself publicly as just a "backroom boy" who knows "his place." The magic hour is too soon for him, although Francis appreciates the value of cultivation: "A man of state needs

helpers--little elves and sprites to do his bidding. Even
unwitting pawns who don't know who they serve." Francis has
nurtured the ability to promote a fastidiously loyal self-image
to whomever claims the power, while scheming adroitly to
implicate that very same whomever in political scandal.

Francis Urquhart portrays the master manipulator in a
psychopath's paradise: the political animal who preys on his
rivals' weaknesses. Typically, psychopaths must fend off the
police using one hand and execute their devilish plots with the
other. But malevolent personalities clever enough to make the
system work for them more closely approximate a complete
evil, as does Kevin Spacey's John Doe in *Seven* and Spacey's
characterization of Keyser Söze in *The Usual Suspects*. And
politics, in particular, with its veiled fang and velvet claw
proves a comfortable medium for the carnivore's skullduggery.

Urquhart occasionally encounters failure, and he displays
the psychopath's intemperance to such unaccustomed defeats.
One scene finds him entering the office of Henry Collingridge
(David Lyon) to coach the new prime minister on selecting a
slate of candidates for the administration's cabinet posts. But
an old political warhorse, Lord Billsborough (Nicholas Selby),
already has the prime minister's confidence, and neither man
accepts Urquhart's recommendations. Pretending to acquiesce
to their judgment, we observe a closeup of the chief whip's
hands: clenched tightly, knuckles popping, a "gripping"
expression of the psychopath's rage.

Francis engages the covert services of an ambitious
journalist, Mattie Storin (Susannah Harker), who finds herself
enthralled at receiving inside information from Urquhart.
Francis, who delivers no damaging statements directly, leaks
hints of wrongdoing to Mattie, allowing her reporter's brain to
draw the obvious conclusions. When she voices her
interpretations to him for confirmation, Francis responds with
his trademark reply, "Mattie, you might very well think that.
You know I couldn't possibly comment."

Mattie does not realize that Urquhart orchestrates the
wrongdoings he passes on as "inside" information. Neither
does she comprehend the depth of his evil, nor the complicity
of Urquhart's wife, Elizabeth (Diane Fletcher), who aids her

husband's grand cause. Francis smiles at Elizabeth after his initial meeting with Mattie: "Interesting girl. Clever." Elizabeth inquires, "Not too clever." Francis replies, "No, no. Just clever enough, I should say." He means just clever enough to do his bidding, but not so clever as to discover the true scope of his mission.

Lest we forget the base nature of these political sophisticates, occasional glimpses of gutter rats flash on screen as symbolic comparisons. The image between the two species proves increasingly blurred when Francis (1) engages in blackmail, (2) engineers a financial scam to discredit the prime minister, (3) directs the character assassination of influential figures who threaten his plans, (4) arranges the prostitution of a political strategist to compromise a rival candidate for prime minister--and (5) commits two murders. Francis Urquhart manages these machinations with the ease of a veteran kingmaker, even as he continues to serve Collingridge, who views him as the epitome of a loyal supporter.

What a psychopath! The rationalizations for his misdeeds and his murders are especially enlightening. When Prime Minister Collingridge finally resigns because of Urquhart's deft manipulations to bring him down, Francis feels no remorse. Indeed, he assesses Collingridge as having no "bottom": "His deepest need was that the people should like him. An admirable trait that, in a spaniel or a whore, not, I think, in a prime minister."

But how well can Francis justify murder? Roger O'Neill (Miles Anderson), a political player and cocaine addict, comes under Urquhart's dominion as someone to blackmail and use for various dirty tricks. Roger, unfortunately, has become unstable emotionally, a risk to Urquhart's grand calling. So, as Francis mixes rat poison with Roger's stash of cocaine, he eulogizes the "necessity" of Roger's demise: "He's begging to be set free. He's had enough. And when he's finally at rest, then we'll be free to remember the real Roger. The burning boy in the green jersey with that legendary, fabulous sidestep, and the brave, terrified smile." Francis confides all this to the camera--to us--and he believes every word.

Mattie's murder, however, comes as a jolt to the habitual

Urquhart composure. He likes Mattie, has sex with Mattie, and trusts her as he dare trust anyone (save his wife) in the political game. She calls him "Daddy" and he allows her an intimacy that only makes his quest more precarious. He even wonders about his desires for the responsibilities that attend the position of prime minister: "Why should I yearn to be everybody's 'Daddy'?"

But he does. And Mattie, too close to the truth, becomes a liability. She finds him on the roof garden, where he goes for solitude. She knows of his manipulations, yet she must hear him say so. He does, and then queries her: "Mattie?" "What?" Softer, this time: "Mattie?" "What?" "Can I trust you?" "You know you can." Francis disagrees: "Oh, Mattie, you give me such pain to say this, but I don't believe you. I don't believe I can trust you." And with these words, Urquhart heaves his beloved Mattie off the roof, to her death.

Our next glimpse of Francis Urquhart comes in a limousine as he rides to begin his ministerial duties. He gives the camera a cold, hard stare, a countenance that complements the man's true character. Urquhart tries to explain that he eliminated Mattie to defend his mission, yet he does so without the hogwash of rationalizations that accompanied Roger's eulogy. Finally, disgusted with "our" lack of understanding, he reverts to his trademark conscience: "You might very well think that. I could not possibly comment."

One oversight remains, however. Unknown to Francis, Mattie has lovingly recorded her encounters with him. When she learns of his evil, she carries the recorder with her one last time. Someone finds the machine near her body, after the fall. Now what? Rarely does such a discovery prove accidental in movie parlance. Finding the recorder means something forbidding for the new prime minister--another crisis in need of resolution.

Francis Urquhart returns in *To Play The King* (1994), disturbed by replays of Mattie's murder, but also busy with the chores of a material psychopath: He must keep his adversaries away, and worry over the trust that he invests in his allies. Getting the power comprises one strategy; keeping the power, quite another.

Francis soon learns that his primary irritation is the King of England (Michael Kitchen), a monarch who not only thinks, but one who yearns to do more for the homeless and the disadvantaged. Francis, of course, sees no reason to assist the slackers of society, or to step aside for royalty. Instead, he works to subvert His Highness, and win another election for himself.

To help in this cause, Francis retains the queasy loyalty of Tim Stamper (Colin Jeavons), now his chief whip, and of young Sarah Harding (Kitty Aldridge), a new protégé and successor to Mattie. The Prime Minister succeeds in challenging the King, but Urquhart's coarse, subterranean tactics create problems within. Francis senses his subordinates' unrest. Indeed, he perseveres because of his keen vigilance to the state of mind of those closest to him: "As the cat's eyelids flicker, some part of us must stay awake, always. Ready, as the coil spring is ready."

He is more ready than his disaffected intimates realize. Stamper wants power for himself, and Sarah begins to wonder about Mattie's mysterious death: two dangerous courses of inquiry that ultimately lead to two car explosions--one for Stamper, one for Sarah. These drastic resolutions become necessary, to Francis, because each victim possesses a copy of the tell-tale recording made by Mattie Storin.

The incineration of this evidence should permit Francis clear sailing, and afford him relief from the recurring memory of Mattie's great fall ("Am I still the man who did that thing?"). So, in *The Final Cut* (1995), we visit a Francis Urquhart who has won three elections, and who wishes to leave a profound legacy of his reign: "I've been here so long now that, love me or hate me, it's hard for you to imagine anyone else in my place...isn't it?"

He may say so, but we could not possibly comment. One glaring weakness that a psychopath long in power will not overcome concerns his past. The thin civility of public decorum simply fails to squelch accelerating rumors of the blackguard's surreptitious misdeeds. And Francis Urquhart knows better than anyone what can happen to the dominating figure when powermongers detect a whiff of vulnerability: He is history.

Despite the mounting odds against him, and against his wife's wishes, Francis vows to stay in power. But Elizabeth Urquhart, the silent, steadfast force behind her husband's most visible triumphs, has other plans. She consults secretly with Corder (Nick Brimble), the Urquhart's menacing, all-purpose handy man. Later, she tells Francis, "He's going to arrange something very special on Margaret Thatcher Day."

Something "special," at a ceremony, on Margaret Thatcher Day. Hmmm. Given Francis Urquhart's oft-used practices of intimidation, betrayal, and murder, he has too little time and too many leaks in the dike to cleanse his wavering public image. For Elizabeth, the topside of this public image must be preserved, whatever the sacrifice.

And the sacrifice, as you may well suspect, is Francis Urquhart. Consider: What one act can spontaneously salvage a covertly despicable character and his bloody longevity from the jaws of justice? What one political transaction can catapult the longstanding psychopath from an unsavory manipulator to a revered statesman? What one dramatic event can usher Francis Urquhart into the hallowed halls of eternal statesmanship? There is only one way: assassination.

To die honorably, especially when one does not expect it, carries the windfall of minimizing and possibly reconstructing past misdeeds. Francis and Elizabeth used to kiss the Judas kiss, their seal of approval for committing otherwise unconscionable acts, such as murdering Roger O'Neill. Now, Elizabeth engages in the same principle with Corder; not to betray her husband, but to embrace the only resolution possible for exalting Francis Urquhart's reign as prime minister. He must die the glorious death of the political beast: immortalized to the public in a captivating, lightening moment of violence. Francis Urquhart must pay the ultimate price of a public servant to his country.

A psychopath is not known for his patience. Instead, he characteristically behaves impulsively, and fails to learn profitably from his mistakes. How does Francis Urquhart overcome the psychopath's usual deficiencies and still meet the rigorous demands of the 3/2 model? Francis begins his quest as a cautious, erudite observer of the political scene. He **maintains a series of secret ploys reasonably well**, confiding fully only in his wife. Had Francis professed publicly his desire to be prime minister, yet done nothing to compromise Collingridge, the position would have eluded him. The question of whether his ruthlessness proved necessary in the quest--particularly since Prime Minister Collingridge did not express this trait--becomes arguable. It also becomes a moot point: Francis never hesitates to use any means in gaining a political edge.

As a **master of misdirection**, the man's gracious, subservient demeanor permits him to fool his most adept political colleagues. Initially thought to personify the loyal image of a benevolent supporter, Francis parlays that image into a public shield to mask his covert callousness. Francis Urquhart's most mesmerizing quality as a psychopath concerns his talent at misdirection. Time and again he deflects suspicion from himself by assuming a most respectable and modest comportment. The facade works remarkably well early in his career, although later this deception suffers the erosion of too many skeletons and too little closet space.

Francis's **abdication of responsibility** runs mostly a smooth course, except for recurring memories of Mattie Storin. Other memories haunt Francis but they flicker in and out, hardly showing the intrusiveness necessary to dampen his relentless onslaught for political attainment. The man's mercilessness knows few boundaries, enforced by the facile rationalizations that encourage him to condone murder for God and country. This renunciation of responsibility, whether through character assassination or by physical violence, arises as a formidable attitude for securing political advancement. Francis never ceases to forge ahead, regardless of the human cost.

Nor does Francis's passion to become prime minister permit him **to long suffer a guilty conscience** over bodies strewn hither and yon. He falters here with his repetitive dreams of killing Mattie, a shocking act that even the usual political dismissal fails to obliterate. Francis never quite relinquishes his remorse over Mattie, but this singular episode does not keep him from savoring many triumphs.

He marks these triumphs with a ceremony of quiet joy. A English gentleman's exuberance hardly invokes the shouting of Yahoos! and the clicking of heels, although Francis Urquhart's **admiration of himself** seems rather evident. He delights in tormenting underlings and playing them one against the other ("Select a scapegoat and enact token mounting"). He does so while sitting above the fray, haughty, bemused, sporting the superior smile. He feels the psychopath's magic, an awe-inspiring emotion of godliness.

But in *The Final Cut*, Francis finds the "magic" slipping away: "I had a peculiar feeling in the House this afternoon, as if I couldn't quite...smell the mood." Desperation replaces confidence, and Francis Urquhart can not scheme enough, betray enough, murder enough to continue in power. He has overstayed his time, a much longer time of evil than most psychopaths enjoy.

Does his assassination constitute a fitting punishment for crimes rendered? Or does his "honorable" death give him one last hurrah in defiance of an ignoble end? Prime Minister Francis Urquhart's timely demise affords him the opportunity to be remembered for his selfless service to England. The one resolution that Urquhart does not engineer, becomes the one resolution that provides him a shot at fortifying his niche in English history. Time and historians may eventually bring the man's stately image down, but Francis no longer can (or must) witness this possibility. Perhaps, in that sense, he has already won the game.

JUSTICE *IN ABSENTIA*

Francis Urquhart and Keyser Söze portray psychopaths of such scope and versatility that to label them exclusively material or spiritual in orientation seems inadequate. Francis proves more human than Keyser, and, by necessity, more visible in his quest to attain power and finesse the lives around him. Both men, however, transcend reality with abandon, unless you choose to believe that, in Urquhart's case, the Brits really do run a corrupt and murderous political machine.

But psychopaths, to entertain, need not loom larger than life or compile an impressive body count. Charming scoundrels exist more abundantly in real life who give no thought to risking murder, yet who prove very keen on advancing themselves even if it occurs at a cost to "close colleagues." Reprising the classic psychopath from Lesson 5, for instance, brings us a man more believable than Francis Urquhart or Keyser Söze, although a man capable in his own slippery way of keeping justice at bay.

"Life is for the taking, is it not?" These words summarize the philosophy of a middle-management malcontent named Chad (Aaron Eckhart), as he speaks to Howard (Matt Malloy), his immediate superior. Both men are 10 years out of the university, and Chad finds himself wary of ambitious interns who desire, as he puts it, "to feed on my insides."

The males' pressing priority, however, concerns women who have done them wrong. Howard's grievance involves the lover who rejected him, and the wrestling match that followed to retrieve his ring from her finger. Chad, in turn, relates that his girl-in-residence, Suzanne (Emily Cline), left him with nary a fare-thee-well. Chad wants to get even, and urges Howard to join him and "Restore a little dignity to our lives."

Hence, *In The Company Of Men* (1997) begins with the motto "Let's do it. Let's hurt someone," with Christine (Stacy Edwards) as the victim, a deaf beauty of shy ways and pure motives. Written and directed by Neil LaBute, the story begins when Chad and Howard are assigned to a branch office for six weeks, just time enough to wine, dine, and bed Christine--before waving *adieu* and leaving her in the lurch. No attempts occur to terrorize or cause bodily harm, no, nothing so crude. Instead, the plan calls for a psychological game of manipulation and reprisal: Do unto her as she would eventually do unto them. But do it unto her first.

The film chronicles Christine's seduction by marking each week with a burst of shrill, discordant music, a signature of the baseness that human nature has to offer. Chad underscores the game's dark spirit when he expresses his contempt for Christine's speaking disability: "In fact, one of the kindest people I've ever had spray spit in my face." A series of dialogues commence between Chad and Howard, held in restrooms, diners, and other mundane locales--all designed to monitor the males' "progress." Both men arrange to date Christine and profess their trust in her. This false sentiment places the now-troubled woman in a dilemma of receiving too much attention, whereas before she received too little.

But Howard, never comfortable with the game, feels genuine affection for Christine and learns rudimentary sign language to show his feelings. Even Chad tells Howard that "She's definitely got something," although this fleeting admission does not forego Chad's basic creed about the other sex: "Women--the nice ones, the most frigid of the race--it doesn't matter in the end. Inside they're all the same: meat and grizzle and hatred, just simmering."

Fearful of the emotional devastation that Christine will suffer, Howard pulls rank and arranges for Chad to leave town on business. Chad, ever the opportunist, takes advantage of Howard's preoccupation with Christine and uses the trip to promote himself--at the expense of his boss's trust. Howard, meanwhile, realizes that the game has gone too far. He confesses to Christine, only to find that she still loves Chad. Thus, a stunned and bewildered Christine finally experiences the anguish that Chad desires: She finds herself torn between her love for him and the cruel truth of his deceit. Howard, more than a little anguished himself, exclaims "Can't you see, I'm the good guy, I'm the good person here..."

But the "good guy" finds himself unable to handle another rejection and still manage what Chad calls the game's key: maintaining control. Howard erupts in a fury of words, all to no avail. Christine is lost to him. When she confronts Chad, he attempts to continue the ruse, then begins laughing and asks her his favorite question: How does it feel to be hurt? Christine slaps him, an action that would humiliate and possibly enrage many men, but, for Chad, the slap verifies his badge of honor. He wins, and he causes her pain. Chad lacks the sensitivity, however, to realize how deeply his game shatters her trust.

Weeks later, Howard, now demoted and working under Chad, visits him to talk out his agony over Christine. Chad beckons his former boss into the bedroom. The camera waits outside as the door closes. When Chad and Howard return, Howard is perplexed. He sees Suzanne in Chad's bed, but does not understand. Chad makes him understand as only a psychopath can: Suzanne never left; it-had-all-been-a-lie. Howard asks the obvious question: "Then why...why, Chad?" And Chad answers, "Because I could."

The answer, of course, proves more complex than Chad's self-congratulatory response. He smoldered under the working necessity of subordinating himself to someone of the same age and education. He, Chad, coveted the superior position, yet he always veiled his aspiration by "praising" Howard for his leadership ability. Thus, Christine became the pawn in a lofty scheme (1) to dupe her for the joy of it, but (2) to do so by playing with Howard's wavering self-confidence as well, and (3) to reap whatever benefits may fall Chad's way because of Howard's disorientation.

Chad's performance attains a mastery of calculated secrecy and misdirection. He entices Howard to help him deceive Christine, while effectively shielding his grander objective of exercising a business savvy to displace Howard. Chad raises no problems of conscience in shirking responsibility for his actions, or in lacking remorse: after all, he warns Howard to "Watch his back," does he not? Howard, naturally, fails to realize that he should have killed the messenger. Chad emerges victorious as the better man, professionally and sexually.

A lurking intelligence arises since, initially, *In The Company Of Men* centers on misogyny--a hatred of women-- as its apparent theme. Indeed, that hatred may be on target for Chad, although not the main target. Only when Chad discloses his lie about Suzanne to Howard does the psychopath's true intent lurch into awareness. Chad depicts a classic psychopath, a chameleon of charm, of earnestness, of betrayal; a character all the more frightening for his assumed credibility.

The distinctive psychopathic feature, however, remains Chad's exuberance over his triumphs. He truly enjoys the pretense of drawing unsuspecting creatures--like Christine and Howard--into his heartless grasp. He knows of his talent for subterfuge, and he glories in that talent. Yes, somewhere, somehow, Chad will court disaster, become careless with his authority, and take the Great Fall. But for now, business ethics, or the lack of them, give him a platform of power for all kinds of psychopathic shenanigans. (One scene illustrates Chad's humiliating use of power when he intimidates a black intern to lower his pants and show him his testicles. Chad does so under the ruse of what it takes--balls!--to become a decisive entrepreneur.)

Momentarily, then, Chad relishes his state of bliss. Our last glimpse shows Suzanne kissing him lavishly. As she works her way down to paradise, Chad's countenance reflects an arc of luxurious contentment. Clearly and without dissent, his countenance seems to say, this interlude of sensual pleasure is surely a fitting tribute for a god. And justice? Justice fails to materialize for Christine or Howard. At best, any equity that will plunge Chad into his toilet of hell serves as a promissory note: The payoff, when it happens, will come in time...just not tomorrow.

THE ESCAPE CLAUSE

Recall the chronology of 44 films listed in Lesson 9, beginning in 1919 with *The Cabinet Of Dr. Caligari* and ending in 1997 with *Kiss The Girls*. These films cover almost 80 years of serial murderers, predators who kill at least three or more victims over an extended time period, as contrasted with mass murderers and spree murderers who become highly visible for a briefer time span.

How many serial killers from this sample of 44 films escape to possibly kill another day? Excluding films involved in series revivals like *The Texas Chainsaw Massacre*, *Halloween*, and *Nightmare On Elm Street*, a total of seven titles remain in which the serial killer either vanishes, or the film's climax fails to indicate capture or termination: *Pretty Maids All In A Row* (1971); *A Shock To The System* (1990); *Henry: Portrait Of A Serial Killer* (1990); *The Silence Of The Lambs* (1991);

Raising Cain (1992); *Serial Mom* (1994); and *The Usual Suspects* (1997). Counting seven films of escapees against the serial killers punished, a figure of 17 percent arises, which increases to 23 per cent when adding in the three series revivals.

These disproportionate percentages indicate that the ruling trend favors punishing the psychopath, usually in dramatic fashion. And a first impression leads to the simple conclusion that death brands the malevolent personality a total failure. Goodness triumphs again, stamping the villain into a benign puddle of urine and feces. No more cunning and deceit, no more misdirection, no more threat to others' life and limb. Now, all that remains is another misguided soul, brought crashing to earth by an inflated ego, a lazy ignorance of reality, or, cinematically, just plain, bad luck.

Many psychopaths meet an abject ending in films that dote on action instead of character, on special effects rather than a plausible story line. The villains' humiliation appear absolute in that these scumbags finally reap the punishment they so richly deserve. And yet we also know that sometimes psychopaths win, not just in eluding justice momentarily like Hannibal Lecter and Keyser Söze, but by flaunting their ego as they enter death's door.

It seems as if those who walk proudly with evil view themselves as possessing an **escape clause** from complete annihilation. They steal goodness from others by taking the lives of innocents, and they leave a stench of themselves for survivors to combat and overcome. The exit of a malevolent being is not a clean exit. The loss of a victim's purity is mourned, and the offender's evil spoor remains to cause distress and prompt tragic reminders.

The psychopath's gesture may be **vain and glorious**, as occurs with Bruno Antony (Robert Walker) in Alfred Hitchcock's *Strangers On A Train* (1951), from the screenplay by Raymond Chandler, Czenzi Ormonde, and Whitfield Cook. Bruno, crushed and dying under a collapsed merry-go-round, can right wrongs and exonerate the film's hero, Guy Haines (Farley Granger), from further persecution. But Bruno refuses and maintains his lying ways, even unto death: "I'm-I'm sorry,

Guy. I-I-I want to help you, but I-I don't know what I can do." Only when he dies does evil recede and justice come forth to relax Bruno's hand and reveal a lighter that will ultimately free Haines.

Vain and glorious also describes the classic denouement in the 1946 western *Duel In The Sun*. Pearl (Jennifer Jones) and Luke (Gregory Peck) are tempestuous lovers. Pearl bears a love/hate relationship with Luke, who has wrought much despair and destruction in exercising his psychopathic bravado. She rides, inescapably, to kill him, and she does-- but he delivers a fatal bullet to her as well. The final scene shows the two lovers in a dying kiss, a fatal embrace that carries them to the only tumultuous arc of their passion not yet experienced.

David Thomson (1997), in his chapter on "How People Die in Movies," observes that "It is so often our killers now who are blessed with wisdom and insight" (p. 168). Discussing the villainous Mitch Leary (John Malkovich) versus the veteran Secret Service agent Frank Horrigan (Clint Eastwood) in *In The Line Of Fire* (1993), Thomson (p. 169) improvises a scene about death between the two adversaries:

> It would not be out of order if Malkovich crooned into the phone, "Frank, don't be petulant. You know, and I know, we're just playing checkers for the audience and they love to think about killing, and you're there just to waste me at the end so they feel OK about it. I've told you all along I'm ready to die for the picture--but, Frank, are you really ready to stop a bullet?"

No, Frank is not, nor does the audience wish to condone such heresy. But in reiterating the old hero/villain formula, do not overlook the malevolent personality's lusty embrace of death as an option. Mitch Leary shows himself more conversant with the notion that relinquishing life becomes part of the game. The exuberant psychopath enjoys the odds stacked against him, making the possibility, yea, the probability of death the grandest risk of all. "Vain and glorious" does not denote an empty expression for the psychopath; vain and glorious epitomizes the evildoer's exuberant view of life...and death.

Indeed, imagine the malevolent individual's fascination with the quintessential Mystery that awaits beyond death's passage. Excepting those resilient monsters who discover the knack of resurrecting themselves for still another sequel, the Mystery of death's afterlife poses the most frightening, most intriguing challenge of all to the compleat psychopath.

Just ask Keyser Söze.

Bibliography

Anderson, J. (1995). *A clockwork orange.* In P. Keough (Ed.), *Flesh and Blood* (pp. 179-182). San Francisco, CA: Mercury House.

Baumeister, R., Smart, L., & Boden, J. (1996). Relation of threatened egotism to violence and aggression: The dark side of high self-esteem. *Psychological Review,* 103(1), 5-33.

Bergman, P., & Asimow, M. (1996). *Reel justice.* Kansas City, MO: Andrews and McMeel.

Berkowitz, L. (1993). *Aggression.* New York: McGraw-Hill.

Bizony, P. (1994). *2001 filming the future.* London, England: Aurum Press.

Bok, S. (1982). *Secrets.* New York: Pantheon Books.

Boorstin, J. (1990). *The Hollywood eye.* New York: Harper Collins.

Brill, L. (1988). *The Hitchcock romance.* Princeton, NJ: Princeton University Press.

Brown, E. (1989). *Public justice, private mercy.* New York: Weidenfeld & Nicholson.

Brown, R. (1994). *Overtones and undertones.* Los Angeles, CA: University of California Press.

Caine, M. (1990). *Acting in film.* New York: Applause Theatre Book Publishers.

Carey, G. (1997). Mankiewicz on 'Eve.' *Scenario,* 3(3), 105-109, 202-203.

Carr, J. (1995). Henry: Portrait of a serial killer. In P. Keough (Ed.), *Flesh and Blood* (pp. 340-341). San Francisco, CA: Mercury House.

Christopher, N. (1997). *Somewhere in the night*. New York: Free Press.

Clark, L., Watson, D., & Reynolds, S. (1995). Diagnosis and classification of psychopathology: Challenges to the current system and future directions. *Annual Review Of Psychology*, 46, 121-153.

Clarke, J. (1990). *On being mad or merely angry*. Princeton, NJ: Princeton University Press.

Clover, C. (1992). *Men, women, and chain saws*. Princeton, NJ: Princeton University Press.

Crane, J. (1994). *Terror and everyday life*. Thousand Oaks, CA: Sage.

Dahmer, L. (1993). *A father's story*. New York: William Morrow.

Delbanco, A. (1995). *The death of Satan*. New York: Farrar, Straus and Giroux.

Denby, D. (1995). Pulp fiction. In P. Keough (Ed.), *Flesh and Blood* (pp. 227-231). San Francisco, CA: Mercury House.

Dennett, D. (1997). When HAL kills, who's to blame? Computer ethics. In D. Stork (Ed.), *HAL's Legacy* (pp. 351-365). Cambridge, MA: The MIT Press.

Detmer, A. (1995, June 26). The reality of make-believe. *Newsweek*, p. 10.

Ebert, R. (1996). *Roger Ebert's video companion* (1997 Edition). Kansas City, MO: Andrews and McMeel.

Fox, J., & Levin, J. (1994). *Overkill*. New York: Plenum Press.

Gardner, G. (1987). *The censorship papers*. New York: Dodd, Mead & Co.

Geberth, V. (1996). *Practical homicide investigation* (3rd Edition). New York: CRC Press.

Gould, S. (1998, February 6). The great asymmetry. *Science*, 279, 812-813.

Greene, G. (1995). The genius of Peter Lorre. In D. Parkinson (Ed.), *The Graham Greene Film Reader*, pp. 403-404. New York: Applause.

Hare, R. (1993). *Without conscience*. New York: Pocket Books.

Harris, T. (1981). *Red dragon*. New York: G. P. Putnam's Sons.

Harris, T. J. (1987). *Courtroom's finest hour in American cinema*. Metuchen, NJ: Scarecrow Press.

Haskell, M. (1987). *From reverence to rape* (2nd Edition). Chicago, IL: University of Chicago Press.

Henderson, J. (1964). Ancient myths and modern man. In C. Jung (Ed.), *Man And His Symbols* (pp. 104-157). Garden City, NY: Doubleday.

Henry, B. (1996). *To die for* screenplay. *Scenario*, 2(2), 108-149.

Hickey, E. (1997). *Serial murderers and their victims* (2nd Edition). Pacific Grove, CA: Wadsworth.

Holmes, R., & De Burger, J. (1988). *Serial murder*. Newbury Park, CA: Sage.

Holmes, R., & Holmes, S. (1996). *Profiling violent crimes* (2nd Edition). Thousand Oaks, CA: Sage.

Kaufmann, H. (1970). *Aggression and altruism*. New York: Holt, Rinehart and Winston.

King, S. (1981). *Danse macabre*. New York: Everest House.

Kirwin, B. (1997). *The mad, the bad, and the innocent*. Boston, MA: Little, Brown and Company.

Klama, J. (1988). *Aggression*. New York: John Wiley & Sons.

Kohn, A. (1990). *The brighter side of human nature*. New York: Basic Books.

Kunen, J. (1983). *"How can you defend those people?"*. New York: Random House.

Lang, F. (1997). Fritz Lang. In P. Bogdanovich (Ed.), *Who the devil made it*, pp. 170-234. New York: Alfred A. Knopf.

Lanzmann, C. (1985). *Shoah*. New York: Pantheon Books.

Latane, B., & Darley, J. (1970). *The unresponsive bystander: Why doesn't he help?* New York: Appleton-Century-Crofts.

Leitch, T. (1991). *Find the director*. Athens, GA: University of Georgia Press.

Lesser, W. (1993). *Pictures at an execution*. Cambridge, MA: Harvard University Press.

Lewis, C. (1982). *The Screwtape letters*. New York: Collier Books.

Lippy, T. (1995a). Adapting *The silence of the lambs*: A talk with Ted Tally. *Scenario*, 1(1), 196-203.

Lippy, T. (1995b). Writing and directing *Heavenly creatures*: A talk with Frances Walsh and Peter Jackson. *Scenario*, 1(4), 217-224.

Lippy, T. (1996). Adapting *To die for*: A talk with Buck Henry. *Scenario*, 2(2), 150-153, 201-206.

Lippy, T. (1997). Writing *Scream*: A talk with Kevin Williamson. *Scenario*, 3(1), 140-142, 145, 216-220.

Lubin, M., & Coe, P. (1982). *Good guys, bad guys*. New York: McGraw-Hill.

Lumet, S. (1995). *Making movies*. New York: Alfred A. Knopf.

Lyyken, D. (1995). *The antisocial personalities*. Hillsdale, NJ: Lawrence Erlbaum.

Macdonald, J. (1986). *The murderer and his victim* (2nd edition). Springfield, IL: Charles C. Thomas.

Mactire, S. (1995). *Malicious intent*. Cincinnati, OH: Writer's Digest Books.

Malcolm, J. (1990). *The journalist and the murderer*. New York: Alfred A. Knopf.

Mankiewicz, J. (1997). *All about Eve* screenplay. *Scenario*, 3(3), 56-103.

Masters, B. (1993). *Killing for company*. New York: Random House.

May, R. (1972). *Power and innocence*. New York: W. W. Norton.

McQuarrie, C. (1995). *The usual suspects* screenplay. *Scenario*, 1(3), 7-49.

Nash, J., & Ross, S. (1986). *The motion picture guide* (Volume 4: H-K). Chicago, IL: Cinebooks (pp. 1139-1562).

Nash, J., & Ross, S. (1987). *The motion picture guide* (Volume 8: T-V). Chicago, IL: Cinebooks (pp. 3257-3710).

Nash, J., & Ross, S. (1987). *The motion picture guide* (Volume 9: W-Z). Chicago, IL: Cinebooks (pp. 3711-4181).

Nettler, G. (1982). *Killing one another*. Cincinnati, OH: Anderson.

Norris, K. (1996). *The cloister walk*. New York: Riverhead Books.

Pagels, E. (1995). *The origin of Satan*. New York: Random House.

Palmer, R. (1994). *Hollywood's dark cinema: The American film noir*. New York: Twayne Publishers.

Parisi, P. (1998). *Titanic and the making of James Cameron*. New York: Newmarket Press.

Paul, W. (1994). *Laughing screaming*. New York: Columbia University Press.

Pearson, P. (1997). *When she was bad*. New York: Viking.

Picard, R. (1997). Does HAL cry digital tears? Emotions and computers. In D. Stork (Ed.), *HAL's Legacy* (pp. 279-303). Cambridge, MA: The MIT Press.

Radzinowicz, L., & King, J. (1977). *The growth of crime*. New York: Basic Books.

Ray, R. (1985). *A certain tendency of the Hollywood cinema, 1930-1980*. Princeton, NJ: Princeton University Press.

Ressler, R., & Shachtman, T. (1992). *Whoever fights monsters*. New York: St. Martin's Press.

Revitch, E., & Schlesinger, L. (1981). *Psychopathology of homicide*. Springfield, IL: Charles C. Thomas.

Rumbelow, D. (1988). *Jack the ripper*. Chicago, IL: Contemporary Books, Inc.

Rushing, J., & Frentz, T. (1995). *Projecting the shadow*. Chicago, IL: University of Chicago Press.

Samenow, S. (1989). *Before it's too late*. New York: Times Books.

Sammon, P. (1996). *Future noir: The making of Blade runner*. New York: HarperPrism.

Sanford, J. (1982). *Evil: The shadow side of reality*. New York: Crossroad.

Saposnik, I. (1983). The anatomy of *Dr. Jekyll and Mr. Hyde*. In H. Geduld (Ed.), *The Definitive Dr. Jekyll and Mr. Hyde Companion* (pp. 108-117). New York: Garland Publishing.

Schaefer, J. (1949). *Shane*. New York: Bantam Pathfinder.

Schama, S. (1995). *Landscape and memory*. New York:

Alfred A. Knopf.

Schank, R., & Childers, P. (1988). *The creative attitude.* New York: Macmillan.

Schechter, H. (1994). *Depraved.* New York: Pocket Books.

Sennett, R. (1994). *Setting the scene.* New York: Harry N. Abrams, Inc.

Skal, D. (1993). *The monster show.* New York: W. W. Norton.

Slotkin, R. (1992). *Gunfighter nation.* New York: Atheneum.

Solomon, S. (1976). *Beyond formula.* New York: Harcourt Brace Jovanovich, Inc.

Spoto, D. (1992). *The art of Alfred Hitchcock* (2nd Edition). New York: Anchor Books.

Stanford, P. (1996). *The devil.* New York: Henry Holt.

Staub, E. (1989). *The roots of evil.* Cambridge, MA: Cambridge University Press.

Stevenson, R. (1983). Strange case of Dr. Jekyll and Mr. Hyde. In H. Geduld (Ed.), *The Definitive Dr. Jekyll And Mr. Hyde Companion* (pp. 17-52). New York: Garland Publishing.

Symons, J. (1985). *Bloody murder.* New York: Viking.

Tally, T. (1995). *The silence of the lambs* screenplay. *Scenario*, 1(1), 147-175.

Tannen, D. (1998). *The argument culture.* New York: Random House.

Tarantino, Q. (1994). *Pulp fiction.* New York: Miramax Books.

Tavris, C. (1982). *Anger.* New York: Simon and Schuster.

Telotte, J. (1987). Through a pumpkin's eye: The reflexive nature of horror. In G. Waller (Ed.), *American Horrors*, pp. 114-128. Chicago, IL: University of Illinois Press.

Thomson, D. (1977). *America in the dark.* New York: William Morrow.

Thomson, D. (1997). *Beneath Mulholland.* New York: Alfred A. Knopf.

Trivers, R. (1971). The evolution of reciprocal altruism. *The Quarterly Review of Biology*, 46, 35-57.

Tucker, W. (1985). *Vigilante: The backlash against crime in America.* New York: Stein and Day.

Twitchell, J. (1985). *Dreadful pleasures*. New York: Oxford University Press.

Twitchell, J. (1989). *Preposterous violence*. New York: Oxford University Press.

Walsh, F., & Jackson, P. (1995). *Heavenly creatures* screenplay. *Scenario*, 1(4), 180-216.

Watson, L. (1995). *Dark nature*. New York: HarperCollins.

Weiner, T. (1994, July 31). Ames espionage case shatters CIA's morale. *Dallas Morning News*, p. A-8.

Williamson, K. (1997). *Scream* screenplay. *Scenario*, 3(1), 101-139.

Wilson, W. (1994). *Sexuality in the land of Oz*. Lanham, MA: University Press of America.

Wilson, W. (1996). *Good murders and bad murders* (Revised Edition). Lanham, MA: University Press of America.

Wilson, W., & Hilton, T. (1998). *Modus operandi* of female serial killers. *Psychological Reports*, 82, 495-498.

Winslade, W., & Ross, J. (1983). *The insanity plea*. New York: Charles Scribner's Sons.

Wise, D. (1995). *Nightmover*. New York: HarperCollins.

Wolf, L. (1980). *Bluebeard*. New York: Crown Publishers.

Wuntch, P. (1997, October 18). As roles go, the old goat is sin-sational. *Dallas Morning News*, p. 5-C.

Zillmann, D., & Bryant, J. (1991). Responding to comedy: The sense and nonsense in humor. In J. Bryant & D. Zillmann (Eds.), *Responding to the Screen* (pp. 261-279). Hillsdale, NJ: Lawrence Erlbaum.

Film Index

Person Index

Subject Index

About The Author

Wayne J. Wilson is professor of psychology at Stephen F. Austin State University in Nacogdoches, Texas (wwilson@sfasu.edu). He received B. A. and M. A. degrees from Southern Methodist University, and the Ph.D. degree from Texas Christian University. His previous works with the University Press of America include *Sexuality In The Land Of Oz*, published in 1994, and a revised edition of *Good Murders And Bad Murders*, published in 1996. *The Psychopath In Film* derives from the author's teaching and research interests in the study of aggression and film.